SCOTLAND
& WALES

Aberdeen
SCOTLAND
Glasgow
Edinburgh
IRELAND
Shrewsbury
Aberystwyth
ENGLAND
WALES
LONDON
Cardiff

Daytrips
SCOTLAND & WALES

37 *one day adventures by car, rail or bus*

JUDITH FRANCES DUDDLE

HASTINGS HOUSE
Book Publishers
Fern Park, Florida

While every effort has been made to insure accuracy, neither the author nor the publisher assume legal responsibility for any consequences arising from the use of this book or the information it contains.

ISBN: 0-8038-2055-0

Printed in the United States of America
10 9 8 7 6 5 4 3 2 1

Cover design and book layout by Mark Salore, Digital Design Services
Edited by Earl Steinbicker
Peter Leers, Publisher

Comments? Ideas?

We'd love to hear from you. Ideas from our readers have resulted in many improvements in the past, and will continue to do so. And, if your suggestions are used, we'll gladly send you a complimentary copy of any book in the series. Please send your thoughts to Hastings House, Book Publishers, 2601 Wells Ave., Fern Park, FL 32730, or fax us at 407-339-5900, or e-mail to Hastings_daytrips@earthlink.net. Visit us at www.DaytripsBooks.com

Contents

INTRODUCTION   7

SECTION I   **DAYTRIP STRATEGIES**   9
Getting Around   9
Food and Drink - Scotland   13
Food and Drink - Wales   14
Restaurants and Pubs   15
Practicalities   15
Tourist Information   18

SECTION II   **DAYTRIPS IN SCOTLAND**   19
1. Edinburgh   20
2. Linlithgow   27
3. Dunfermline   31
4. Stirling   35
5. Dunbar   39
6. St. Andrews   43
7. Dundee   48
8. Blair Atholl   52
9. Aberdeen   55
10. Inverness & Loch Ness   61
11. Aviemore & the Cairngorms   65
12. Nairn   69
13. Elgin   73
14. Wick   78
15. John O' Groats   82
16. Glasgow   84
17. Paisley   89
18. Ayr - Rabbie Burns Country   93
19. Lanark   98
20. Oban   102
21. Fort William   105

SECTION III   **DAYTRIPS IN WALES**   109
22. Shrewsbury   110
23. Aberystwyth   114
24. New Quay   122
25. Aberaeron   127
26. Llandudno   131
27. Conwy   136
28. Bangor   140
29. Caernarfon   144
30. Porthmadog   149
31. Portmeirion   154
Isle of Anglesey   159
32. Beaumaris   161
33. Benllech   166
34. Holyhead   170
Daytrips from Cardiff   174
35. Cardiff   174
36. Newport   179
37. Tenby   183

SECTION IV   **APPENDIX**   188
Scottish Timeline   188
Welsh Timeline   190
Scottish Glossary   194
Welsh Glossary   195
ACKNOWLEDGEMENTS   196
INDEX   197

Introduction

Scotland is 31,510 square miles in area, 274 miles long from north to south and varies in breadth between 24 and 154 miles. Scotland also has 787 groups of islands known as the Hebrides, Orkney, and Shetland; with only 62 of these small Isles exceeding 3 square miles in area.

The total area of Wales is 8,020 square miles and is 143 miles from north to south, varying between 34 and 114 miles in breadth. Wales also has one island known as Anglesey, which has a total area of 276 square miles.

Due to the sheer magnitude of Scotland and Wales, there are many desirable locations and attractions to visit. From Neo-Classical cities and historical towns to the beautiful, untouched countryside and tranquil villages — there is something for everyone. There is no language barrier as everyone speaks English, and getting around on your own is as easy as it is back home.

The main base cities or towns (Edinburgh, Glasgow, Shrewsbury, Aberystwyth, and Cardiff) have been suggested due to their close proximity to all the major transport facilities including airports, an extensive railway network, and motorways. These in turn will take you effortlessly to all the other daytrip destinations mentioned in this book.

The beauty of daytrip travel is that once you have selected a base that appeals to you, you can rest assured that the area has already been carefully tried out and tested. Instead of having the hassle of changing your hotel from town to town, packing and unpacking every day, you can be comfortable and just stay in the one hotel, safe in the knowledge that all the work in preparing the routes, itinerary, transportation, where to eat, what to see, the cost of attractions, meals and so on has all been eliminated. All you have to do is to sit back, read this book and enjoy your holiday.

The destinations should appeal to a wide variety of interests. Apart from the usual cathedrals, art galleries, stately homes, castles, museums and monasteries, there are such attractions as country walks, famous literary trails, walled cities, craft centres, distilleries, glass making factories, medieval streets, great seaports, resorts, quaint little hamlets, maritime attractions, scenic narrow-gauge railway travel, some wildlife expeditions, copper mines, a honey farm, an Italian Village, the Hogwarts Express (from

Harry Potter), a Millennium stadium, a 9-meter-high collapsible clock, the mecca of golf courses, and even the smallest house in the world. Not only does this mirror a charming sense of bygone days, but several daytrips actually illustrate how well Scotland and Wales are adapting to their future roles in the Devolution process.

As is with every travel experience, dining (and drinking) well is vitally important. For this reason, included in every Daytrip chapter is a selection of particularly enjoyable pubs, tea rooms, cafés, and restaurants. These are price-keyed, with an emphasis on the medium-to-low range.

Every trip can be made via rail or car, and specific transportation information is given in the "Getting There" section of each daytrip. In the "Practicalities" section of each trip, you will find information about the population of a particular town or city, the location, telephone number and Internet site of the local Tourist Information Centre, and days when the colourful outdoor farmers' markets are held.

As you probably would expect, the majority of attractions have an entrance fee to assist with the upkeep of their buildings — this is indicated in the text. These are of course subject to change slightly, but at least the listings will provide a guide to anticipated expenses. Cathedrals and churches are the exception; although they do not charge an entrance fee they do welcome donations,however small, to help pay their maintenance costs.

Along with the entrance fees, and wherever possible, we have also included opening times, a telephone number, and an Internet site where applicable. Be advised that places, phone numbers and Internet sites have a way of changing without any warning, and errors do creep into print. If you have your heart set on a particular sight, just check first with the local Tourist Information Centre (TIC) to see if the opening times are still valid, and that it isn't closed for any refurbishment. TICs are always the best source of up-to-the-minute information, and their friendly staffs are always willing to help in any way, whether finding you accommodation or simply by pointing you in the right direction.

On a final note — don't worry if you can't visit every attraction at any one destination. Be selective. Your daytrips around Scotland and Wales should be fun, not a chore. If you start to feel that way, take a step back and wander over to the nearest café, tea shop, or pub and have a minute. There is always another day!

Happy Daytripping!

Section I

DAYTRIP STRATEGIES

GETTING AROUND

Scotland and Wales's modern transport infrastructure and communications makes getting around easy, as naturally befits two nations whose sons invented the telephone, television, macadam roads, the wireless, the automobile, and the compression ignition engine! Indeed, air, rail, and ferry links are on the increase and competitive economy fares have encouraged many new visitors. Still, the best way to get around the cities and towns, and see all the wonderful sights, is on foot; that is unless you intend to visit an attraction farther afield, then you will require public transport or a self-drive car.

If you opt for the latter mode of transport, remember to drive on the left-hand side of the road and don't park your car on a street where you see double yellow lines, or you may find that a "jobsworth" Traffic Warden has left you a present of parking ticket on your windscreen upon your return.

There are 32 unitary authorities that make up Scotland, and 22 unitary authorities that make up Wales. The townsfolk in every single area make you feel right at home. Understanding the Scots and the Welsh isn't too difficult, for the vast majority of speakers are bilingual in both Gaelic and English. There are estimated to be around 85,000 people who still speak the Gaelic/Scots language, and 750,000 people who speak Welsh; therefore many various regional dialects have developed. At the end of this book, I have listed some everyday Scottish and Welsh words and phrases along with their English equivalent.

BY RAIL:

There are two main train service operators in Scotland — **ScotRail** and **Railtrack**. ScotRail provides rail transport for the business, commuter, leisure, and tourist markets and operates 2,000 daily services to the main suburban routes around Glasgow and Edinburgh, interurban routes linking Glasgow, Edinburgh, Aberdeen, and Inverness, and on its rural routes covering the North and West Highlands as well as the South West of Scotland. Railtrack owns and maintains railway lines all over Great Britain. For information visit **W**: scotrail.co.uk and **W**: railtrack.co.uk.

In Wales there are five rail companies operating, the main one being **Central Trains**, **W**: centraltrains.co.uk. The other four include: **First Great Western**, **Valley Lines**, **Virgin Trains**, and **Wales and Border Trains**. The Internet search engines will easily pick out their web addresses for you, or just pop into a travel agent for further information.

BY BUS:

Scottish Citylink is Scotland's largest provider of coach service, linking over 200 towns and cities across the country with a fleet of modern and comfortable coaches, all in distinctive blue and yellow livery. Advance booking is not usually required, although you are advised to do so for longer journeys. You can buy tickets at the local station or depots or on the bus on the day. **W**: citylink.co.uk.

While in Wales, **Arriva** is the main operator of bus and coach service. **W**: arriva.co.uk.

RAIL / BUS PASSES:

If you intend to use public transport often while staying in Scotland, there are various good value passes that you should consider. All can be purchased in advance of a visit from a travel agent or from the rail and bus companies. Here are the options:

Freedom of Scotland Travelpass, providing unlimited travel on all scheduled train services within Scotland, all Caledonian MacBrayne scheduled ferry services, and various Citylink services. Valid for any 4 out of 8 consecutive days — £89, or any 8 days out of 15 consecutive days. This Travelpass is great for any independent travellers of all ages — with it you are free to roam across Scotland by train, coach, and ferry, all for a fixed price.

Highland Rover Ticket, includes rail travel between Glasgow and Oban, Fort William, and Mallaig. Travel between Inverness and Wick, Thurso, Kyle of Lochaish, Aberdeen, Aviemore, and intermediate stations. Also includes Scottish Citylink bus travel between Oban/Fort William and Inverness. The ticket is valid for any 4 out of 8 consecutive days and costs £59, but is not valid on trains arriving before 9 a.m. at Aberdeen or Inverness on Mondays to Fridays.

Central Scotland Rover Ticket includes rail travel between Edinburgh, Glasgow Queen Street, North Berwick, Bathgate, Stirling, the Fife Circle, Falkirk and all intermediate stations. Also included is unlimited travel on Glasgow Underground. The ticket is not valid between Glasgow Central and Edinburgh via Motherwell and on trains timed to depart before 9.15 a.m. Monday to Friday.

City Link Explorer Pass offers maximum flexibility at a minimum price

— you can use any service at any time within the validity of the Pass; the choices are: 3 days consecutive travel for £35; 5 days travel out of 10 for £55; 8 days travel out of 16 for £85. Citylink have teamed up with other bus, coach, and ferry companies so you have the opportunity to visit almost every part of Scotland.

Smart Card is a Citylink Discount Card for full-time students aged between 16–25. It allows you to travel on all Scottish Citylink services, saving you up to 30% on most adult fares. The card costs £6 for one year.

Senior Smart Card is the same as a Smart Card except that it is for the over 50's, again saving the card holder up to 30% on adult fares. The card costs £6 for one year.

All information on train and bus timetables in Scotland can be obtained from: **Scotrail, W**: scotrail.co.uk, ☎ (08457) 550-033; **Railtrack, W**: railtrack.co.uk, ☎ (08457) 484-950; and **Citylink, W**: citylink.co.uk, ☎ (08705) 505-050.

Central Trains operating throughout Wales offer the **Rangers Ticket** and the **Rovers Explorer Ticket**, similar to the Highland Rover Ticket and the Central Scotland Rover Ticket. Central asks anyone interested in either of these two tickets to call their telesales on ☎ (0870) 000-6060 for further information on the areas they cover.

Arriva offer the **Red Rover Ticket** — Buy a rover on the first bus you board and use it all day on buses 1 to 99 in the Gwynedd and Anglesey timetables. Adult: £4.80, child: £2.40.

Freedom of Wales Flexi Pass, a rail/bus combination pass — valid after 9 a.m. on all trains (Central included) as far as Crewe and Shrewsbury. Valid at all times on buses 1 to 99 in the Gwynedd and Anglesey timetables plus Arriva Cymru buses throughout the company's operating area. Also valid on the Ffestiniog Railway. The pass is valid for 8 days of travel out of 15 consecutive days. Adults £75, child and Railcard holders £49.50. ☎ (0870) 608-2608 for further information.

Persons residing outside of Great Britain should ask their travel agent about the various economical **BritRail Passes**, valid for virtually all rail services in England, Scotland, and Wales. Some of these include car rentals along with train travel. These bargains must be purchased overseas in advance of your trip, and must be validated before the first use. Contact a travel agent or the nearest office of the British Tourist Authority for information, or visit **W**: raileurope.com.

BY CAR:

Scotland and Wales both have excellent road networks with motorways (superhighways) and dual carriageway roads (divided highways) linking many of the main cities and towns. The primary road network extends over most of the countries except for a few remote areas, where single-track roads with passing places predominate (this means you have to pull in to let others pass or overtake). It is a pleasurable experience driving on the quiet roads of Scotland and Wales, but keep in mind that you should be driving on the left — it won't take you long to re-program the old grey matter.

Speed limits for different classes of roads are as follows: 30 mph (48kph) — towns, cities, built up areas (unless otherwise sign posted). 50 mph (80kph) — out of town. 60 mph (96kph) — single carriageways. 70 mph (112kph) — dual carriageways, motorways. Note that the speed limit for caravans, RV's, and camper vans etc., is 60 mph (96kph). Also note that 70 mph is the maximum legal speed at which you can drive in the UK. Exceed the speed limit and you risk a heavy fine (the higher the speed, the higher the fine).

Pedestrians have the right of way, especially at Pelican and Zebra Crossings (black and white stripes on the road).

All drivers and passengers must "belt up;" anyone caught not wearing a seat belt will have to face an "on-the-spot" fine of £20 — these can be issued by either a Police Officer, a Police Traffic Warden, or a local Council Parking Attendant.

Although wheel clamping is illegal for parking on public highways in Scotland, private car owners are still allowed to clamp your car if you park your car in their car park without permission or paying the appropriate parking fee. When parking your car in any car park, check to see if there is a fee for parking and make sure you pay it.

Scotland and Wales have strict rules against drinking and driving; don't risk it!

CAR RENTAL:

Many companies offer competitive car hire rates including: **Arnold Clark**, ☎ (0141) 848-0202, **W**: arnoldclark.com; **Avis**, ☎ (0870) 606-0100, **W**: avis.co.uk; **Budget**, ☎ (0870) 156-5656, **W**: budget.co.uk; **Europcar**, ☎ (0800) 800-227, **W**: europcar.co.uk; **Hertz**, ☎ (08708) 448-844, **W**: hertz.co.uk; **National Car Rental**, ☎ (0870) 600-6666, **W**: nationalcar.co.uk; to name but a few.

Most companies require the driver to be between 23 and 75 years old, with a current driving license having been held for at least one year. When you pick up a car in one town and drop it off in another, there may be a surcharge. Be sure to check if you are required to fill the tank full or to the same level as when you hired the car, otherwise you will have to pay a re-fuelling fee.

BY AIR:

In Scotland there are four international airports (Edinburgh, Glasgow, Aberdeen, and Inverness), two regional airports (Dundee and Prestwick), and another 23 smaller airports located around the Highlands and Islands.

In Wales, the only major airport is in Cardiff. Cardiff International Airport is situated just 12 miles from the City Centre and 10 miles from the

M4 motorway. ☎ (01446) 711-111, **W**: cardiff-airport.co.uk. Direct flights from USA via Amsterdam can be made with KLM, ☎ 1-800-447-4747. Alternatively, you can fly straight into London and then catch a train from Paddington Station to Cardiff — the journey can be made in two hours.

If Shrewsbury is your base, you can fly directly to Manchester Airport from the USA by using US Airways, ☎ 1-800-428-4322, **W**: usairways.com; **Virgin Atlantic**, ☎ 1-800-862-8621; or **American Airlines**, ☎ 1-800-433-7300. Cars and taxis can be hired at the airport, which will take you the 75-mile journey to Shrewsbury. Depending on the size of car, the hire charge can be anything from £15 to £48 per day.

An American carrier offering flights to Glasgow and Edinburgh Airports is **Continental Airlines**, ☎ 1-800-231-0856 or **W**: continental.com, from their New York area hub located in Newark, NJ.

Both Edinburgh and Glasgow Airports are only 8 miles to the City Centre — taxis from the airports to the town centres cost £15 and £12 respectively. To contact **Edinburgh Airport** ☎ (0131) 333-1000 or **W**: baa.co.uk/edinburgh; and to contact **Glasgow Airport** ☎ (0141) 887-1111 or **W**: baa.co.uk/gasgow.

FOOD AND DRINK IN SCOTLAND

Scotland has a distinctive cuisine, often based on very traditional foods. "Haggis" is the first food that often springs to mind when associating a traditional dish with Scotland. Don't really know what a Haggis is? Well, I'll tell you, as long as it doesn't put you off tasting it. Haggis is made from sheep's offal (or pluck). The windpipe, lungs, heart, and liver are boiled and then minced. This is mixed with beef suet and lightly toasted oatmeal. The mixture is placed inside the sheep's stomach, which is sewn closed. Lastly, the haggis is traditionally cooked by boiling it for up to three hours. The Haggis is traditionally served on January 25 — Burns Night. The story of Robert (Rabbie) Burns can be found in the "Ayr-Rabbie Burns Country" chapter of this book.

Another good old Scottish traditional food is porridge! This simple dish made of oatmeal, boiled slowly and stirred continuously with a spirtle — a 12" long wooden stick. In days gone by, crofters in the Highlands of Scotland would make a large pot of porridge at the beginning of the week, allow it to cool, then cut it up into slices and take a piece with them every day in their pocket for lunch — sounds "yummy" doesn't it? Today, porridge is eaten as a nourishing and filling breakfast by people all over the country, although you still wouldn't catch a true Scot adding any sugar or syrup to the recipe — just salt is used.

The list of native and unusual dishes could go on and on — Tatties, Scotch Pies, Black Bun, Colcannon, Bannocks etc., but now it's time to mention the more contemporary cuisine served in Scotland. The unspoilt environment and climate without extremes mean a wide range of foodstuffs originate within the country, such as Wild Red Deer, Scottish Salmon and trout, grouse, partridge, pheasant, pigeon, monkfish, mussels, sole and scallops.

To wash down this glorious food, try the Water of Life or Uisge-Beatha in Gaelic — to you and I, Scotch Whisky. "Scotch" is certainly the best known Scottish drink — it's distilled from barley liquor and flavoured with peat tainted water. Alternatively, you have the traditional Scottish beers, which include the Indian Pale Ale (IPA). On a chilly day, there is nothing like a Hot Toddy to get the circulation going again. This is a teaspoon of sugar and a teaspoon of Scottish heather honey in a warm glass, add a measure of Scotch whisky (not Malt), then topped up with boiling water and gently stirred with a silver spoon.

FOOD AND DRINK IN WALES

The majority of restaurants across Wales provide wonderful examples of Welsh cuisine, ranging from cawl and laverbread to succulent, traditional Welsh lamb. Which traditional Welsh food you are served depends on which part of Wales you are visiting. For an example, if you are in Aberystwyth, you are more than likely to be offered "Ceredigion Cawl" to eat — in other words "soup." The cawl is made from meat, root vegetables, herbs, and leeks and is prepared and cooked over 2 days. A bowl of warming cawl should be served with a wooden spoon.

"Stwns Rwdan A Iau" is a popular North Wales dish using liver, onions, swedes (rutabagas), and potatoes. The "Stwns" is the swede and potato mashed together.

The "Trout wrapped in Bacon" recipe comes from traditional rural Wales — local trout (possibly poached) sitting in a dish wrapped in fat bacon from last year's family pig.

Portmeirion prides itself in developing the "Fillet of Beef with Beetroot and Truffle," but the two best-known foods of all to come from Wales is the "Laver Bread" (Bara Lawr) and "Bara Brith" (Currant or speckled Bread). Laver is a kind of edible seaweed — an excellent source of dietary iron, while the Bara Brith is a traditional rich cake that is the centrepiece of many Welsh tea tables — served sliced with salted butter and some tasty farmhouse cheddar cheese.

You have a variety of home-made wines and drinks served in Wales, including Mead and Welsh Ginger Beer. The Mead recipe is made from Honey, Ginger, Hops, and Allspice, and is a traditional drink found in Tenby and surrounding areas. To make Welsh Ginger Beer, take a 10-pint saucepan half-filled with dandelions and nettles in equal proportions, together with two sticks of rhubarb and four sticks of ginger which have previously been pounded. You also need a handful of currant leaves, white sugar, water, and yeast.

RESTAURANTS AND PUBS

Several choice restaurants and pubs are listed for each destination in the book. The majority of these are long-time favourites of experienced travellers, while some are new and worth trying. The approximate price range per person appears as:

£   -   Inexpensive, but may have fancier dishes available.
££   -   Reasonable. These establishments may also feature daily specials.
£££ -   Expensive.
X   -   Days closed.

To help you with your selections, The **Taste of Scotland**, (who in 2002 gained the Scottish Tourist Board's Food Grade assessment scheme award) publish The Taste of Scotland Guide. The guide includes over 300 of the best establishments in Scotland, all condensed into a handy compact book. Web visitors can purchase the Guide at a special online price by accessing **W**: taste-of-scotland.com

Although you cannot purchase A Taste of Wales in booklet or guide form, you can actually download all the recipes free of charge by accessing **W**: visitwales.com

In some restaurants, a service charge is already added to the bill so there is no need to tip, unless the meal and the service was out of this world. Where no service charge is added, the waiter expects a gratuity of 10–15%, but you can use your own discretion on this one, as it much depends on the service you received.

In pubs, tipping is neither expected or encouraged. Pubs are usually open on Mondays through Saturdays at 11 or 11.30 a.m. to 11 p.m., and on Sundays from noon to 3 p.m. and 7–10.30 p.m. Meals stop being served after 2 p.m., although this can vary from pub to pub.

Informal types of restaurants can be found in the guise of cafés, pubs, coffee and tea shops. All serve an à la carte style of picking and choosing your meal. If you are not that hungry, a salad will suffice as your main course; on the other hand, if you are ravenous you can choose a "starter" (appetizer) and a main course.

PRACTICALITIES

WHEN TO GO:

The weather in Scotland and Wales, like the rest of the UK, is unpredictable. The best time to visit is between Spring and Summer; most visitors choose July and August, the height of Summer, when all the flowers are in bloom. From October on there is more chance of the weather becoming cool and wet, so always carry a folding umbrella.

HOLIDAYS:

Legal holidays in Scotland are:
New Year's Day (January 1)
Holiday (January 2)
Good Friday
Easter Monday
May Bank Holiday (first Monday in May)
Spring Bank Holiday (last Monday in May)
August Bank Holiday (first Monday in August)
Summer Bank Holiday (last Monday in August)
Christmas Day (December 25)
Boxing Day (December 26)

Legal Holidays in Wales are:
New Year's Day (January 1)
Good Friday
Easter Monday
May Bank Holiday (first Monday in May)
Spring Bank Holiday (last Monday in May)
Summer Bank Holiday (last Monday in August)
Christmas Day (December 25)
Boxing Day (December 26)

MONEY MATTERS:

Banks are open from 9 a.m. to 4 p.m. Monday to Friday. Most have autotellers (ATMs) with credit-card cash advance facilities. This service is open 24 hours a day — but check with your own bank before leaving home to make sure that your PIN code will work. Bank Notes are issued in 100 GBP (Great British Pound), try to avoid 50 GBP, instead go for 20 GBP, 10 GBP and 5 GBP. The highest denomination coin is the 2 GBP, followed by the 1 GBP, and then the large 50p and the compact sized 20p, 10p, 5p, 2p and 1p. Scotland has its own bank notes, printed by The Bank of Scotland, but are still the exact equal value as the pound sterling (£).

Travellers Cheques are the safest way of carrying large amounts of money around and can be cashed at any bank (remember proof of ID) or at any exchange. Credit Cards are widely accepted but not for cab fares or small purchases.

A word about prices: Prices (and opening times) quoted in this book were believed to be current at the time of research, but are of course subject to change. They rarely go down — expect in many cases to pay a bit more. Still, the quoted prices serve as a guide to the relative costs of different attractions.

MAIL:

Postcards and stamps can be bought from either a Post Office or a Newsagent. A Postcard with a 1st class stamp sent to America costs about

56p and will take approximately 5–6 days to arrive. All parcels must be taken to the Post Office to be correctly weighed and labelled.

TELEPHONES:

Two types of **public telephones** are used in Scotland and Wales, often paired together so you have a choice. The first uses coins of 10, 20, or 50 pence, or £1 and do not make change although unused coins are returned to you. The second is the Charge/Credit Card. Due to the increase number of people using mobile phones, British Telecom (BT), phased out the Phonecard in 2002 and the service completely ceased to operate in 2003.

Scotland and Wales are divided into **area codes**, which are dialed only when calling from outside that area. All phone numbers in this book indicate the area code in parentheses. Other dialing codes are: (080x)= free call; (084x)= local rate; (087x)= national rate; (090x)=premium rate — note that the x can be any digit. 077, 078, and 079 are for mobile service. **Cellular** (mobile) phones may be rented, although if you're staying for a while it may be better to purchase a prepaid-service phone, to which you can add minutes as you go along. These are sold just about everywhere.

INTERNET:

Website URLs were current at the time of writing, but are subject to change at the discretion of their hosts. They are indicated by the symbol **W**; replace this with www. when typing in the address. If you can't find the one you're looking for, use a search engine such as Google, Yahoo, or Freeserve.

SUGGESTED TOURS:

The do-it-yourself walking tours in this book are relatively short and easy to follow. They always begin at the local train station, or bus depot since most readers will be using public transportation. Those going by car can park in the stations' car parks and start from the same point. Suggested routes are shown by heavy broken lines on the maps, while the circled numbers refer to major attractions or points of reference along the way, with corresponding numbers in the text. Remember that the tour routes are only suggestions — you may prefer to wander off on your own using the maps as a guide.

Trying to see everything in any given town could easily become an exhausting marathon. You will certainly enjoy yourself more by being selective and passing up anything that doesn't catch your fancy. Vindication will be granted if you fail to visit every church.

Practical information, such as the opening times and admission charges of various attractions, is as accurate as possible at the time of writing, but everything is subject to change. Before setting out on a visit, always check with the local Tourist Information Centre, or call the attraction itself to find out if there have been any unexpected changes.

*OUTSTANDING ATTRACTIONS:

An * asterisk before any item, be it an entire daytrip, an object of beauty, or just one exhibit in a museum or gallery, denotes a special treat that in the author's opinion should not be missed.

TOURIST INFORMATION

There are over 160 Tourist Information Centres in Scotland and approximately 82 in Wales. The sign for the Tourist Information Centre (TIC), both in Scotland and Wales, is a big **i**. This symbol is white, slanted, with a little right flick at the bottom of it, and is set in a pale blue square. Each destination has its own Tourist Information Centre, whose address, phone number, and where possible web address, are listed in the Practicalities section for that trip. Ask the TICs in Scotland about the "Historic Scotland's" Explorer Pass — this provides entry to over 60 top attractions.

ADVANCE PLANNING INFORMATION:

The British Tourist Authority, which covers England, Ireland, Scotland, and Wales, has branches throughout the world to help plan your trip. Some of these are located at:

551 Fifth Avenue, **New York**, NY 10176-0799, USA, ☎ (800) 462-2748 or (212) 986-2200, Fax (212) 986-1188.

625 North Michigan Avenue, **Chicago**, IL 60611-1977, USA ☎ (800) 462-2748.

5915 Airport Road, Suite 120, Mississauga, Ont. L4V 1TI, **Canada**, ☎ (888) VISIT UK or (905) 405-1840.

Level 16, Gateway, 1 Macquarie Place, **Sydney**, NSW 2000, Australia, ☎ (02) 9377-4400.

3rd Floor, Dilworth Building, Queen and Customs St., **Auckland** 1, New Zealand, ☎ (09) 303-1446.

Lancaster Gate, Hyde Park Lane, Hyde Park, Sandton 2196, **South Africa**, ☎ (011) 325-0343.

And on the **INTERNET** at **W**: visitbritain.com and **W**: visitscotland.com.

Section II

DAYTRIPS IN
SCOTLAND

Most of the daytrips in this section may be taken from either Edinburgh or Glasgow, as noted in the text.

Trip 1

Edinburgh

"Edinburgh is what Paris ought to be" said Robert Louis Stevenson, and how right he was! Edinburgh features a winning combination of magnificent architecture, spectacular countryside, and exhilarating nightlife; all within an historical setting in Southeast Scotland. This beautiful city is Scotland's capital — fortified for over 2000 years since the Iron Age and steeped in history. It represents the essence of modern-day nationhood.

The ideal way to explore Edinburgh is on foot. A stroll down the famous Royal Mile or through the elegant streets of the 18th-century New Town captures the atmosphere and wonderful views of this remarkable city. The Royal Mile is host to many attractions, including Edinburgh Castle; the Tartan Weaving Mill & Exhibition; the Camera Obscura & World of Illusions; the Scotch Whisky Heritage Centre, and Gladstone's Land. Just a "stones throw" away you will find many more exciting places to visit; places mentioned a little later in this book. These are just few of the reasons why Edinburgh should be used as your base city.

GETTING THERE:

Trains from **London's Kings Cross Station** take as little as 4-1/2 hours. Waverley Station serves the North and East Coast and is situated in Edinburgh's City Centre. If you intend to stay in the West End of Edinburgh, a train from King's Cross Station to Edinburgh's Haymarket Station is the better option for you. Check timetables by ☎ (08457) 484-950 or **W**: rail.co.uk

Trains from **Glasgow's Queen Street Station** run every 15 minutes to Waverley Station, with a journey time of 49 minutes. Again, if you intend to stay in Edinburgh's West End, head instead for Edinburgh's Haymarket Station. For up-to-date travel information, contact the train operator ScotRail Railways, **W**: scotrail.co.uk

By Car from **London**, Edinburgh is 412 miles to the northwest via the M1 and A1 motorways.

By Car from **Glasgow**, take the M8 and A8 motorways. The distance is 45 miles, with a travelling time of just one hour — at a leisurely 50 mph.

By Air, Edinburgh is connected to London's Heathrow Airport by British Airways Shuttle. This jaunt at present takes 1 hour 15 minutes. To check on flight schedules contact **British Airways** ☎ (0845) 773-3377 or **W**: britishairways.com. The **Airlink Express Bus** runs between Edinburgh Airport and the City Centre every 10 minutes during the day.

GETTING AROUND:

Although the suggested tour can easily be covered by foot, you may decide that the more hilly parts of Edinburgh should be seen by bus, taxi or even by chauffeur-driven car. The local Tourist Information Centre (see below) will gladly provide you with all the information you need.

PRACTICALITIES:

The **Edinburgh & Scotland Tourist Information Centre** (TIC) is situated at 3 Princes Street, ☎ (0131) 473-3800 or **W**: edinburgh.org. Public Transport throughout Edinburgh is excellent and inexpensive. Bus companies offer daily, weekly, and monthly passes, some of which include discounts for local sightseeing. These can be purchased at the above TIC address.

Edinburgh is buzzing all year round, but if you want to catch some of the traditional festivals that are held in the city, such as the Edinburgh Military Tattoo, Highland Games, Edinburgh Festival, International Fringe Festival, and the famous Hogmanay you are better planning your trip from the beginning of August to December/January.

FOOD AND DRINK:

You will find all manner of transatlantic cuisine in Edinburgh — American, French, Mexican, Italian and, of course, Scottish fare.

Hard Rock Café (near to the Royal Mile at 20 George Street) Internationally known American restaurant and bar offering a varied menu, excellent service and upbeat atmosphere. ☎ (0131) 260-3000 ££

Littlejohns Restaurant (104 Hanover St., just a couple of streets from the Royal Mile) Quality family dining experience, with a pleasant and relaxed atmosphere. Superb kids menu. ☎ (0131) 226-6300, **W**: little johns.co.uk. £

The Pompadour Restaurant (Princess Street) Offering superb views over the castle while sampling French cuisine. ☎ (0131) 222-8888. £££

La Lanterna Restaurant (83 Hanover Street) A very warm and hospitable Italian welcome is assured in this family-run restaurant. Freshly-cooked cuisine to order. ☎ (0131) 226-3090. X: Sun. ££

The Tower Restaurant and Terrace (Museum of Scotland, Chambers Street) Unique rooftop restaurant offering unmissable views of Edinburgh Castle. ☎ (0131) 225-3003, **W**: tower-restaurant.com. ££

Creelers Seafood Bar Bistro and Restaurant (3 Hunter Square, Royal Mile) À la carte and bistro menus of Scottish fish, meat, and vegetarian dishes. ☎ (0131) 220-4447. ££

The Elephant House (21 George IV Bridge) Finest quality coffee & teas, with over 600 elephants on view. ☎ (0131) 220-5355. **W**: elephants.bun.com. X: Sun. £

Henderson's Salad Table (94 Hanover Street) Vegetarian restaurant with cosmopolitan atmosphere and live music. ☎ (0131) 225-2131. **W**: hendersonsofedinburgh.co.uk. X: Sun. except during festival. ££

Martins (70 Rose Street North Lane, between George and Princes St.)

Specialising in fresh Scottish foods, wild and organic fish, shellfish, and game. ☎ (0131) 225-3106. X: Sun., Mon. ££ and £££

SUGGESTED TOUR:

Circled numbers correspond to numbers on the map.

Begin your day's sightseeing outside the Tourist Information Centre on Princes Street, next to Waverley Train Station ❶. Follow the street in a westerly direction until you see East Princes Street Gardens, where you will find the:

*SCOTT MONUMENT ❷, ☎ (0131) 529-4068 or 529-3993. *Opening times vary throughout the year, phone and check. £2.50.*

The monument is a 200-foot-high marble statue, completed in 1844, of Novelist Sir Walter Scott and his dog.

At the corner of West Princes Street Gardens, you will find the **Floral Clock**, built in 1903 and reputed to be the oldest in the world. It is almost 12 feet in diameter and filled with 250,000 flowers — hence its name.

The nearby **National Gallery of Scotland ❸** can be found at The Mound. It is home to a wonderful collection of masterpieces from the Renaissance to Post-Impressionism; works by Raphael, Rembrandt, Turner, and Van Gogh. ☎ (0131) 624-6200, **W**: natgalscot.ac.uk. *Open Mon.–Sat. 10–5, Sun. noon–5. Free; charges for special exhibitions.*

If you now follow the map uphill, you will reach:

*EDINBURGH CASTLE ❹. ☎ (0131) 225 9846, **W**: historic-scotland.net. *Open April–Sept., daily 9:30–6; Oct.–March, daily 9:30–5. Last admission 45 minutes before closing. Adults £7.50, child £2.00, concessions £5.50.* ♿

Home of Scottish Kings and Queens from centuries past, the castle dominates the city from its high perch of volcanic rock. This magnificent royal fortress houses the Crown Jewels of Scotland, the Stone of Destiny, and the Scottish National War Memorial. The best way to view the castle is to either take a guided tour or to purchase an illustrated guide book at the gift shop inside.

Leave the castle and begin your leisurely stroll down one of the most fascinating thoroughfares in Europe, the **Royal Mile**. Actually a straight succession of several streets, it leads downhill to the Palace of Holyroodhouse, the official Scottish residence of Her Majesty the Queen, but also open to tourists. This stretch of road during the Middle Ages was an overcrowded slum, where the poor townspeople eked out a living as best they could. After the 18th century, Edinburgh prospered and so the Royal Mile was considerably improved and today presents a thoroughly delightful mixture of buildings.

The parade ground just in front of the castle is called the Esplanade, built in the early 19th century and now used for the famous Military

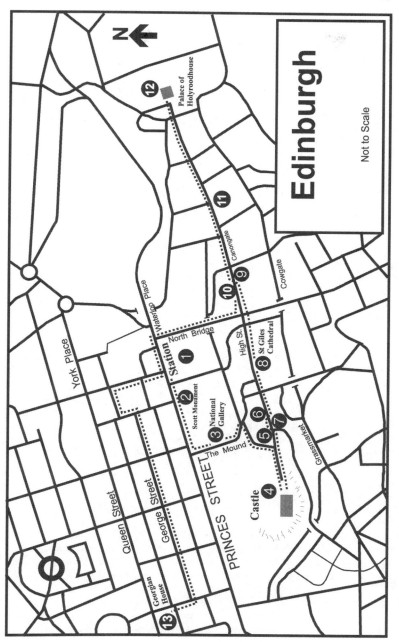

Tattoo. Nearby is the:

*CAMERA OBSCURA & WORLD OF ILLUSIONS ❺. ☎ (0131) 226-3709, **W**: camera-obscura.co.uk. *Open April–Oct., daily 9:30–6; Nov.–March, daily 10–5. Adults £4.25, child £2.10, seniors £2.70, students £3.40, and family £12.00.*

This is an observation tower situated on Castlehill. It is worth your while to climb the steep steps of the tower, because at the top you will find a breathtaking rooftop view of the city. You will also be treated to a "Light Fantastic" and holography.

Where Castle Hill becomes Lawnmarket you will find **Gladstone's Land ❻**, an early 17th-century six-story tenement belonging to the National Trust. This atmospheric building shows living conditions of old Edinburgh and contains remarkable painted ceilings. ☎ *(0131) 226-5856,* **W**: *nts.org.uk. Open April–Oct., Mon.–Sat. 10–5, Sun. 2–5. Adults £3.50, concession £2.50, and children £2.50.*

Beside the Edinburgh Castle is the **Scotch Whisky Heritage Centre ❼**. This particular visit will be well received by those of you who are fine malt whisky connoisseurs. The mystery of whisky is revealed. A barrel car travels through 300 years of history, complete with sound effects and aromas. You can learn about malt, grain, and blends — and of course there is free tasting for adults. ☎ *(0131) 220-0441,* **W**: *whisky-heritage.co.uk. Open daily, 10–5. Closed Dec. 25. Adults £6.50, students/seniors/disabled £4.50, child £3.25, and family (2 adults and up to 4 children) £14.00.*

Practically next door to the Whisky Centre is **The Hub**, Edinburgh's Festival Centre. Situated within a spectacular A-listed building, it serves as a ticket centre, café, shop, information centre, and even rental function space. ☎ *(0131) 473-2000,* **W**: *eif.co.uk/thehub. Open daily from 9.30 a.m.*

On the opposite side of the street is the entrance to **The Writer's Museum**, once called Lady Stair's House. This museum is solely devoted to Scotland's greatest literary figures: Robert Burns, Sir Walter Scott, and Robert Louis Stevenson. ☎ *(0131) 529-4901,* **W**: *cac.org.uk. Open Mon.–Sat. 10–5; also Sun. during Edinburgh Festival, 2–5. Free.*

*ST. GILES' CATHEDRAL ❽. ☎ (0131) 225-9442, **W**: *stgiles.net. Open Easter to Sept., Mon.–Fri. 9–7, Sat. 9–5, Sun. 1-5; Oct.–Easter, Mon.–Sat. 9–5, Sun. 1–5. Free.*

St. Giles' is more correctly known as the High Kirk of Edinburgh and dates mainly from the 15th century. The tiny Thistle Chapel is dedicated to the Order of the Thistle, Scotland's highest order of chivalry, and features two carved bagpipe-playing angels.

Just behind St. Giles' is Parliament House. Built in 1632–39, it was the seat of the Scottish Government until 1707, when that was abolished under the Act of Union with England. It is now the home to the Supreme

Law Courts of Scotland.

Continue down High Street to the **Museum of Childhood** ❾. This fun-filled museum is solely devoted to the history of childhood. There is a vast collection of historic toys, dolls, games, books, and costumes. ☎ *(0131) 529-4143*, **W**: *cac.org.uk. Open Mon.–Sat. 10–5, also on Sun. from July–Aug., noon–5. Free.*

On the opposite side of the street and just off the Royal Mile, you will find the **Brass Rubbing Centre** at Trinity Apse, Chalmers Close. Those wishing to take a little bit of old Scotland home can make rubbings of rare Scottish brasses and medieval church brasses. ☎ *(0131) 556-4364. Open April–Sept., Mon.–Sat. 10–5. During the Edinburgh Festival it is also open on Sun., noon–5. Free entry; small charge for brass rubbing.*

Now retrace your footsteps, so that you are back on High Street. Just a few yards away you will find **John Knox House** ❿, a 15th-century house turned into a museum. It has elaborate carvings, numerous gables, and outside stairs. ☎ *(0131) 556-9579. Open Mon.–Sat. 10–5, also on Sun. from July–Aug. Adults £2.25, senior/students £1.75, child (15 & below) 75p, under 7 free.*

The Royal Mile now narrows into Cannongate and leads downhill to a former Cannongate Tollbooth, now called **The People's Story Museum.** The 1591 building used to be a courthouse and prison, but the houses have now been turned into an exhibition illustrating the life and works of Edinburgh citizens, from the late 18th century to the present date. Almost directly opposite The People's Story, you will find **The Museum of Edinburgh** ⓫, packed with collections from Edinburgh's colourful past. *Open Mon.–Sat. 10–5; also on Sun. 2–5 during the Edinburgh Festival. Free.*

Continue walking down Cannongate until you reach the end of the Royal Mile. Here you will find the:

*PALACE OF HOLYROODHOUSE ⓬. ☎ (0131) 556-1096, **W**: the-royal-collection.org.uk. *Open April–Oct., daily 9:30–6; Nov.–March, daily 9:30–4:30. Closed during royal residences in late May and late June to early July. Adults £6.50, under 17 £3.30, over 60 £5.00, family ticket £16.30.*

Often referred to as Holyrood Palace, this is the official Scottish residence of the Queen. Dating back to the 15th century, it was only when James IV transformed the original building from a guest house that it became a palace. Unfortunately, most of this has since been destroyed. Mary Queen of Scots lived here for six tragic years, starting in 1561. For it was here she witnessed the barbaric butchery of her Italian secretary and alleged lover, David Rizzio, most likely at the hand of her over-jealous husband Lord Darnley.

The State Apartments relate to Queen Mary house tapestries, paintings, and furniture, while the Picture Gallery has portraits of 89 Scottish Kings.

Adjoining the palace is **Holyrood Park,** a place rich in animal and plant life where you can soak up the fresh air and catch your breath.

We have one last visit before ambling back to Waverley Station. As we head for Charlotte Square, we can stroll down Princess Street and pop into some of the many interesting shops enroute. Once you reach the most elegant square in town, you will see the splendid **Georgian House** ⓭ at number 7, now owned by The National Trust for Scotland. Designed by Robert Adam in 1791, it was fully restored and furnished between 1790 and 1810 and is now opened to the public. ☎ *(0131) 226-3318. Open March–Oct., Mon.–Sat. 10–5, Sun. 2–5; Nov.–Dec. 24, Mon.–Sat. 11–4, Sun. 2–4. Adults £5, children £4, concessions £4.*

Now walk back down to Princess Street and return to the starting point at Waverley Station by strolling through the magnificent Princess Street Gardens.

The Palace of Holyroodhouse

Linlithgow

A Daytrip from Edinburgh or Glasgow

This historic county town of West Lothian — Linlithgow — is located just 18 miles west of Edinburgh, just off the M9 motorway and right on the Edinburgh - Glasgow rail line.

The ruined splendour of Linlithgow tells a story of a massive fortified palace, where Mary Queen of Scots was born on December 8, 1542. Its dramatic setting at the edge of a small lake, or loch, makes it one of the most romantic visions of old Scotland.

Today, the small quiet place that grew up around the palace is now a popular dormitory town with electronics as its main industry. In 1994 it was named "Scottish Tourism Town of the Year."

This very easy and rather short trip could be combined in the same day with one to Stirling (see page 35) as there is a direct train service between them.

GETTING THERE:

Trains depart **Edinburgh's Waverley Station** every half-hour for the 20-minute ride to Linlithgow.

Trains leave **Glasgow's Queen Street Station** at half-hourly intervals for the 31-minute run to Linlithgow.

By Car from Edinburgh, take the A8 and M9 roadways west to the Linlithgow exit, then the A803 into town. The total distance is 20 miles.

By Car from Glasgow, take the M8, M80, A80, M9 and the A803 into town. The total distance is 35.5 miles.

PRACTICALITIES:

The local **Tourist Information Centre**, ☎ (01506) 844-600, **W**: edinburgh.org, is in the Burgh Halls at the cross, just off High Street. Early shop closing is on a Wednesday. Linlithgow's population exceeds 12,500.

FOOD AND DRINK:

Cameron's Traditional Tea Room & Coffee Shop (276A High Street) serves home-cooked light meals and snacks. ☎ (01506) 848-599. £

The Four Marys (65–67 High Street) Historic inn and bistro set in a 16th -century building. ☎ (01506) 842-171. £ and ££

Champany Inn (Champany, Linlithgow, 2 miles northeast on the A803 where it meets the A904) Pub, restaurant and hotel, offering a wide variety of Scottish and traditional fare. Pub open daily, restaurant Mon.–Fri. for lunch, Mon.–Sat. for dinner. (01506) 834-532. ££ and £££

SUGGESTED TOUR:

Circled numbers correspond to numbers on the map.

Leave the **train station** ❶ and stroll down the High Street to **The Cross** ❷, the focal point of Linlithgow, which was once a market place and is now a square in front of the magnificent Town House. Built in 1668–70, the house replaced the original tolbooth, which was demolished on the orders of Oliver Cromwell. Now, altered over the years, it accommodates the Burgh Halls and the local Tourist Information Centre. Directly in front, you will find the Cross Well, a replica of the 1628 original stone fountain (part of which can be found at Pitmedden Garden, Aberdeenshire), which was created by a one-handed stonemason named Robert Gray.

Kirkgate leads steeply uphill through the oldest part of town to the splendid 16th-century gateway of the palace. Continue through and into the grounds of **Linlithgow Palace** ❸. While paying the small entrance charge, you would do well to purchase a copy of the illustrated guide brochure, which describes all of the rooms and outlines an interesting tour.

Since at least the 12th century, a royal residence has stood on this site. The present palace was started for King James I of Scotland in 1425 and was a favoured home of James IV and James V. The latter's daughter, Mary Queen of Scots, was born here in 1542. In 1746 the palace was gutted by a fire, leaving it as it stands today in semi-ruins. ☎ *(01506) 842-896*, **W**: *his toric-scotland.net. Open April–Sept., daily 9:30–6:30; Oct.–March, Mon.–Sat. 9:30–4:40, Sun. 2:30–4:30. Adults £2.80, concessions £2. and children £1.*

St. Michael's Church ❹, just south of the palace, is one of the most interesting churches in Scotland. The motto of the Royal Burgh of Linlithgow is "St Michael is kind to strangers," which is an extremely comforting thought when new to a foreign country. The first mention of the church was in 1138, when King David I gave the land, chapel, and other rights to the Cathedral of St. Andrews, but it was only on May 22, 1242, that the Church of St. Michael of Linlithgow was consecrated by Bishop David de Bernham. ☎ *(01506) 842-188*, **W**: *stmichaels-parish.org.uk. Open April–Sept., daily 10–4:30; Oct.–March, Mon.–Fri. 10–3. Free.*

The town of Linlithgow itself has some interesting old houses. A stroll down High Street will bring you to **Linlithgow Museum and Heritage Centre** ❺, Annet House, 143 High Street. Run by the Heritage Trust, the museum celebrates Linlithgow's past and present. ☎ *(01506) 670-677*, **W**: *linlithgow story.org.uk. Open Easter–Oct., Mon.–Sat. 10–5, Sun. 1–4. Adults £1, concession 60p, and family £2.*

For your final visit of the day, why not go on a relaxing boat trip on the Union Canal. The **Linlithgow Canal Centre** ❻, situated on Manse Road Basin (just before the train station) operates the *Victoria* and the *St.*

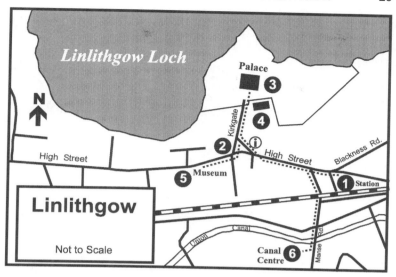

Linlithgow Palace

Magdalene for public cruising. The centre has also created a museum from canal stables, and turned a canal cottage into a warm, cosy tea room. Well worth the visit! ☎ *(01506) 671-215,* **W**: *lucs.org.uk. Open Easter through Oct., weekends 2–5, also daily July–Aug. Museum free. Cruises on the St. Magdalene: Adult £6, child/concession £3. The cruise is to Avon Aqueduct and takes 2-1/5 hours. Short boat trips are available on the Victoria.*

From here it is only a short walk back to the station.

View of the Palace from the Park

Dunfermline

A Daytrip from Edinburgh or Glasgow

The name Dunfermline means "fortress by the crooked stream," which seems to suggest that it was the site of an early fortified settlement, although there is very little evidence to support this theory. It was during 1060 that Malcolm Canmore (Malcolm III to friends) chose the town as the site for his new royal residence and together with his second wife — Queen Margaret — set up a religious community in Dunfermline under the aegis of the Church of Rome. For 500 years, Dunfermline was at the centre of court and monastic life in Scotland.

Today, as you walk around this beautiful, ancient town you will discover many unexpected treasures; from the birthplace of philanthropist Andrew Carnegie to the ornate city chambers in the French Gothic style. You, too, will be walking in the footsteps of monarchs and monks.

GETTING THERE:

By Train from Edinburgh's Waverley Station into Dunfermline Town takes 30 minutes. Trains leave the station at regular intervals.

Trains depart Glasgow's Queen Street Station every 20 minutes for the 85-minute journey to Dunfermline Town.

By Car from Edinburgh to Dunfermline, cross the Forth Bridge and follow the signs for the M90 and A823. The total distance is 17 miles.

By Car from Glasgow, take the A814, A8, M8, M80, A985, and A994 roadways into the town. The total distance is 40 miles.

PRACTICALITIES:

The local **Tourist Information Centre** is at 1 High Street, ☎ (01383) 720-999, **W**: standrews.com. As there isn't a direct bus service to the local attractions from the train station, for this particular daytrip fine weather and a stout pair of walking shoes is essential — having said that, all the attractions are only a 15-minute walk away.

FOOD AND DRINK:

Abbots House Heritage Centre Coffee Shop (Maygate, inside the Heritage Centre) Serves light snacks — homemade soup, coffee, salads, etc. ☎ (01383) 733-266. £

Chalmers (5 Chalmers Street, near St. Margaret's Cave) Coffee house and restaurant, serves Scottish and French cuisine. ☎ (01383) 724-327. £ and ££

McDonalds Fast Food Restaurant (106 High Street) For those with children (or not) — the famous fast food restaurant. £

SUGGESTED TOUR:

Circled numbers correspond to numbers on the map.

From the **Train Station** ❶, follow the map across the bridge and onto Comely Park and Priory Lane. Follow the Lane around onto Moodie Street where you will find the **Andrew Carnegie Birthplace Museum** ❷. This is the cottage where Andrew Carnegie was born during 1835. The son of a jacquard loom weaver, Andrew entered into self-education, which following his emigration to America in 1848 helped make his millions in the steel industry. Carnegie never forgot his roots and in 1903 he founded the Carnegie Dunfermline Trust because, in his own words, he wanted "to bring into the monotonous lives of toiling masses of Dunfermline, more sweetness and light." The trust was responsible for some marvellous work, which is explained in greater detail by the museum. ☎ (01383) 724-302. Open April–Oct., Mon.–Sat. 11–5, Sun. 2–5. £2.

Back to the map, stroll along Monastery Street and past the splendid ruins of **Dunfermline Palace** ❸. Follow the road around until you reach the Abbey, which is situated on St.Catherine's Wynd and St. Margaret Street. The Abbey as it stands today consists of two churches — the **Nave** ❹ of the medieval monastic church erected by David I, the son of Margaret and dedicated in 1150 — and the modern-day parish **Abbey Church** ❺, dedicated in 1821, which is the final resting place of the remains of King Robert the Bruce. *Open daily April–Oct. at the usual worshipping times. Free. The **Dunfermline Abbey Nave and Palace Visitor Centre** ❹, ☎ (01383) 739-026, is open April–Oct., Mon.–Sat. 9.30–6.30. £2.*

Now, at this point, you can either turn left on St. Catherine's Wynd and head for the peace and tranquillity of Pittencrieff Park and the **House Museum** ❻, or turn right onto Maygate to visit the **Abbot House Heritage Centre** ❼. Within a 14th- to 16th-century historic house you will find the Heritage Centre, Café, and shop. See 1,000 years of Fife's history from the Picts (ancient people of Northern Britain) to the present day. ☎ *(01383) 733-266, **W**: abbothouse.co.uk. Open all year, daily 10–5. Adults £3, seniors £2. Children free if accompanied by an adult, otherwise charged £1.25.*

A good little tip if you are visiting between April and October: buy a Saver Ticket for £5, which grants you admission to the Birthplace Museum, the Nave and Palace Visitor Centre, and the Abbot House.

On leaving Abbot House, turn left and walk towards Kirkgate, as indicated on the map. Keep following the road to the left until you reach Chalmers Street, where **St. Margaret's Cave** ❽ is located. The cave was originally on the banks of the Tower Burn — but it is now 86 steps below a municipal car park. It was used in the 11th century by Saint Margaret,

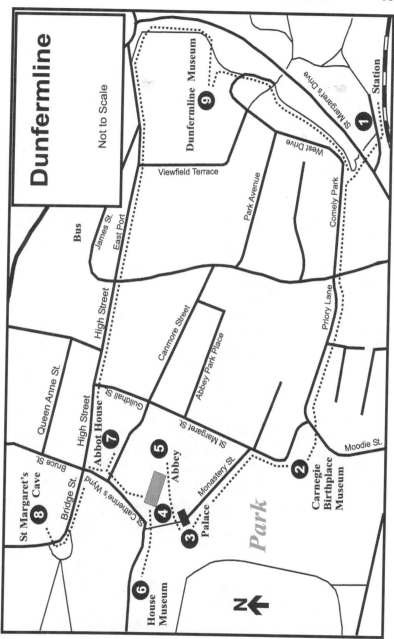

Dunfermline

Not to Scale

Queen of Scotland, to pray. ☎ *(01383) 313-838. Open Good Friday to the last weekend in Sept., 11–4. Free.*

Before heading back to the train station, but only if you have already telephoned the enquiry line 24 hours in advance to book, why not call into the **Dunfermline Museum** ❾. Just follow the map down High Street and East Port, then turn right onto Viewfield Terrace. Apart from being West Fife Museums Headquarters, the museum displays the history of Dunfermline and the linen and silk industries that were so important to the town from the early 19th to mid-20th centuries. ☎ *(01383) 313-838. Open all year, Mon.–Fri. by appointment. Free.*

You can return to the train station by following the map down West Drive and onto Comely Park.

Statue of Robert the Bruce at Stirling's Bannockburn

STIRLING

A Daytrip from Edinburgh or Glasgow

Stirling has been described as a "huge brooch clasping the Highlands and Lowlands together." Whoever held Stirling Castle, controlled the Scottish nation. Although the site was probably inhabited by Ancient Britons and possibly later by Romans and even, according to legend, by King Arthur, the earliest known record of a castle here dates from the 12th century. This was taken by the English in 1296 and recaptured by the great Scottish hero William Wallace after the Battle of Stirling Bridge.

From the ramparts of Stirling Castle, the sites of no less than 7 Scottish battles can be seen. It's hardly surprising then, given the history of the castle, that Stirling means "Place of Strife."

This trip can easily be combined in the same day with one to Linlithgow as they are both on the same rail line.

GETTING THERE:

Trains leave Edinburgh's Waverley Station every 25 minutes for the 50-minute run to Stirling.

Trains depart Glasgow's Queen Street Station frequently for the 40-minute ride to Stirling.

By Car from Edinburgh, take the A8, A71, M8, M9, and A91 roadways to Stirling, a distance of 39 miles.

By Car from Glasgow, the quickest route to Stirling is via the A8, M80, A80, and A91 roads. The total distance is 29 miles.

PRACTICALITIES:

There are two ports of call for information in Stirling, the first **Tourist Information Centre** is based at 41 Dumbarton Road, ☎ (08707) 200-620, and the second is located at the **Royal Burgh of Stirling Visitor Centre**, Castle Esplanade ☎ (08707) 200-622, **W**: visitscottishheartlands.org. Stirling's population is 37,000.

FOOD AND DRINK:

Sportsters Sports Bar and Diner (52–54 King St.) American food served in a lively bar and restaurant. ☎ (01786) 409-000. £ and ££

Golden Lion Milton Hotel (8 King St.) A full restaurant with Scottish food, set in an historic building. ☎ (0808) 100-5556, **W**: miltonhotels.com. £ and ££

Portcullis Hotel (Castle Wynd, near the castle) An old pub that goes well back into Stirling's history. Full restaurant and bar meals. ☎ (01786) 472-290. £ and ££

SUGGESTED TOUR:

Circled numbers correspond to numbers on the map.

Leave the **train station** ❶ and follow the map around the Thistle Shopping Centre, then turn right on King Street, soon becoming Spittal Street. The continuation of this, St. John Street, leads uphill past some old houses to the interesting **Church of the Holy Rood** ❻ and the Old Town Jail, which you can visit later.

For the moment, turn right on Castle Wynd and stroll uphill to **Argyll's Lodging** ❷. This is the finest and most complete surviving 17th-century townhouse in Scotland. It was built by Sir William Alexander, the Principal Secretary for Scotland and founder of the Scottish Colony of Nova Scotia in the New World. When this was ceded to the French in 1632, Sir William turned his interests southward and took possession of parts of Maine and all of Long Island, which he intended to rename Isle of Sterlinge. Fortunately for New Yorkers this did not happen and Sir William died heavily in debt. His coat-of-arms, above the main entrance, depicts an Indian, a beaver, and a mermaid. The house later passed to the Earl of Argyll, thus the name. ☎ *(01786) 431-319. Open April–Sept., daily 9:30–6; Oct.–March, daily 9:30–5. Adults £3, seniors £2.25, and children £1.20.*

Continue uphill to the **Royal Burgh of Stirling Visitor Centre** ❸, where you will discover the story of Royal Stirling from the Wars of Independence through life in the mediaeval burgh to the present day, with the aide of a multilingual audiovisual show. Also housed here is one of the Tourist Information Centres. ☎ *(01786) 462-517. Open April–June & Sept., daily 9:30–6; July–Aug., daily 9–6:30; Nov.–March, daily 9:30–5. Closed Dec. 25–26, Jan. 1. Free.*

Straight from here, you can wander up to:

*STIRLING CASTLE ❹, ☎ *(01786) 450-000. Open April–Sept., daily 9:30–6; Oct.–March, daily 9:30–5. Adults £6.50, seniors £5, children £2.*

The castle is mounted high on an old volcanic outcrop, with historical records showing that it was first built somewhere in between 1370 and 1750. The attractions include the restored Great Hall and a medieval kitchen reconstruction. Be sure to explore the battlements, especially Lady's Hole Terrace, which has some fabulous views.

Now follow the map down the steps and around the Back Walk to the **Guildhall** ❺, a lovely 17th-century almshouse for "decayed breithers," as unsuccessful merchants were called. Next to this is the **Church of the Holy Rood** ❻, a medieval church dating from the 15th century. This is where the infant James VI (son of Mary Queen of Scots and James I) was crowned in 1567 and where John Knox preached the sermon. ☎ *(01786) 475-275. Open*

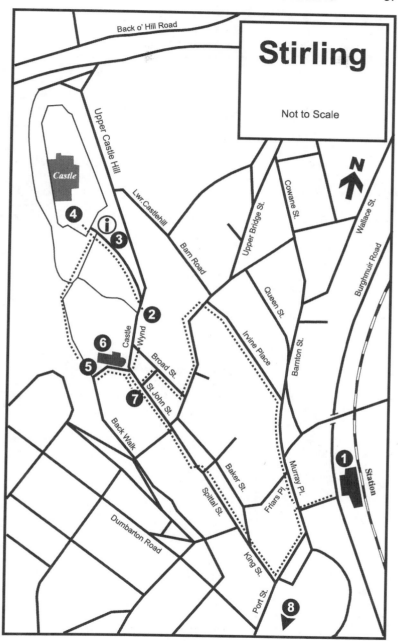

May–Sept., daily 10–5. Free.

Turning left behind the apse of the church brings you to the remains of a Renaissance palace, commissioned by the Earl of Mar in 1570. The building work was never completed and later became a workhouse for vagrants. During a siege of the castle in 1746 it was badly damaged, but the intriguing façade was left standing to serve as a windbreak.

Now stroll down St. John Street where you will find the **Old Town Jail** ❼. The jail paints a frightening picture of what it would have been like to be imprisoned in the 1800s. As you walk round the dingy corridors inspecting the cells, you can soak in the atmosphere of jail life — creaking hinges, a shuffle of feet, an eerie silence. Without warning you may even witness an attempted jailbreak! (Don't worry, it isn't a ghost, just an actor giving one of his "Living History Performances"). ☎ *(01786) 450-050. Open April–Sept., daily 9:30–6; Oct. and March, daily 9:30–5; Nov.–Feb., daily 9:30–4. Adults £3.30, children, seniors, and students £2.45, family ticket £9.15.* From here you can follow the map back to the train and bus stations.

ADDITIONAL ATTRACTION:

You should not visit Stirling without seeing the famous battlefield of Bannockburn. From the bus station, located next to the train station, catch the Guide Friday Bus, which runs every 40 minutes starting at 9.55 a.m. for the 2-mile journey to Glasgow Road, and the **Bannockburn Heritage Centre** ❽. The battle of Bannockburn was undoubtedly one of the most spectacular battles of the Scottish Wars of Independence. Although the struggle against the English was to continue for some 13 years more, the Scottish victory was of enormous importance as it secured the future of the throne for Robert Bruce, King of Scots. At the centre, attractions include an audiovisual presentation of the battle, an informative "Kingdom of the Scots" exhibition and a striking equestrian statue of King Robert. ☎ *(01786) 812-664. Site open all year. Heritage Centre and Shop open April–Oct., 10–5.30; March and Nov. to Dec. 23, 10.30–4. Last audiovisual half an hour before closing. Heritage Centre & Shop (incl. audiovisual): Adults £2.50, concessions £1.70, family £7.*

Dunbar

A Daytrip from Edinburgh or Glasgow

By now you may have been on a few daytrips, so perhaps you feel it's time to unwind a little and take life at a slower pace? Dunbar is a resort with a difference. It provides all the amenities of a seaside town combined with historic buildings and spectacular landscapes. It has an Old World charm that has been preserved since 1370.

The renowned conservationist John Muir (1838-1914) once said "...all my life I've been growing fonder and fonder of wild places and wild things. Fortunately, around my native town of Dunbar by the stormy North Sea, there was no lack of wildness though most of the land lay in smooth cultivation."

GETTING THERE:

Trains depart from Edinburgh's Waverley Station every 3 hours, with a journey time of just over 20 minutes.

Trains leave Glasgow's Queen Street Station every 2 hours and arrive at Dunbar's station 1 hour and 20 minutes later.

By Car from Edinburgh take the A1 and A1087 routes. The total distance is 29 miles and usually takes 44 minutes without any delays.

By Car from Glasgow, turn off at Junction A814 and then follow roads A8, M8, A720, A1, and A1087 to Dunbar. The total distance is 77 miles, with a journey time of 1 hour and 33 minutes.

PRACTICALITIES:

Choose a fine day to visit Dunbar, as you will be walking through the town to the harbour. As Dunbar is renowned for its high sunshine record, this shouldn't be a problem. The local **Tourist Information Centre** is situated at 143 High Street, ☎ (01368) 863-353, **W:** visitscotland.com

FOOD AND DRINK:

Country Café (High Street) Serves traditional Scottish fare. ☎ (01368) 863-604. £ and ££

Umbertos (High Street) Serves Italian and British cuisine. ☎ (01368) 862-354. ££ and £££

Smiths & The Tasty Bite (High Street) Local bakers with adjoining café serving cakes, scones, teas and coffees. ☎ (01368) 862719. £

Central Café (West Port, just off High Street) Award-winning fish and chip shop with sit-in facilities. ☎ (01368) 863-755. £

SUGGESTED TOUR:
Circled numbers correspond to numbers on the map.

Leave the **train station** ❶ and follow the map past the Bowling Club and onto High Street. This is the main shopping street in Dunbar, so take your time and perhaps pop into a shop that takes your fancy — it costs nothing to browse. A little farther on, on the corner of Silver Street and High Street, you will come across the **Dunbar Town House Museum** ❷. Dating from around 1620, this is Dunbar's oldest building. Now home to an archaeology and local history centre, its hands-on collections include 20th-century toys, games, clothes, music, and entertainment. You can also test your own skills as an archaeologist by planning and drawing an excavation of a real site, then check out your findings with fact. ☎ *(01368) 863-734*, **W**: *dunbarmuseum.org. Open daily April–Oct., 12.30–4.30. Admission is free.*

Follow the map along High Street, past West Port until you reach the **John Muir Birthplace** ❸. John Muir, born in 1838, is known as the founding father of the National Parks movement in the USA. His boyhood was spent in Dunbar, but he and his family emigrated to America in 1849. The house where he was born has now been developed into a museum and centre recalling the story of Muir and the importance of his conservation message. ☎ *(01368) 860-187. Open April–July, Mon.–Sat., 11–1 and 2–5; Sun. 2–5. Admission free.*

Follow the map to the harbours, **Cromwell** and **Victoria** ❹. By the 17th century Dunbar became an important fishing port. In 1655 the town's small quay was severely damaged by a storm, so Cromwell's government was asked to pay £300 towards building a pier and harbour. It was duly named Cromwell's Harbour. By 1839 many new industries had developed, such as shipbuilding, sail cloth and cordage manufacturing, herring curing, and soap making. Due to the influx of these new businesses, a second harbour had to be built. They named the harbour Victoria after the reigning queen.

Not too far away, you will find the ruins of the **Castle** ❺. Although the castle is not much to look at now, in the very early period of the Christian era it emerged as a powerful fortress. The castle's location on one of the main routes between England and Scotland made it a desirable strategic asset for any ruler.

In 1214 King John of England invaded Scotland and seized Dunbar Castle. During his rule he wasted the surrounding countryside before returning home. After that Edward I decided to invade Scotland in 1296, assisted by the eighth Earl of Dunbar. The person who thwarted their plans was "Black Aggie," Agnes the Countess of Dunbar, who secured possession of the castle and gave it back to the Scots. The next 37 years saw

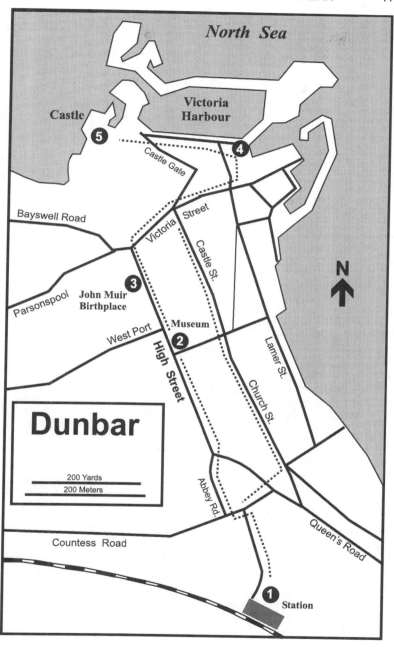

North Sea

Castle

Victoria Harbour

⑤

Castle Gate

④

Bayswell Road

Victoria Street

Castle St.

③

John Muir Birthplace

Parsonspool

West Port

Museum

②

High Street

Lamer St.

Church St.

Dunbar

200 Yards
200 Meters

Abbey Rd.

Queen's Road

Countess Road

① Station

the castle demolished and rebuilt by Edward III, who forced the ninth Earl of Dunbar to rebuild it at his own expense and sent English troops to garrison it.

Follow the map down Castle Street and Church Street, back to your starting point at the train station.

Ruins of St. Andrews Cathedral

St. Andrews

A Daytrip from Edinburgh or Glasgow

On May 14 1754, twenty-two "Gentlemen of honour, skilful in the ancient and healthful exercise of Golf," founded the Royal and Ancient Golf Club of St. Andrews — which is the world's most celebrated golf course.

St. Andrews is a picturesque Royal Burgh at the centre of the golf world and boasts several fine courses, including the famed Old Course, beloved of champions past and present.

The Golfing Mecca is renowned for more than the game it gave the world — overlooking the sea but now standing in ruin, St. Andrews Castle is a lasting epitaph of a distant past. Founded in 1200, the castle was the dramatic wave-swept backdrop of many of the bloodiest episodes of the Reformation. Another building left in ruin is that of St. Andrews Cathedral, although it is still possible to this day to climb the daunting St.Rules Tower.

As the golf course is practically in the town and the public footpaths cut right through it, you can follow a round of golf from start to finish — even if you're not a player.

GETTING THERE:

Trains marked for Dundee leave **Edinburgh's** Waverley Station at hourly intervals for the 95-minute journey to Leuchars, the nearest station to St. Andrews. From there catch a bus or taxi into St. Andrews, a distance of 5 miles.

Trains from **Glasgow's** Queen Street Station via Edinburgh's Waverley Station, will arrive in Leuchars after a 2-1/4-hour journey.

By Car from Edinburgh, take the routes A8, A90, A91, and A915 to St. Andrews. The total distance is 55 miles.

By Car from Glasgow, take the A80, M80, M9, and A91 routes. The total distance is 74 miles.

PRACTICALITIES:

The local **Tourist Information Centre** is situated at 70 Market Street. ☎ (01334) 472-021, **W**: visit-standrews.co.uk. Taxi ranks are at the Bus Station on City Road and outside the Holy Trinity Church.

If arriving by car, watch out for St. Andrews town centre's peculiar "voucher parking system." To be able to park up to 2 hours, you have to buy 80-pence vouchers from participating shops.

The open-top bus runs from May 25 to October 1 — starting point is in Church Street.

FOOD AND DRINK:

Russell Hotel (26 The Scores, near to the Golf Course) Bar food and restaurant, serving Scottish and International dishes. ☎ (01334) 473-447. £ and ££

St. Andrews Golf Hotel (40 The Scores) Bistro food and à la carte restaurant. ☎ (01334) 472-611, **W**: standrews-golf-co.uk. £ and ££

North Point Café (24 North Street, near to the castle, harbour, and cathedral) Sandwiches and daily changing specials. Extensive coffee menu. ☎ (01334) 850-004. £

La Posada (St. Mary's Place) Mexican restaurant. Magician on Wednesday evenings. ☎ (01334) 470-500. ££

SUGGESTED TOUR:

Circled numbers correspond to numbers on the map.

Leave the **bus station** ❶ and follow City Road and Golf Place to the **Royal and Ancient Golf Club** ❷. In 1457 James II banned the game of golf because he feared men would stop practising archery and be unable to defend his kingdom, but thankfully this did not see the end of golf, just its beginning. The famous clubhouse is not open to visitors, and women guests are welcome only on St. Andrews Day. Luckily, if you do feel the urge to have a game there are five other courses in town, and plenty of golf shops that hire clubs out to visitors. Just opposite the Golf Club, you will find the:

*BRITISH GOLF MUSEUM ❸. Bruce Embankment, ☎ (01334) 460-046, **W**: britishgolfmuseum.co.uk. *Open Easter to mid-Oct., daily 9.30–5.30; mid-Oct. to Easter, Thurs.–Mon. 11–3. Adult £3.75, child £1.50, senior citizens £2.75, family £9.50.*

The Golf Museum traces the history of British golf from the Middle Ages to the present day. You can discover how a golf ball is made as well as sharing the experiences of great players of the past.

Now walk easterly down The Scores until you reach the Castle Visitor Centre and:

ST. ANDREWS CASTLE ❹, ☎ (01334) 477-196. *Open April–Sept., daily 9.30–6; Oct.–March, daily 9.30–4. Adult £2.80, child £1, seniors £2.*

The castle started life in 1200 as a bishop's palace, but before it turned into ruins it was used as a prison for religious reformers. Though in ruin, the castle is quite fascinating and steeped in historical importance. Be sure to see the strange bottle dungeon, hollowed out of solid rock, and the Kitchen Tower. Agile travellers may want to probe the Mine and Counter Mine, used in the 16th-century taking of the castle.

A path from here leads to the quaint little **Harbour** ❺, one of the old-

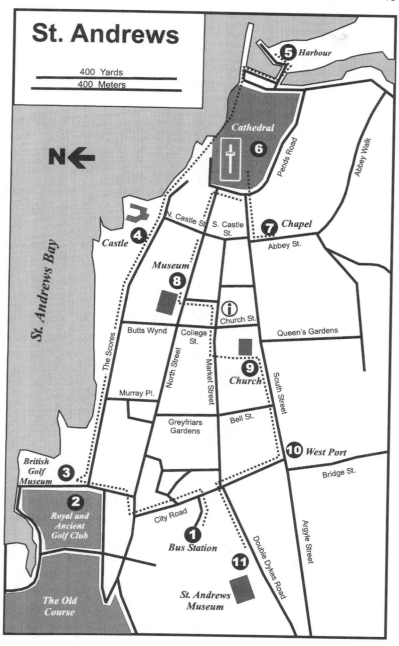

St. Andrews

400 Yards
400 Meters

N

5 Harbour

Cathedral

6

Pends Road

Abbey Walk

Castle **4**

N. Castle St.

S. Castle St.

7 *Chapel*

Abbey St.

Museum

8

The Scores

Butts Wynd

College St.

i Church St.

Queen's Gardens

North Street

Market Street

9

Church

South Street

Murray Pl.

Greyfriars Gardens

Bell St.

10 *West Port*

Bridge St.

British Golf Museum **3**

2

Royal and Ancient Golf Club

City Road

1

Bus Station

11

St. Andrews Museum

Double Dykes Road

Argyle Street

The Old Course

St. Andrews Bay

est in Scotland. Celtic Monks built the church of St. Mary on The Rock, whose remains stand near to the harbour.

Follow the map to:

*ST. ANDREWS CATHEDRAL and ST. RULE'S TOWER ❻, The Pends. ☎ (01334) 472-563. *Open April–Sept., daily 9.30–6.30; Oct.–March, Mon.–Sat. 9.30–4.30, Sun. 2–4.30. Adult £2, child £0.75, seniors £1.50.*

Though the cathedral is now in ruin, the remains still impress upon you the scale of what was once the largest cathedral in Scotland. Close to the southeast angle stands St. Rule's Tower. This 100-foot-high tower has survived intact and can still be climbed to this very day for a magnificent view of the town.

The route now leads past The Pends, a 14th-century vaulted gate-house, to the priory precinct. Just down South Street stands the hand-some 16th-century Queen Mary's House, which according to tradition sheltered Mary, Queen of Scots in 1563. The house is open to the public every year on St. Andrews day, 2 to 4 p.m. Continue around to **St. Leonard's Chapel ❼**, built in 1512 for St. Leonard's College and now well restored. Visitors may look around the college, but by appointment only.

Retrace your steps and turn left on North Street. The first group of buildings on the left is known as Dean's Court, dating from the 16th and 17th centuries and now used as a student residence. A few steps beyond is the small **Preservation Trust Museum**. The Trust has created a fascinating museum in an old fisherman's cottage near the cathedral. The ground floor concentrates on two old shops, a chemist and a grocer's shop, dating from 1837. Upstairs houses a changing series of exhibitions on a variety of subjects. *12 North St.* ☎ *(01334) 477-629. Open daily, 2–5 during Easter, then from May–Sept. and on St. Andrews Week. Free, although donations are welcome.*

The entrance arch to **St. Salvator's College ❽** is just down North Street. Go inside and examine this central part of the ancient university. The oldest structure, dating from 1450, is the Chapel. Tours of the university are offered from early July to mid-Sept., at 10.30 and 2.30. They start at the porter's lodge in the quadrangle.

Now follow the map through Market St. with its interesting 19th-century fountain. The very narrow Logie's Lane leads to Church Square and then onto South Street, where across the way is **Holy Trinity Church ❾**, founded in 1410 but considerably altered since. It was here that John Knox preached his first sermon in public. Surprisingly, there is an intricate monument to a Catholic archbishop who was brutally murdered nearby in 1679.

Continue down South Street, past the ruins of Blackfriars Chapel to the **West Port ❿**. Dating from 1589, it is the only fortified gateway in Scotland to survive. Pass through it and turn right onto City Road. Then turn left at the mini-roundabout and follow the map along Double Dykes

Road to **St. Andrews Museum** ⓫. The museum is located in Kinburn Park and was built as a private residence in 1855 and named after a Crimean battle of the same year. Kinburn Castle became home to St. Andrews Museum in 1991 and is now owned and operated by Fife Council. The museum explores St. Andrews' heritage from medieval times right through to the 20th century, and offers imaginative displays using interesting artifacts to tell the town's story through the ages. Along with a changing programme of temporary exhibitions on a wide variety of topics, the museum is host to lectures and children activities. When you have finished absorbing all that information, you can pop into the museum's café for a light meal and a cup of tea or coffee. ☎ *(01334) 412-690. Open April–Sept., daily 10–5; Oct.–March, Mon.–Fri. 10:30–4, Sat.–Sun. 12:30–5. Free.*

Retrace your steps back along Double Dykes Road, turn left at the second roundabout and this will bring you back to the bus station.

Trip 7

Dundee

A Daytrip from Edinburgh or Glasgow

Just as you're about to sit down to your breakfast of toast and marmalade, please give a thought to the City of Dundee. For it was Dundonian Janet Keiller who in 1797 invented a recipe for marmalade after trying to find a use for a load of bitter Seville oranges.

The fourth city of Scotland, Dundee has known prosperity since the 12th century, when flax, linen, and wool became a flourishing trade. Textiles were the major industries — most importantly linen, and the growth was so strong that by the time of the American War of Independence, Dundee had become the principal centre for the production of sailcloth in Europe.

This fascinating city is also the homeport of the Antarctic exploration vessel, the Royal Research *Discovery*, which took the ill-fated Captain Robert Scott and his crew on their first voyage to Antarctica in 1901.

During the year, Dundee is host to some major events, such as the Maritime Battle re-enactment, a model railway exhibition, many festivals and open-air fairs.

GETTING THERE:

Trains leave Edinburgh's Waverley Station every hour for the 75-minute run.

Trains depart Glasgow's Queen Street Station every hour for the 1-1/2-hour ride to Dundee.

By Car from Edinburgh, follow the M8, A8, and A90 roads to Dundee, a distance of 61 miles.

By Car from Glasgow, the quickest route to Dundee is to turn off at Junction A814 and then follow the road signs for A8, A80, A85, and M90. The total distance is 82 miles.

PRACTICALITIES:

The local **Tourist Information Centre** is situated at 21 Castle Street, ☎ (01382) 527-527, **W**: angusanddundee.co.uk. Dundee has a population of 143,000.

FOOD AND DRINK:

Cornerstone Coffee House Ltd. (118 Nethergate) Coffees, teas, snacks, lunches. ☎ (01382) 202-121. £

Pizza Express (31A Albert Square) Live music in bar and restaurant. A contemporary menu. ☎ (01382) 226-677. £ to ££

Nosey Parkers (160 Nethergate) Bistro and café bar. Contemporary and exotic menu. ☎ (01382) 322-515. ££ to £££

SUGGESTED TOUR:

Circled numbers correspond to numbers on the map.

Your starting point is **Dundee Train Station ❶**. Turn right and head towards the quay, which is not that far away. You can't miss it because moored there is the:

*RRS *DISCOVERY* and DISCOVERY POINT ❷. ☎ (01382) 201-245, **W**: rrsdiscovery.com. *Open April–Oct., Mon.–Sat. 10–5, Sun. 11–5; Nov.–March, Mon.–Sat. 10–4, Sun. 11–4. Closed Dec. 25, Jan. 1–2. Adults £5.95, seniors/concessions/students £4.45, child £3.85, and family (2 adults & 2 children) £17.*

This is a brilliant opportunity to travel back in time to 1901 and experience the life of the polar hero — Captain Scott.

Re-trace your steps back towards the train station. Keep on the left-hand side and then turn left down Green Market, walking straight to the end. Here you will find:

*SENSATION ❸. ☎ (01382) 228-800, **W**: sensation.org.uk. *Open daily from 10 a.m. Adults £5, children and concessions £3.50.*

This is a unique, hands-on attraction, based on senses. It even has an Internet area, café, and souvenir shop.

Talking of souvenirs, if you fancy a bit of shopping you must visit **Overgate ❹**. *City Square, Nethergate,* ☎ *(01382) 314-201. Open daily.* Follow the map back along Green Market and turn left onto West Marketgait. Over the road you will see a two-storey, glass-fronted mall, housing every type of commodity you can imagine - excellent for the discerning shopper.

Next door to the new Overgate stands Scotland's highest surviving tower, the **Old Steeple ❺**. *Nethergate,* ☎ *(01382) 206-790.* Guided tours give an insight to Dundee's past, today's bell-ringing chamber, and working ancient belfry. Also, admire the breathtaking views from the top of the tower.

Follow the map on to High Street, then turn left onto Reform Street. Directly at the bottom of this street is Albert Square — here you will find:

*McMANUS GALLERIES ❻, Albert Square. ☎ (01382) 432-084, **W**: dun deecity.gov.uk. *Open Mon.–Sat. 10:30–5 p.m., closing at 7 on Thurs. Closed Dec. 25–26, Jan. 1–2. Free. Café. Shops.*

This museum covers art, history, and the environment. It contains col-

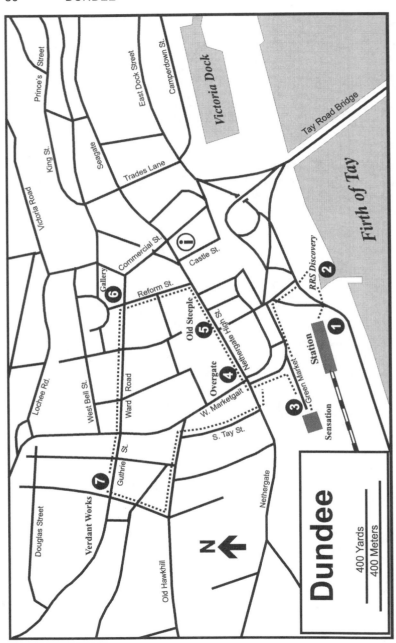

lections of local history, archaeology, decorative arts, and material from ancient Egypt; all which is housed in a fine Victorian Gothic building. For the animal lovers amongst you, there is a wide range of local birds and mammals, including the famous Tay Whale on display. You could easily spend the majority of your daytrip visiting this particular museum!

Before returning to the train station, why not pop in at the **Verdant Works** ❼. This attraction remains a working jute mill, a fascinating industrial museum where you can experience how the people of Dundee really had to live over a century ago. Definitely well worth a visit. *West Hendersons Wynd,* ☎ *(01382) 225282.* To get to the museum on leaving the McManus Galleries, turn right onto Ward Road. Walk along, crossing over West Marketgait and onto Guthrie Street. Walk to the end where you will find Verdant Works. *Open April–Oct., daily 10–5. During Nov.–March you will have to phone for winter opening times. Adults £5.95, seniors/concessions £4.45, child £3.85, family of 4 £17.*

To return to the train station, turn right onto Horsewater Hunter, left down Southstay Street, left again at Nethergate, and finally right onto West Marketgait. Continue walking until you reach your starting point, the train station.

Blair Atholl

A Daytrip from Edinburgh or Glasgow

Nestled quietly in the Central Highlands is the whitewashed and majestic Blair Castle. When Queen Victoria visited here in 1844, she was so captivated by the 200 Athollmen, who formed the royal bodyguard, that she presented them with regimental colours. Now known as the Atholl Highlanders, they form Europe's only private army.

This 1746 castle opens 30 rooms to visitors, all of which are filled with a sweeping history of Scottish aristocratic life from the 16th century to the present, a treat not to be missed by anyone visiting Scotland.

In addition to the castle, there are a few nice attractions in the village itself as well as some very interesting country walks that can be taken, using a guide map available from the castle.

GETTING THERE:

Trains depart Edinburgh's Waverley Station every 2 hours for the 2-hour ride to Blair Atholl.

Trains leave Glasgow's Queen Street Station every 2 hours for the 2-hour journey.

By Car from Edinburgh, take the A90 across the Forth Bridge (toll), the M90, and then the A9 to Blair Atholl. The total distance is 77 miles.

By Car from Glasgow take the A8, M80, A80, and A9 to Blair Atholl. The total distance is 95 miles.

PRACTICALITIES:

The nearest **Tourist Information Centre** to Blair Atholl is at Pitlochry, 22 Atholl Road, ☎ (01796) 472-215 / 472751, **W**: perthshire.co.uk.

FOOD AND DRINK:

Atholl Arms Hotel (near the train station) A country inn with a pub and restaurant. ☎ (01796) 481-025. £ and ££

Castle Restaurant (located in the castle itself) An attractive self-service cafeteria with good food. ☎ (01796) 481-207. £

SUGGESTED TOUR:

Circled numbers correspond to numbers on the map.

Leave the **train station** ❶ and follow the map to the castle, a distance of less than a mile, travelling through parkland most of the way. Those

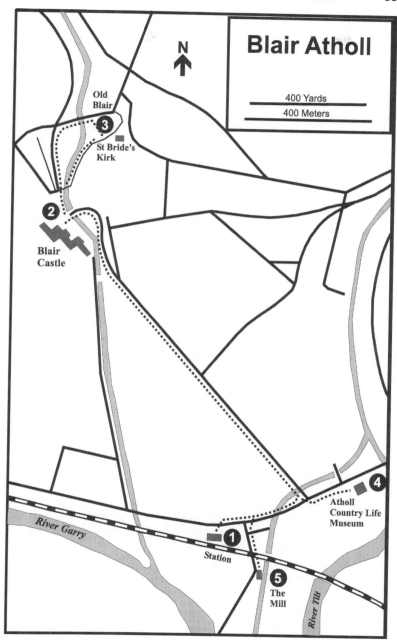

Blair Atholl

400 Yards
400 Meters

Old Blair

St Bride's Kirk

Blair Castle

Atholl Country Life Museum

River Garry

Station

The Mill

River Tilt

with cars can, of course, drive there.

BLAIR CASTLE ❷. ☎ (01796) 481-207, **W**: blair-castle.co.uk. *Open late March–Oct., daily 10–6. Castle and Grounds: Adult £6.25, child £4, concession £5.25, disabled £2, family £18.*

In 1269, while the Earl of Atholl was away in England for an extended period, a neighbour, John Comyn, started to build a castle on the earl's land. Upon Atholl's return, he complained to King Alexander III, got his land back and incorporated the usurping tower into his own castle. It is still there, called **Comyn's Tower**.

During the 18th century, Blair Castle had been completely altered and lowered in order to make into a mansion, but in 1872 architect David Bryce remodelled and recastellated the building. It contains an enormous wealth of furniture and decorative arts from the 16th century onwards, as well as armour, tapestries, china, paintings and many historical artefacts. A well-illustrated guide book, describing everything of interest in great detail, can be obtained at the entrance of the castle.

The grounds of the castle is a great place for a short **country stroll**. One particularly attractive route is shown on the map in this book, while a trail map covering a larger area is available.

Head north from the castle, passing through a gate and across the little stream. The path leads to the romantic ruins of **St.Bride's Kirk** and its churchyard. Close to this area are the bare remains of **Old Blair ❸**, dating from before the moving of the village to its present site during the 18th century.

Return to town and the:

*ATHOLL COUNTRY LIFE MUSEUM ❹, ☎ (01796) 481-232. *Open Easter and end of May–June and mid-Sept. to mid-Oct., daily 1.30–5 p.m.; July, Aug. to mid-Sept., Mon.–Fri. 10–5, Sat.–Sun. 1:30–5. Adults £3, school children £1.*

This museum holds a unique and lively display of working life in Atholl. There are some fascinating artefacts from days gone by, including farm implements and tools, the old post office, an 1880's kitchen, and local wild flower photographs.

Heading back to the station, try and visit **The Mill ❺**. This is a restored working water-driven mill, bakery, café, and flour and oat suppliers. ☎ *(01796) 481-321. Open Easter–Oct., Mon.–Sat. 10–5:30, Sun. noon–5:30.*

From here it is only a few steps back to the station.

Aberdeen

A Daytrip from Edinburgh or Glasgow

This is the granite or silver city, so called because of its traditional industries, not only in granite quarrying, but also in fishing, paper making, and textiles. Situated on the North Sea coast at the mouth of the rivers Don and Dee, this port is Scotland's third-largest town in terms of population. The North Sea oil boom of the 1970's brought new importance and prosperity to the city.

The architecture of Aberdeen is both striking and impressive. The Aberdonians are extremely proud of the mile-long and 70-foot-wide granite-faced buildings which line the city's Union Street, for it represents a neo-classical era long gone but not forgotten.

GETTING THERE:

Trains depart Edinburgh's Waverley Station at regular intervals for the 2-1/2-hour journey.

Trains leave Glasgow's Queen Street Station frequently for the 2-1/2-hour ride to Aberdeen Station.

By Car from Edinburgh take the M8, A8 and A90 routes to Aberdeen. The total distance is 125 miles.

By Car from Glasgow follow the A77, M80, M90, and A90 routes. The total distance is 147 miles.

PRACTICALITIES:

The local **Tourist Information Centre** is based in Provost Ross's House, Shiprow. ☎ (01224) 288-828, **W**: castlesandwhisky.com

FOOD AND DRINK:

The Coffee Club (363 Union St.) Light menu—coffee, cakes, sandwiches. £

The Howff (365 Union St.) Serves bar food on Sunday—all-day breakfast for just £4. £

Yangtze River Chinese Restaurant (8 Bridge St.) Established over 34 years, serves a wide variety of Chinese dishes. On Thursday and Fridays buffet lunches and dinners are served. £ and ££

Harry Ramsden's (Esplanade, Sea Beach, close to the City Centre) Famous fish-and-chip take-away and restaurant. £ and ££

SUGGESTED TOUR:

Circled numbers correspond to numbers on the map.

Leave the **train station** ❶ and follow the map along Guild Street, turning right onto Market Street. Here you will find **Aberdeen Harbour** ❷ and the Fish Market. The Fish market used to be open to visitors, but now only the fish merchants have access to this part of the dock. However, you will still have the opportunity of watching, close-up, ships from all over the world coming and going, and carrying on with their daily business. The harbour has continually evolved since the 12th century and has been extensively rebuilt during the past two decades, with completely up-to-date facilities today.

Your seafaring mood can be continued by following the map to the nearby **Maritime Museum** ❸, situated on the old cobbled street of Shiprow. The museum has recently been much extended, incorporating Provost Ross's House, the third oldest building in Aberdeen, constructed in 1593. The £4 million development highlights the drama of the North Sea industries using models, paintings, touch-screen consoles, and an audiovisual theatre. *Open Mon.–Fri. 10–5, Sat. noon–3. Free.*

A few more steps up Shiprow will bring you to Castlegate and the 17th-century **Mercat Cross** ❹, a small stone shelter in the middle of the open square, embellished with portraits of the Scottish sovereigns from James I to James VII. Opposite the cross on Broad Street stands the castellated **Town House**, incorporating the 17th-century tower of Tolbooth, a former jail outside of which public executions took place until 1867.

Americans may be interested in strolling up King Street to **St. Andrew's Cathedral** ❺, the Mother Church of the Episcopal Communion in America, where the first bishop of the United States was consecrated in 1784. Note the coats of arms of the American States above the north aisle.

Now retrace your steps back to Broad Street to the Neo-Gothic **Marischal College** ❻, the second-largest granite building in the world, founded in 1593. The college also houses an interesting **Anthropological Museum**, which covers civilisations throughout the world from ancient to modern times, with a focus on Scotland. *Open Mon.–Fri. 10–5. Free.*

You are ready to explore **Old Aberdeen**, until 1891 an independent burgh, which lies one-and-a-half miles to the north. Using a number 20 bus, or any bus going north on Kings Street, it will only take you 15 minutes to get to Old Aberdeen.

Ask the bus driver to drop you off at **King's College Chapel** ❼, which was founded by the Bishop William Elphinstone in 1495. The chapel is diminutive but most impressive with the original carved stalls lining the chancel and nave, and an intricately-carved rood screen. Adjacent is the **King's College Visitor Centre**, which presents 500 years of the University's history.

Following the map along High Street and then onto the cobbled Chanonry, you will come to **St. Machar's Cathedral** ❽, an extremely attractive stone church dating from 1130. It is named after the saint who first

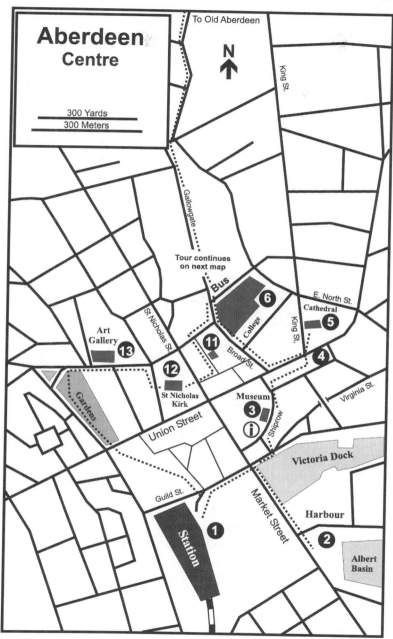

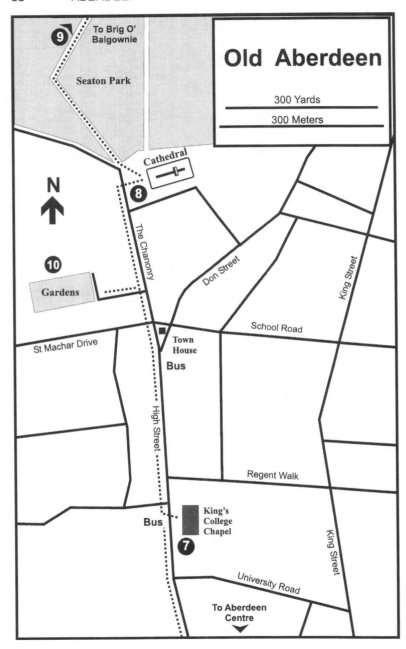

St. Machar's Cathedral in Old Aberdeen

Aberdeen Harbour

brought Christianity to this area in the 6th century and established a chapel on this site. Enter from the south porch to examine the renowned heraldic ceiling, emblazoned with the shields of 16th-century leaders.

St. Machars sits on the edge of Seaton Park, where you will find the 13th-century **Brig O' Balgownie** ❾, Scotland's oldest medieval bridge, which was the only means of crossing the River Don until the 19th century.

On the way back, be sure to visit the **Cruikshank Botanical Gardens** ❿ with its extensive collection of rare plants, operated by the university. You can catch the number 20 bus back to the city centre from the Town House.

Hop off the bus at **Marischal College** ❻ and head for **Provost Skene's House** ⓫, which is situated between Broad Street and Flour Mill Lane. This is a restored domestic building dating from 1545, which is now a museum of civic life, with furnished period rooms and a painted chapel. *Open Mon.–Sat. 10–5, Sun. 1–4. Free.*

The route now leads to **St.Nicholas Kirk** ⓬, in its tranquil park-like setting. Once the largest parish church in Scotland, it dates back to the 12th and 15th centuries. The interior is well worth exploring, particularly the medieval crypt of the East Church, where witches were once imprisoned and which was later on used as a soup kitchen to feed Aberdeen's poor. *Open May–Sept., Mon.–Fri. noon–4, Sat. 1–3. All year round, visitors can also gain admittance 10–1 by ringing the bell at the office door.*

Just a short distance away, on Schoolhill, is the **Aberdeen Art Gallery** ⓭, which houses an excellent collection of 18th-through 20th-century art. Special exhibitions and events keep the place lively. *Open Mon.–Sat. 10–5, Sun. 2–5. Free.*

The best way back to the station is through the Union Terrace Gardens and the Trinity Shopping Centre.

Inverness and Loch Ness

A Daytrip from Inverness or Glasgow

S trategically positioned on the Caledonian Canal and the River Ness, the "Capital of the Highlands" is an important road and rail hub. Its 19th-century castle stands on the site of a medieval fortress. Through the centuries Inverness has been razed to the ground several times. Among the few tangible remnants of its past is the curious Ciacha-Cudainn, a stone on which the womenfolk used to set tubs of water filled from the river—according to legend, Inverness will prosper for as long as the stone remains in the city.

The quaint town of Drumnadrochit sits closely to the 754-feet-deep Loch Ness and is only a 23-minute bus ride from Inverness. Not only do you get a chance of catching a glimpse of the infamous "Nessie"—the resident monster of Loch Ness, but you can also pay a visit to the Loch Ness Exhibition Centre and Urquhart Castle.

The Highlands, brimming with wildlife, is a beautiful and peaceful place, so just enjoy the scenery around you and relax! Inverness would make an excellent base for visiting Loch Ness, Nairn, and Elgin.

GETTING THERE:

Trains leave Edinburgh's Waverley Station every 2 hours or so and takes 3-1/2 hours to arrive at Inverness Station.

Trains depart Glasgow's Queen Street Station at 2-hourly intervals and also takes 3-1/2 hours to arrive at Inverness Station.

By Car from Edinburgh, take the A8, A90, M90, A9, and A82 roads to Inverness and Loch Ness. The total distance to Inverness is 158 miles, and to Loch Ness just add an extra 15 miles.

By Car from Glasgow, take the A814, A8, M8, M90, A80, M80, M9, A9, and A82 route to Inverness and Loch Ness. The total distance to Inverness is 177 miles, and to Loch Ness 192 miles.

PRACTICALITIES:

This trip can be taken at any time, although some shops close for half day on Wednesday. The local **Tourist Information Centre** is based at Castle Wynd, next to the Castle, ☎ (01463) 234-353, **W**: visitscotland.org. **City Link,**

☎ (08705) 505-050, runs a bus service from Inverness to Loch Ness at regular intervals. The bus numbers are: 917, 918, and 919. The local population is about 45,000 in the city, plus another 60,000 in the surrounding districts.

FOOD AND DRINK:

Inverness has a wide selection of restaurants and pubs in all price ranges, including:

The Castle Restaurant (41–43 Castle Street, near the castle) Serving multi-cultural and traditional cuisine. ☎ (01463) 230-925. £ and ££

Blackfriars Pub (Academy Street, next to the station) Great selection of home-cooked bar meals. ☎ (01463) 233-881. £ and ££

The Italian Coffee Shop (Inglis Street, between the railway station and the High Street) Take out—sandwiches, soup, tea. £

SUGGESTED TOUR:

Circled numbers correspond to numbers on the map.

From the **Train Station** ❶ follow the map onto Strothers Lane, turn left, walk across Academy Street, Church Street, and then turn left to walk down Bank Street. Just before Ness Bridge, turn left onto Bridge Street. On your left-hand side, on the corner of Bridge Street and Church Street you will see a 16th-century steeple that belonged to the old jail. Virtually opposite the steeple, on the corner of Bridge Street and Castle Street, stands the 19th-century Gothic-style **Town House** ❷. Although the building is now used as local government offices, you can still have a little look around—nobody minds, really. Go inside and admire the ornate staircase.

From this point, you can see **Inverness Castle** ❸. The earliest known castle in Inverness was MacBeth's on the Crown Hill, where the murder of King Duncan is said to have taken place in 1039. Duncan's son, Malcolm of Canmore avenged his father's death by destroying MacBeth's castle, and in 1057 built another castle for himself on the present site, which today is known as Castle Hill.

Although there has been a castle in Inverness for many centuries, the present one is a relatively modern structure. It was erected in two parts in 1834 and 1846 and is used today as the Sheriff Court House and administrative offices. At the **Castle Garrison Encounter** you can journey back in time to 1745, enlist in the regiment, and meet some of its other characters live. Visits take about 40 minutes. *Open daily during the tourist season, 10.30–5.30. From 7 p.m. to 7.30 during June–Sept. a piper plays the bagpipes every evening.*

Take Castle Street, which winds its way up around the rear of the castle and past some pretty floral displays to get to the statue of Flora MacDonald, the heroine who smuggled "Bonnie" Prince Charlie (Charles Edward Stuart, the Young Pretender) to the Isle of Ulst, away from George II and his supporters.

Close by, on Castle Wynd you will find the **Tourist Information Centre and Inverness Museum and Art Gallery** ❹. A variety of exhibitions and

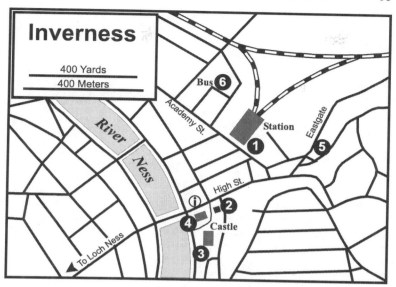

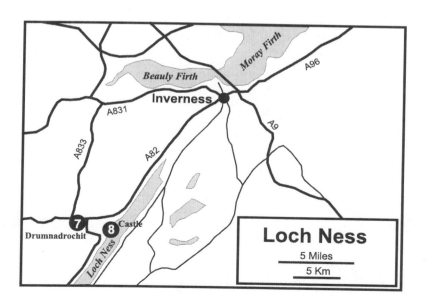

events are on display, ranging from archaeology and art to natural and local history. You can experience the newly opened "Hands on the Highlands." ☎ (01463) 237-114. *Open Mon.–Sat., 9–5. Free.*

Now retrace your steps back onto High Street and walk towards Eastgate. The next place we stop at is for the discerning shopper—**Eastgate Shopping Centre ❺**. Sometimes you need a bit of light relief after absorbing so much knowledge when visiting historic sites, and there's no better therapy than shopping—right girls? All under one roof, you can mooch around as many shops as possible and if your shoes start to pinch a bit, grab a cup of coffee and a sit down at Starbucks.

Once you are fully rejuvenated, follow the map back along Academy Street and Strothers Lane, turning left for the **Bus Station ❻**. Here you can catch either the 917, 918, or 919 bus to Loch Ness (Drumnadrochit). The **Loch Ness Monster** is infamous and has been immortalised forever in an American film starring Ted Danson. Since the first sighting of "Nessie" in 1933, tourists have flocked to this area in the Highlands in the hope of photographing the dinosaur-type mammal. We are going one step better by obtaining our information from the **Loch Ness Exhibition Centre ❼**. The centre is a huge complex incorporating an exhibition, hotel, restaurants, field centre, and cruises. ☎ *(01456) 450-573,* **W:** *loch-ness-scotland.com. Opening times vary throughout the year, but during peak season (July and Aug.) open from 9 a.m. to 8 p.m. Adults £5.95, students £4.50, seniors £4.50, children (7–16) £3.50, family ticket (2 Adults & 3 children 7–16) £14.95.*

Our last visit of the day is to **Urquhart Castle ❽**, one of the largest castles in Scotland and only 2 miles walking distance away from Drumnadrochit. Now owned by Historic Scotland, the castle sits on a rocky peninsula on the banks of Loch Ness. Some visitors with walking problems may find access to the castle difficult due to the uneven ground on which it was built. For those able to make it, it will be a fascinating visit. ☎ *(01456) 450-551,* **W:** *historic-scotland.net. Open April–Sept., daily 9:30–6:30; Oct.–March, daily 9:30–4:30. Adults £3.80, concessions £2.80, children £1.20.*

It's now time to stroll back to the little village of Drumnadrochit, where you can catch one of the many buses back to Inverness station (Train or Bus depending where you are off to next—Elgin, Nairn?).

Aviemore & the Cairngorms

A Daytrip from Edinburgh or Glasgow

One of the great things about Aviemore and the Cairngorms is that it is easy to get out and explore even if you haven't brought your own car. You can get about on foot, bike, by hired car, train, or bus. Aviemore is still a fairly small place, but its main attraction is its location as the nearest sizeable village to the ski slopes of the Cairngorm Mountains, the largest range in the British Isles—a mass of granite, flora and fauna 160 square miles in extent—and a popular destination in both summer and winter. Paths along the range take energetic walkers through moss, campions, and creeping rhododendrons; golden eagles, capercaillies, deer, ptarmigan and wildcats. It's a great place for walking, cycling, skiing, birding, fishing, golf and pony trekking—whatever your hobby or interest, there are plenty of good local services to help kit yourself out with the right gear.

Historically, Aviemore the village was initially a crofting area and then became a stopover for drovers driving livestock south to the lowlands. With the advent of the railways it became a railway junction with a line branching off from the main Inverness line through the distilling area of Speyside to Keith, where it joined the Inverness–Aberdeen line. A great deal of whisky used to pass through the village at one time.

Aviemore Village is centrally located for the Badenoch and Strathspey areas and can offer plenty of accommodation with fine views of the Cairngorms and lots of outdoor activities.

GETTING THERE:

Trains leave Edinburgh's Waverley Station every hour for the 3-hour journey to Aviemore. The earliest train leaves at 5.55 a.m. and arrives in Aviemore at 9.41 a.m. The last workable train leaves Aviemore at 5.28 p.m., arriving back in Edinburgh at 8.30 p.m.

Trains depart Glasgow's Queen Street station every couple of hours for the 3-hour ride to Aviemore. The earliest train leaves Glasgow at 7.08 a.m. and arrives in Aviemore at 9.41 a.m. The last workable train departs Aviemore Station at 5.28 p.m. and arrives back in Glasgow at 8.30 p.m.

Always check train timetables for last-minute changes to the service by phoning Railtrack on ☎ (08457) 484-950 or on the Web at **W**: rail.co.uk

By Car from Edinburgh take the A8, A90, M90, and A9 roads to Aviemore. The total distance is 125.5 miles, with a journey time of 3 hours; but always allow for delays.

By Car from Glasgow follow the A8, M8, M80,A80, and A9 signs to Aviemore. The total distance is 144 miles, with a travelling time of 3-1/2 hours.

PRACTICALITIES:

The total population of Aviemore is about 2,800. The **Tourist Information Centre** is on Grampian Road, ☎ (01479) 810-363, **W**: highland-freedom.com. In order to visit the Cairngorms, you need to take with you comfy, sturdy footwear—and sensible clothes—just in case of cold or adverse weather. Always "Be Prepared," as the Scouts would say.

FOOD AND DRINK:

Café Mambo (Unit 12/13 Grampion Road) Serves Tex-Mex and American food with a Scottish twist. Famous for hot chocolate, cocktails, and shooters. Children eat for just 99p. Food served from 12 noon until 9 p.m., although the café only closes late on. ☎ (01479) 812-475. £ and ££

Littlejohns Restaurant (LJ's) (Grampian Road) Serves a variety of traditional Scottish and English food. Open all year, daily 10–10. ☎ (01479) 811-633. £ and ££

Glenmore Visitor Centre Café (Glenmore) Serves light meals and snacks—cakes, tea, coffee, sandwiches etc. ☎ (01479) 861-220. £

SUGGESTED TOUR:

Circled numbers correspond to numbers on the map.

On leaving the **train station** ❶, our first visit has to be to the **Cairngorm Reindeer Centre** ❷, as we can make the daily visit to Britain's only reindeer herd free-ranging in their mountain habitat at 11 a.m. During the summer season, a special bus is in operation, running from the Aviemore Railway Station to the Cairngorm Mountains. Passengers just have to inform the driver of their destination, i.e. the Reindeer Centre and the bus will stop there. The ride only takes about 25 minutes and will only cost a few pence or even a pound. If you decide to visit outside the summer months, there is an alternative bus you can catch from the train station and that is the bus heading for Coylumbridge, which runs every 30 minutes.

As the little town of Coylumbridge is only 2.3 miles from Aviemore, it might be easier just to walk—it won't take you long to reach the Reindeer Centre, but be sure to wear some sturdy footwear. *Open Jan.–Dec. Daily visit at 11 a.m. and from Easter through September an extra visit at 2.30 p.m. Closed Dec. 25 and Jan. 1. Admission fee: £6 which includes being taken to feed the herd on the slopes of Cairn Gorm.* ☎ *(01479) 861-228.*

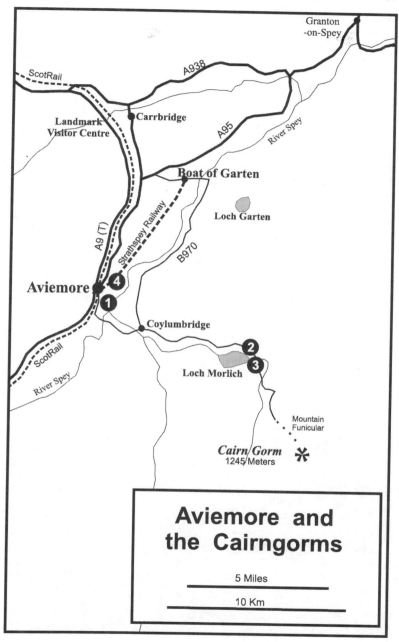

Granton
-on-Spey

ScotRail

A938

Landmark
Visitor Centre

Carrbridge

A95

River Spey

Boat of Garten

Loch Garten

Strathspey Railway

A9 (T)

B970

Aviemore

④

①

Coylumbridge

②

③

Loch Morlich

ScotRail

River Spey

Mountain
Funicular

Cairn Gorm
1245 Meters

✳

Aviemore and
the Cairngorms

5 Miles

10 Km

Next to the Reindeer Centre is our next visit, the **Glenmore Visitor Centre** ❸. The centre is geared towards families, but even those without kiddies will still enjoy the visit. The audiovisual explains about the past, present, and future of the native Caledonian pinewood at Glenmore. Also at the centre is a forest shop, café, and Ranger Service. *Open all year round, 9–5. Admission free.* ☎ *(01479) 861-220.*

While you are up the mountain why not have a relaxing walk in the **Glenmore Forest Park**, trying to spot as many of the habitual wildlife as possible.

It's now time to travel back down the mountain and catch a steam train. The **Strathspey Railway** ❹ is located at the Aviemore Station and sets off on a five-mile journey through scenery virtually unchanged in 100 years. Its destination is the Boat of Garten, a beautiful village, where during the summer months the bagpipes are played and many festivals are held. While you are travelling through the breathtaking Highland landscape, sit back and enjoy morning coffee, luncheon, or afternoon tea. The timetable for the steam train is:

Depart Aviemore:	10.40	12.00	2.00
Arrive B of G:	11.00	12.20	2.20
Depart B of G:	3.00	4.00	5.00
Arrive Aviemore:	3.20	4.20	5.20

Basic return fare: £6.00; with children, family, and senior rates available. ☎ *(01479) 810-725, W: trathspeyrailway.co.uk.*

If you take the last steam train at 5 p.m. back to Aviemore Station, you will be in time to catch the 5.28 p.m. train back to Edinburgh or Glasgow. Safe journey!

Highland Cattle at Aviemore

Nairn

A Daytrip from Inverness, Edinburgh or Glasgow

This town is a Victorian seaside resort, well known for its beautiful harbour, where boat owners offer trips out to see the resident bottlenose dolphins or simply to view Nairn from a different angle. Also, just a mile away from Nairn's East Beach is the Culbin Forest, a fantastic place for walking and seeing nature at its best.

For the historians among you, Nairn has a wonderful museum to visit—there is a lot to see and do, so we better get a move on! As Nairn is on the same train line as Inverness and only 16 minutes away by train, you could make the two trips on the same day.

GETTING THERE:

Trains leave Inverness Station every 15 minutes for the 16-minute ride to Nairn.

Trains leave Edinburgh's Waverley Station every half-hour for the 4-1/2 hour journey to Nairn.

Trains depart Glasgow's Queen Street Station every hour for the 4-hour trip to Nairn.

By Car from Inverness, take the B865, A82, A9, and A96 to Nairn. The total distance is 17 miles.

By Car from Edinburgh, take the A8, M90, A9, and A96 routes to Nairn. The total distance is 170 miles.

By Car from Glasgow follow the A8, A80, M80, M9, A9, and A96 road signs to Nairn. The total distance is 188 miles.

PRACTACALITIES:

The local **Tourist Information Centre** is situated on King Street, which is adjoined on to Academy Street. ☎ (01667) 452-753, **W**: caithness.org. Open 10–5, Monday to Saturday.

Nairn's population is approx. 11,030. Half-day early closing is on Wednesday. Many annual festivals are held in the town, including the Nairn Highland Games (August) and the Nairnshire Farming Society Show (July).

FOOD AND DRINK:

The Longhouse (8 Harbour Street) Coffee shop and licensed restaurant, serving a variety of fresh produce. ☎ (01667) 455-532. £ and ££

Chip Inn (8 Leopold Street, off Academy St.) Traditional fish-and-chips served everyday from April to October. ☎ (01667) 455-544. £

Jacko's Public House (44 Harbour Street) Serves pub grub 7 days a week. ☎ (01667) 452-743. £

SUGGESTED TOUR:

Circled numbers correspond to numbers on the map.

Leaving the **train station** ❶, walk along Chatten Drive and turn right onto Lodgehill Road. Take the third turning on your left, down Leopold Street and turn right again on to Academy Street. Just after the bus stop on the opposite side of the road, turn left into Viewfield Drive. Stroll along the tree-covered drive until you reach the:

*NAIRN MUSEUM ❷. ☎ (01667) 456-791. *Open Easter through Oct., Mon.–Sat. 10–4.30. Adults £1.50, child £0.50p, family ticket (2+2) £2.50, season ticket £7.* ♿.

The first thing you will see as you draw up close to the entrance of the museum is the immortalised bronze statue of Dr John Grigor (1814–86), who took a leading role in enhancing and improving the town, making Nairn "The Brighton of the North." The museum was started in 1858 when it received its first donation of a rattlesnake from "The American Settlement" — given by Miss Grant of Larkfield.

On a local level, the museum has a rich social history collection, and there is the opportunity to relive the hardship which was inherent to the town's key industries of fishing and farming. The Nairn Museum also has a fine collection of minerals and fossils from as far away as Greenland and Scandinavia.

Now retrace your steps and follow the map down Falconers Lane and turn left on to High Street. As you head towards Harbour Street, you will pass house number 79/79a on High St., reputed to be the oldest house in Nairn.

At the end of Harbour Street, you will reach the **Harbour** ❸. The "Old Harbour" was built in 1821 by Thomas Telford, the famous engineer who also built the Caledonian Canal. The present harbour was built in 1932 after much controversy. If you look out to sea from this point, you may see the resident family of bottlenose dolphins, swimming and jumping merrily in the Moray Firth.

Now from the East Beach you can walk the short one-mile distance to our last visit of the day — **Culbin Forest** ❹. This unique forest stretches for 8.7 miles along the southern shore of the Moray Firth and is a peaceful and relaxing way of spending your last hours in Nairn. The mature pine growing in the forest is home to roe deer, red squirrels, crossbills, badgers,

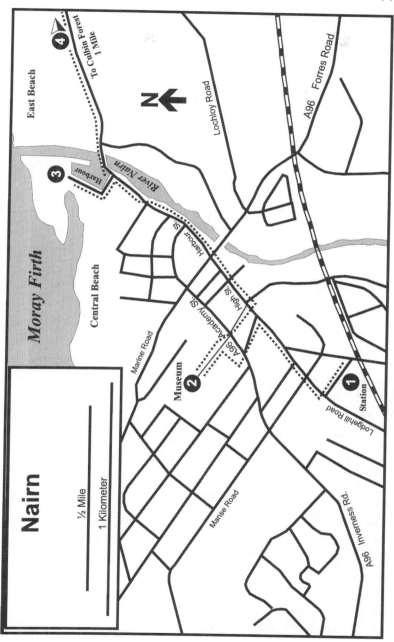

pine martins, frogs, newts, and dragonfly nymphs. Over 500 species of flowering plants, some rare, can be found here, and more than 130 species of lichen—for which Culbin is especially famous. ☎ *(01343) 820-223,* **W:** *forestry.gov.uk/culbin*

Follow the map back to the train station.

Elgin Town Scene

Elgin

A Daytrip from Inverness, Edinburgh or Glasgow

A n hour's drive from Inverness lies the beautiful commercial capital city of Moray—Elgin. Elgin is a very attractive and historical place, which was given the status of a Royal Burgh by Alexander II in the 13th century. You may decide to combine your visit to Inverness with a visit to Elgin.

Despite the unwelcome attentions of various armies and bands of brigands, Elgin grew steadily throughout the medieval period until by the 17th century it boasted many fine buildings reflecting the prosperity of its merchants and craftsmen. Today some 242 important buildings are "listed" by Scottish Ministers as being of architectural or historical interest, including the Cathedral, Ladyhill, High Street, Cooper Hill, and the breathtaking Biblical Garden.

A walk around the town usually takes about an hour and a half, but if it takes longer so what—you're on holiday!

GETTING THERE:

Trains to Elgin leave **Inverness Station** at hourly intervals, making the journey in 42 minutes.

Trains depart Edinburgh's Waverley Station every couple of hours for the 5-hour journey to Elgin.

Trains leave Glasgow's Queen Street Station regularly for the 4-1/2-hour ride to Elgin.

By Car from Inverness to Elgin, take the A82 and the A96 roads. The total distance is 40 miles.

By Car from Edinburgh, take the A8, A90, M90, M9, and A95 routes to Elgin. The total distance is 175 miles.

By Car from Glasgow, follow the road signs for the A8, M80, A80, A9, and A96 to Elgin. The total distance is 194 miles.

PRACTICALITIES:

The local **Tourist Information Centre** is situated at 17 High Street, ☎ (01343) 542-666/543-388, **W**: castlesandwhiskey.com. Although early closing is on a Wednesday, many shops do not adhere to it. The population of Elgin is 23,000.

An indoor market is held every Saturday in the Elgin Auction Centre (opposite B&Q). A Farmers Market is held on the last Saturday of every month and more frequently during the summer months, on the High Street, Elgin.

FOOD AND DRINK:

Elgin has a wide selection of restaurants and pubs in all price ranges, including:

Abbey Court Restaurant (15 Greyfriars St.) Serves an extensive menu of freshly prepared food. ☎ (01343) 542-849. ££

Audrey's Tearooms and Coffee House (15/16 Harrow Inn Close) Serves tea, coffee and light meals — speciality home baking. ☎ (01343) 552-660. £

Littlejohns Restaurant (193 High Street) Serves American, Mexican and Italian food. ☎ (01343) 551-199. ££

SUGGESTED TOUR:

Circled numbers correspond to numbers on the map.

Leave the **train station** ❶ and follow the map in a westerly direction to High Street. At the west end of High Street is the hilltop site of Elgin's original **Royal Castle**, which was occupied by King Edward I of England in 1296 during the Wars of Independence. Only a fragment of the castle now remains. The hill is surmounted by a column, erected in 1839 in memory of the fifth and last Duke of Gordon; the statue was added in 1855. **Lady Hill** ❷ derives its name from the castle's Chapel of St. Mary, which continued in use until the 16th century.

As you now walk in an easterly direction down High Street, you will pass on your right-hand side the **Thunderton Hotel** ❸. The present hotel is all that remains of the most splendid house in Elgin, once a Royal Residence with orchards and a bowling green. In medieval times this was the site of the "Great Lodging" of the Scottish Kings, and in 1746 Bonnie Prince Charlie stayed here on his way to Culloden.

Still on High Street and only a few feet away is **St. Giles Kirk** ❹. There has been a church on this site since the 12th century. The present church, built in 1827–28, was designed in the manner of a Greek Doric temple by Archibald Simpson and is dedicated to the patron saint of Elgin, St. Giles.

To the east of St. Giles Kirk stands the **Muckle Cross** ❺, a 19th-century replacement of a 1365 cross. This part of the High Street was used both as a cemetery and market place for many centuries.

Directly opposite the cross, on the left-hand side of High Street stands a property believed to originally belong to the **Knights of St.John** ❻, but the tower itself is the only portion remaining of the town house built in 1634 by Andrew Leslie of the Glen of Rothes.

Continue to follow the map in an easterly direction — just past Commerce Street on the right you will find **Number 42–46 High Street** ❼, a good example of the arcaded buildings for which Elgin is famous. In the 18th century this was The Red Lion Inn, the only place where Dr. Samuel

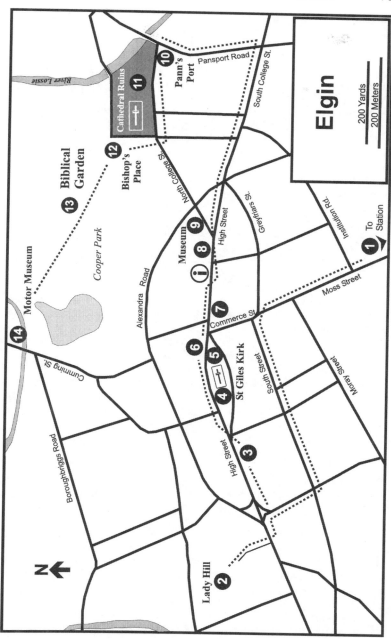

Johnson "found reason to complain of a Scottish table." The close to the rear is a fine example of Scottish Burgh architecture, which has just been restored.

Number 7 High Street ❽ is a well-preserved three-storey house called Braco's Banking House, built in 1694 by John Duncan and his wife Margaret Innes. The building itself takes the name from William Duff of Dipple and Braco, ancestor of the Earl of Fife.

Right at the end of the High Street at number 1, we have the award-winning **Elgin Museum ❾**, built in 1842 to a design by Thomas Mackenzie to house the collections of the Elgin Literary and Scientific Association. This is now run by a registered charity, the Moray Society. The museum houses a major display called "The Story of Moray" (from dinosaurs to the present day) as well as Pictish Sculpture and foreign travellers. Also on display is "The Past is a Foreign Country," covering missionaries, soldiers, and explorers from Elgin, and the "curios" they brought back from the Empire. ☎ *(01343) 543-675,* **W**: *elginmuseum.demon.co.uk. Open Easter through Oct., Mon.–Fri. 10–5, Sat. 11–4, Sun. 2–5. Adults £2, children £0.50, concessions £1, family ticket £4.50. Shop.* &.

Follow the map from High Street, going round the roundabout, along South College Street, and turning left into Pansport Road. As you turn left again at North College Street, you pass by the only survivor of the four gateways set in the precinct wall of the Cathedral. Restored in 1857, the **Panns Port ❿** derived its name from the meadowland lying immediately to the east, known as "le Pannis."

"The Lantern of the North," otherwise known as **Elgin Cathedral ⓫** stands proud on the right-hand side of King Street. Founded in 1224, the cathedral must have been a magnificent building, and even in its ruinous condition, it is still the glory of Elgin, rivalled only by the splendour of St. Giles church which dominates the picturesque and pedestrianised city centre. The cathedral stands as a testament to troubled times and is a poignant reminder of the atrocities carried out by the notorious "Wolf of Badenoch" who, in addition to putting Elgin and Forres to the torch as an act of revenge, burned down the cathedral in 1390. ☎ (01343) 547-171. *Open April–Sept.*

Adjacent to the Cathedral is the **Bishop's Palace ⓬**, a building that was known as the Precentor's Manse (a Ministers House) and is the only one left out of a group of more than twenty manses in the precincts of the cathedral.

Just behind the wall adjacent to the cathedral and set in Coopers Park, is the most spectacular garden I have ever seen — **The Biblical Garden ⓭**. To sit in this garden is shear "heaven" (no pun intended) — the plants grown in the garden, all 110 of them, have been mentioned in the Bible and the bronze-like statues depict the parables, so it has clearly been intended that this garden as well as being of considerable interest to those who study the scriptures, will also encourage anyone who enjoys gardens and gardening to visit. ☎ *(01343) 543-451. Open May–Sept., 10–7.30. Free.*

Our last visit of the day is only a short walk away from Cooper Park. In fact you can reach the **Moray Motor Museum**  by strolling across a bridge on the north side of the park. Housed in an old converted mill building that is light and airy, you are treated to a trip into yesteryear. On show there is a variety of antique cars and motorbikes, such as a 1928 4.5-litre Bentley and a 1939 SS100. ☎ *(01343) 544-933. Open daily Easter–Oct., 11–5. Admission £3.*

Follow the map back to the train station.

Elgin Cathedral

Trip 14

Wick

An Overnight Trip from Edinburgh or Glasgow

I f you are planning on visiting John O' Groats, which is 876 miles from Lands End in Cornwall and the farthest point north on the British mainland, you will have to call in at the most northerly town on the east coast of Britain, Wick. This little town dates back to Viking times, and its name originates from the Norse word Vik, meaning "Bay."

The amazing coastline, a little to the south of Wick, is known to those navigating at sea as "The Old Man of Wick"—a comforting landmark indeed, with a long and noble history. From the cliff top, you see some spectacular scenery—on the south coast is the "Brig O'Trams," a natural archway carved into the cliffs by centuries of pounding waves of the North Sea. Also to the south is the ruin of Oldwick Castle, fortified by the Vikings and now one of the three oldest castles in Scotland.

Today, the town is famous for its collectable Caithness Glass and for the Pulteney Distillery.

This trip cannot be done in one day for obvious reasons, but for many visitors it is worthwhile setting aside two or three days out of your itinerary and stopping over either in Wick or Inverness. Wick makes a fine base for a daytrip to John O' Groats.

GETTING THERE:

It is virtually impossible to travel from **Edinburgh by train** to the town of Wick in one day—the journey time would be a whopping 9-1/2 hours. It would mean setting off at the earliest time possible, 5.55 a.m. and arriving in Wick at 3.19 p.m., leaving you no time whatsoever to look around and visit John O'Groats. The most workable solution would be to leave Edinburgh's Waverley Station at 5.55 a.m. and head for Inverness—arriving at 10.25 a.m. Stop and have a look round Inverness, described on pages 61-64. Ask the local Tourist Information Centre for hotel or B&B recommendations. In the morning catch the 7:21 a.m. train from Inverness to Wick. You will arrive in Wick at 11.14 a.m. The last workable train from Wick to Inverness is at 4.17 p.m., arriving back at 8.07 p.m.

The most workable **train leaves Glasgow's** Queen Street Station at 7.08 a.m., arriving in Wick 8 hours and 11 minutes later at 3.19 p.m. Again, it is advisable to stop over in a hotel or B&B in Wick, as the latest workable train service leaves at 4.17 p.m. and arrives back in Glasgow at 11.34 p.m., giving you no time to explore and visit attractions.

By Car from Edinburgh, take the A8, A90, A9, and A99 routes to Wick. The total distance is 260 miles. Once again, it is advisable to stop regularly en route to prevent tiredness and to book into a hotel or B&B in Wick for the night.

By Car from Glasgow, follow the A8, M80, M9, A9, and A99 roads to Wick. The total distance is 279 miles. Stopping en route applies as before.

By Air from Edinburgh, it is possible to fly to Wick, Monday to Saturday, departing at 11.10 a.m. and arriving at 12.15 p.m. Fares would cost between £108 and £270 depending on the day you fly and availability.

PRACTICALITIES:

The local **Tourist Information Centre** is located in Whitechapel Road, just off High Street, ☎ (01955) 602-596, **W**: caithness.org. Wick has a population of approximately 8,000.

FOOD AND DRINK:

The Home Bakery (97 High Street) Bakery shop, café, and takeaway. Open 9–4.30. ☎ (01955) 602-516. £

The Queens Hotel (16 Francis Street) Serves lunches, dinners, high teas and bar suppers. ☎ (01955) 602-992. £ and ££

Breadalbane House Hotel (Breadalbane Crescent, close to the Heritage Centre) Serves a variety of bar meals and light snacks. ☎ (01955) 603-911. £

SUGGESTED TOUR:

Circled numbers correspond to numbers on the map.

On leaving **Wick Train Station** ❶ follow the map along River Street and onto Harbour Quay Road. Continue walking along Wellington Avenue to our first visit—**Old Wick Castle** ❷. Just 3 miles south of the town you will find the ruins of the castle. It's a lovely scenic route to the cliff top, and once there you will be provided with breathtaking views of the surrounding countryside. There is evidence to suggest that the ancient earls of the Norse line lived in the castle some 800 years ago. After that, Sir Reginald de Cheyne occupied it in the earlier part of the 14th century. Upon his death around 1345 it passed to the Earl of Sutherland by virtue of his marriage to Sir Reginald's daughter. The Oliphants, Sutherlands of Duffus, Glenorchy, and Dunbars of Hempriggs subsequently owned it until it was abandoned in the 18th century.

Now retrace your steps back into town via Wellington Avenue, Battery Road, Roxburgh Road, and Huddart Street. Located on the latter is the **Pulteney Distillery Visitor Centre** ❸. For those of you who enjoy a "little snifter," this is a great place to visit. At the same time you can discover the history and art of Scotch Whisky making, which you may know is a serious business to a Scotsman. As the distillery is still a working concern,

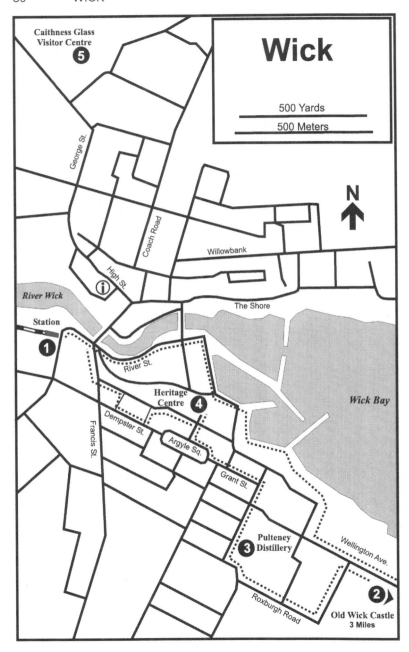

Caithness Glass
Visitor Centre
5

Wick

500 Yards

500 Meters

N

George St.

Coach Road

Willowbank

High St.

River Wick

The Shore

Station

1

River St.

Heritage
Centre **4**

Wick Bay

Dempster St.

Argyle Sq.

Francis St.

Grant St.

Pulteney
3 Distillery

Wellington Ave.

Roxburgh Road

2

Old Wick Castle
3 Miles

it's always a good idea to either telephone them first or pop in to arrange a tour time. ☎ *(01955) 602-371.*

On the map, stroll past Argyle Square, turn right and then take the third left onto Bank Row. Situated here is the **Wick Heritage Centre** ❹, which was founded in 1971 by the Wick Society. The building is a couple of converted terraced houses located quite close to the harbour, and is home to many exhibits about fishing and the local history of Wick. **W:** *caithness.org. Open May–Sept., 10–5, last admission 3.45. Adult £2, child 50p.*

Make your way back to the train station, as indicated on the map, where you will find next to it the bus depot, and bus numbers 77 and 177 to Thurso. We, however, are not going to Thurso so we want to be dropped off at the **Caithness Glass Visitor Centre** ❺ on the Airport Industrial Estate. The buses run at 8.27 a.m., 9.20, 12.40, 2.35, 3.35, and 5.20 p.m., from Wick bus depot and will arrive at the glass centre 10 minutes later. If you prefer, you can walk the short distance; the decision is yours.

Although there are now glass centres located in Perth and Oban, it was here in Wick where Caithness Glass was originally founded in 1961. From start to finish, you can watch how the exquisite glassware is created from sand by a skilled craftsman using only the heat of the furnace and the skill of hand and eye. Also at the centre is a large, well-stocked factory shop, where you can purchase many bargains in glass, crystal, paperweights, jewellery, and ceramics. A comfortable licensed restaurant serves breakfast, morning coffee, lunch, afternoon tea; and an informative exhibition about the "Story of Caithness Glass" should just about round your day off nicely. ☎ *(01955) 602-286. Open all year, Mon.–Sat., 9–5, Sun. (Easter to Dec.) 11–5. Free. Café.* ♿

Follow the map back to the train station.

John O'Groats

A Daytrip from Wick

As mentioned in the chapter about Wick, John O'Groats is the farthest village north on the British mainland—in fact, the greatest distance between Cornwall (the area farthest south in Britain) and John O'Groats is 876 miles. These two points are often chosen as the start and finish for many races. Visitors to the Northern Highlands feel an enormous urge to seek out this little village, not because it has many attractions to see (it doesn't), but just so they can say "I was there."

John O'Groats is named after a Dutchman Jan de Groot who in the 15th century was granted a charter by King James IV of Scotland to run a ferry to the Orkney Islands, the charge being a groat (or 2p a trip).

Today, the village is home to many types of shops, selling knitwear, glass, pottery, and candles. Also, for the adventureous among you, perhaps a trip out to sea on a "High Surf Superiority Rigid-hulled Inflatable boat" or an RIB.

GETTING THERE:

By Bus from Wick Railway Station, catch the numbers 77 and/or 177 to John O'Groats. The service runs from 9.20 a.m., 12.40 p.m., 3.35 p.m., and 5.30 p.m., arriving in John O'Groats at 10 a.m., 1.40 p.m., 4.30 p.m., and 6.10 p.m. respectively. Return journeys from John O'Groats are from 10.05 a.m., 1.50 p.m., 4.45 p.m., and 6.10 p.m., arriving back in Wick at 11.05 a.m., 2.30 p.m., 5.25 p.m., and 7 p.m. For all bus information ☎ (01847) 893-123, **W**: rapsons.co.uk. All fares are only a matter of a pound and a few pence.

PRACTICALITIES:

The local **Tourist Information Centre** is situated on County Road, ☎ (01955) 611-373, **W**: visitjohnogroats.com. The population of John O'Groats is approximately 200 and is mainly employed in the fishing, farming, and tourism industries.

FOOD AND DRINK:

Seaview Hotel (John O'Groats) Serves breakfasts, bar meals, snacks, and dinners. ☎ (01955) 611-220. £ and ££

John O'Groats House Hotel & Groats Inn (John O'Groats) The hotel, established in 1875, is the official starting point for any races from John O'Groats to Lands End (Cornwall). Serves bar meals and snacks. Open all year. ☎ (01955) 611-203. £

SUGGESTED TOUR:

With John O'Groats there is no suggested tour and map, as it is the mere fact of just being here, rather than the places there are to visit. However, I would suggest you visit the **Last House in Scotland Shop** and Museum, where admittance is free and where you can send your post-cards home stamped by the official last house stamp (as the name suggests, it is the last house farthest north—no other houses exist beyond this point). Visitors can enjoy learning about the history of the village and see some interesting artefacts of bygone times. You can also pick up a couple of souvenirs for friends and family from here. *Open all year.* ☎ *(01955) 611-250.*

Most people who visit John O'Groats insist on having their photographs taken in front of the village's famous signpost, which points out the exact distance between John O'Groats and other destinations—for example John O'Groats to London 691 miles. A special photographer will take your photograph and actually put up the country you're from.

For those of you with an adventurous nature and "sea-legs," a "must" is a trip out to sea to view some of the magnificent marine wildlife indigenous to this area. **The Northcoast Marine Adventures** organises such trips in a huge inflatable boat powered by a 450 h.p. engine driving a water jet. The boat is 11 metres long and 4 metres wide, and is fitted with radar, satellite navigation equipment, and marine radio communications—all of which makes it a very safe, comfortable, and stable platform from which to view the marine wildlife. They actually call themselves "The Marine Wildlife Show" and have "cast" members consisting of Atlantic Grey Seals, Harbour Porpoise, Rissos Dolphins, Pilot Whales, Puffins, Guillemots, Gulls, and many more varieties of sea birds. *The Northcoast Marine Adventures operates every 2 hours starting from 10 a.m. to 8 p.m., Easter to the end of October. For charges* ☎ *(07867) 666-273, E-mail: ncexplorer@northcoast.fsnet.co.uk*

It's now time to make tracks back to the bus stop and to Wick.

Trip 16

Glasgow

The engine of Scotland, Glasgow is undoubtedly one of the liveliest and most cosmopolitan destinations in Europe. Boasting world-famous collections, the best shopping in the UK outside of London as well as the most vibrant nightlife in Scotland, this fascinating city is just too good to miss.

Upfront and affable, Scotland's largest city overflows with sheer personality and a sense of style. Its story has always been bound up with trade, first with the Americas (it still has a Jamaica and a Virginia Street), then in the 19th century it became the "Second City of the Empire." Today a symbol of those far-off days is the Tall Ship in Glasgow harbour, S.V. *Glenlee.*

It is the legacy of those times that contributes much to the fine Victorian cityscape of today—arguably the best in the UK and symbolised by the ornate marbled pillars and staircases of Glasgow City Chambers.

A must-see is the Art Nouveau splendour of Glaswegian architect and designer, Charles Rennie Mackintosh. The Glasgow School of Art is his masterpiece, though other venues in the city are also his work, including The Light House, Scotland's Centre for Architecture, Design and the City.

You will also find based in Glasgow the Scottish Opera, Scottish National Orchestra, Scottish Ballet, and the Royal Scottish Academy of Music and Drama.

Although the majority of tourists choose Edinburgh as their base for exploring Scotland, Glasgow is equally convenient for nearly all the Scottish daytrips in this book. It has a wonderful selection of first-class hotels, excellent restaurants, and enough nightlife to keep you busy between probes of the countryside.

GETTING THERE:

Trains depart Edinburgh's Waverley Station frequently for the 50-minute ride to Glasgow's Queen Street Station.

Trains from London's Euston Station usually take 5-1/2 hours to reach Glasgow's Central Station, and 5 hours to reach Queen Street Station. For up-to-date information on rail travel within the UK, contact the 24-hour National Rail enquiries line ☎ (0345) 484-950, **W**: railtrack.co.uk

By Car from Edinburgh take the A1, A8, and M8 for the quickest route into Glasgow. The total distance is 47 miles.

By Car from London take the A4, A40, and M1 for the quickest route into Glasgow. The total distance is 404 miles.

By Air, Glasgow International Airport handles 45 daily flights to and from London's Heathrow and Gatwick airports.

PRACTICALITIES:

The sunniest months for visiting Glasgow are said to be April through to September, with May being the sunniest of all. I would say Scotland's weather is like the UK's—Unpredictable, so always take your umbrella!

The local **Tourist Information Centre** is situated at 11 George Square, ☎ (0141) 204-4400, **W**: seeglasgow.com. Glasgow has a population of 663,000.

FOOD AND DRINK:

The city is blessed with a fantastic range of restaurants and pubs in all categories. Mentioned below, in trip sequence, are a few good choices along the suggested walking tour:

Babbity Bowster (16–18 Blackfriars Street) Meals in trendy pub. £

Old Empire Bar and Diner (66 Saltmarket) Typically home-made Scottish meals made in a family run pub. ☎ (0141) 552-0844. £

Café Gandolfi (64 Albion Street) Traditional Scottish tea room and a European café restaurant. ☎ (0141) 552-6813. X: Dec. 25–26, Jan. 1–2. £ to ££

Café Mao (84 Brunswick Street Merchant City) Serving exciting and healthy food from the Orient and Far East. ☎ (0141) 564-5161. ££

Rogano (11 Exchange Place) Oldest surviving restaurant, café, and bar in Glasgow. Cooking the finest fresh fish and seafood directly from Scottish waters. ☎ (0141) 248-4055. £££

The Willow Tea Rooms (217 Sauchiehall Street) Light meals served in an historic Charles Rennie Mackintosh building. ☎ (0141) 332-0521. X: evenings, Dec. 25, Jan. 1–2. £

SUGGESTED TOUR:

Circled numbers correspond to numbers on the map.

For the convenience of those based in Edinburgh, this walk begins at **Queen Street Station** ❶. Just outside this, you will find the Tourist Information Centre at **George Square** ❷. One of the oldest public squares in Glasgow, it was laid out in the 18th century and named after George III. It probably is host to more statues than any other square in Scotland, including those of Queen Victoria, Prince Albert, Sir Walter Scott, Robert Burns, William Gladstone, James Watt, and Sir Robert Peel (the grandfather of today's policemen). Across its east end stands a massive 1888 Italian Renaissance-style building, the **City Chambers** ❸, featuring a 240ft.-high tower and opulent interiors full of mosaics and maiolica.

Follow the map up Frederick Street and turn right onto Cathedral Street. This will lead you to:

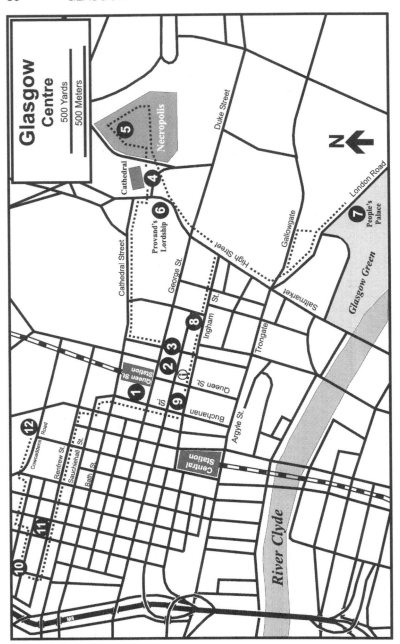

*GLASGOW CATHEDRAL ❹, Cathedral Square, ☎ (0141) 552-6891, **W**: historic-scotland.net. *Open April–Sept., daily 9.30–6; Oct.–March, daily 9.30–2.*
Begun in the 13th century on the site of an earlier church erected in the 6th century by St. Mungo, the founder of Glasgow, this cathedral is the rarest complete survivor of the Great Gothic Churches of South Scotland.

Adjacent to Glasgow Cathedral is the **Glasgow Necropolis ❺**, a spectacular cemetery renowned for its beautifully-designed tombs and excellent views over the city. Cemeteries are not usually tourist attractions, but this is an exception.

Opposite the Cathedral you will find Glasgow's oldest house, **Provand's Lordship ❻**. Built in 1471, it features period furniture and domestic displays dating from 1500 to 1918. *Open Mon.–Thurs. and Sat., 10–5, Fri. and Sun. 11–5. Free.*

Ambitious walkers may want to take a little side trip at this point. Continue down High Street and then turn right onto Gallowgate, which once led you to the gallows but now brings out at the Barras. This is a world-famous flea market founded over 100 years ago and is home to more than 1,000 traders.

Follow the map down London Road and onto Glasgow Green until you see the:

*PEOPLE'S PALACE ❼ , ☎ (0141) 554-0223, **W**: glasgow.gov.uk/cls. *Open Mon.–Thurs. and Sat. 10–5, Fri. and Sun. 11–5. Free.*
This refurbished 1897 red-stone building is now a culture centre for Glasgow's East End. A social history museum, it brings to life the city's past and its people.

Now retrace your footsteps back down London Road and onto High Street. Turn left and walk along Ingram Street, where you will come across **Hutcheson's Hall ❽**. This A-listed building replaced an earlier 1641 hospice founded by George and Thomas Hutcheson. Its newly refurbished ground floor now boasts a multimedia exhibition among the many other attractions. *Open daily, 10–5. Closed public holidays and Dec. 24 to Jan. 5.*

Ingram Street leads to the gigantic Corinthian portico of the **Royal Exchange ❾**, begun in 1775 as a mansion for one of Glasgow's leading tobacco lords. The equestrian statue in front is of the Duke of Wellington. Later used as a business exchange, this fantastic building is now a library.

Turning right on to Buchanan Street, you will see an upmarket shopping street, giving a glimpse of an opulent past. If you still feel that you have plenty of energy to spare you will want to follow Buchanan Street round and admire the many more places of interest, such as the:

TENEMENT HOUSE ❿, 145 Buccleuch Street, Garnethill, ☎ (0141) 333-0183. *Open March–Oct., daily 2–5.*
This Victorian tenement flat, built in 1892, re-creates the living condi-

tions for Glaswegians in the first half of the 20th century and offers a rare glimpse into the domestic lives of ordinary people.

GLASGOW SCHOOL OF ART , 167 Renfrew St. ☎ (0141) 353-4526, **W**: gsa.ac.uk. *Open Sept.–June, Mon.–Fri. 10–5, Sat. 10–1. Guided tours operated Mon.–Fri. at 11 & 2, Sat. at 10.30 and 11.30; July–Aug., Mon.–Fri. 11–5, Sat.–Sun. 10–5. Guided tours operate Mon.–Fri. at 11 and 2, Sat.–Sun. at 10.30, 11.30, and 1.*

Charles Rennie Mackintosh completed this architectural masterpiece in 1907; even to this day it remains a working art school.

MUSEUM OF PIPING ⑫ 30-34 McPhater St., ☎ (0141) 353-0220, **W**: thepipingcentre.co.uk. *Open May–Sept., daily 9–5; Oct.–March, Mon.–Sat. 9–5.*

This is definitely for the music lovers among you—an entire museum dedicated to the history and the music of the great Highland bagpipe.

Glasgow is a wondrous place, with many more attractions to visit, so you may need two daytrips to fit it all in. But hey, what's the rush anyway, you're on holiday!

Glasgow Cathedral from the Necropolis

Paisley

A Daytrip from Glasgow or Edinburgh

Only eight miles away from Glasgow and on the same rail line as Lanark is the largest town in Scotland. Paisley's birthplace was Seedhill, an area of good fertile soil where the River Cart could be easily forded. There was also a waterfall that acted as a natural fish dam.

According to legend, around AD 560, an Irish monk called Mirin came to this settlement and founded a Celtic Church. Mirin was later buried here and canonised. Because of the miraculous tales told about him, St. Mirin's shrine became a popular place of pilgrimage.

During 1163 a community of Cluniac monks set up a monastery near the shrine, between the ford and the waterfall, where by this time there was a working corn mill. The monastery later became Paisley Abbey.

Paisley prospered during the 19th century through its weaving and thread-making industry, lending its name to its most famous export—the Paisley pattern shawl. If you don't have one, don't leave town without buying one—the shawls are beautiful.

Nowadays, Paisley offers excellent facilities to industry, commerce, the public, and of course to students of the University. The town caters to its large population with traditional High Street shopping, modern shopping centres and supermarkets, as well as a vast range of restaurants, bars and nightclubs.

GETTING THERE:

Trains depart Edinburgh's Waverley Station every half-hour for the two-hour journey to Paisley's Gilmour Street Station.

Trains leave Glasgow's Central Station every 10–15 minutes, arriving at Paisley's Gilmour station 10 minutes later.

By Car from Edinburgh follow the A8, A70, A74, M8, and A741 roads to Paisley. The total distance is 55 miles, with a journey time of about an hour.

By Car from Glasgow take the M8 and A741 route to Paisley. The total distance is just 8.4 miles, with a travelling time of 10 minutes.

PRACTICALITIES:

The **Paisley Tourist Information Centre** can be found at 9a Gilmour Street, next to the train station, ☎ (0141) 889-0711, **W**: visitscotland.com. The largest town in Scotland has a population of over 79,000.

Paisley does not have a day for closing early, so can be visited at any time. Paisley does hold a Farmers' Market on the last Saturday of every month on the County Square, directly opposite Gilmour Street. The market is open from 9 a.m. to 1 p.m. and sells fresh produce such as game, beef, ostrich eggs, organic vegetables, seafood, and the like.

FOOD AND DRINK:

Arts Centre Café (Inside Paisley's Art Centre on New Street) Serves a variety of light snacks—sandwiches, coffee, tea, cake. ☎ (0141) 887-1010. £

Anoka Indian Restaurant (5 St. James Street) A licensed restaurant, serving traditional Indian food; either sit-in, take away, or home delivery—buffet, à la carte etc. ☎ (0141) 591-1701/1702 or Freephone (0800) 052-0024. £ and ££

The Bull Inn Public House (7 New Street) A selection of bar meals served from Monday to Saturday, 12 noon–5 p.m. ☎ (0141) 849-0472. £

SUGGESTED TOUR:

Circled numbers correspond to numbers on the map.

Leave the **Train Station ❶** and walk along Gilmour Street, passing the County Square as you do so. Take the second left and then the second right onto Abbey Close. Practically opposite the Town Hall is the 800-year-old **Paisley Abbey ❷**, founded when Walter Fitzalan signed a charter at Fotheringay in 1163. It is a beautiful church, steeped in history, where six High Stewards, Marjory Bruce, Robert II's wives, and Robert III are buried. *Open Mon.–Sat., 10–3:30. Services on Sunday 11 a.m., 12.15 p.m. and 6.30 p.m.* ☎ *(0141) 889-7654.*

Following the map along Bridge Street, turn right onto Orchard Street and walk across Causeyside Street and onto New Street. Standing on your right hand side is **Paisley Arts Centre ❸**, a place which offers a wide ranging programme including leading-edge contemporary dance, alternative comedy, children's puppet shows, film, drama and jazz.

Now turn left onto Shuttle Street and George Place, where the fully restored and furnished 18th-century weavers' cottages stand—called the **Sma Shot ❹**. Within the cottage you will find photographs and artefacts of local interest relating to weavers and mill workers. The cottage also houses a tea room, where you can sit a few minutes in a layout exactly matching written descriptions of other cottages found in the surrounding area—and let your imagination run riot. *Open from April through Sept., Wed. and Sat., noon–4. Admission Free.* ☎ *(0141) 889-1708.*

Now walk along Storie Street past Paisley University and turn left. Directly opposite Townhead Terrace on High Street is the **Paisley Museum ❺**. This is Scotland's first municipal museum, designed by John Honeyman and opened in 1871. Sir Peter Coats, partner in the large firm of thread makers J&P Coats, was a donor to the museum, together with the Paisley Philosophical Society who amassed considerable collections of shawls and pattern books, which made the venture possible. In 1882, art

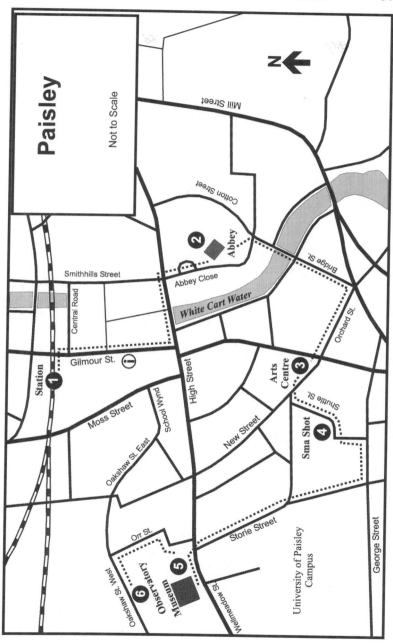

and sculpture galleries were added to the building, again paid for by Peter Coats. The museum has the finest collection of Paisley shawls in the world—naturally! *Open Tues.–Sat., 10–5; Sun. 2–5. Closed Mon. Open Public Holidays 10–5. Admission Free.* ☎ *(0141) 889-3151.*

Behind the museum is **Coats Observatory** ❻, reached by following the map along Orr Street and turning left onto Oakshaw Street West. This substantial Victorian observatory features displays on astronomy, astronautics, seismology, and meteorology. The site where the observatory stands was originally earmarked for possible Museum and Library extensions, but after the 1880 Annual General Meeting of the Paisley Philosophical Institution proposed that the Society should purchase an astronomical telescope, Mr. Thomas Coats offered to buy it for them and house it in the then-new building. Today the observatory sends daily returns to the Meteorological Office of wind speed and direction, barometric pressure, hours of sunshine, visibility, cloud cover, humidity, rainfall, and temperature. Also installed in the early part of the century were two seismic recorders—records from these include readings for the San Francisco earthquake of 1906. *Open Tues.–Sat., 10–5; Sun. 2–5. Late opening Thurs. during winter. Admission Free.* ☎ *(0141) 889-2013.*

Backtrack to Oakshaw Street East and follow the map to your starting point at the train station.

Ayr — Rabbie Burns Country

A Daytrip from Glasgow or Edinburgh

Ayrshire is the birthplace of one of Scotland's most famous sons, Robert Burns. Born January 25, 1759, Burns was the son of a poor tenant farmer who believed in the importance of education. Burns spent his formative years in the vicinity of Ayr where many of his best-loved stories take place. Not only did he love to write poetry, he also had a keen musical ear and rescued some 360 folk songs—polishing old words or writing new ones. His legacy of poems and songs include "To a Haggis," "A Red Red Rose," "Tam O'Shanter," and "Auld Lang Syne"—sung all over the world on New Year's Eve. The original words, written in the poet's own hand, can be seen at the museum.

GETTING THERE:

Trains depart Edinburgh's Waverley Station every 25 minutes, with a journey time of 2-1/2 hours.

Trains leave Glasgow's Central Station every 30 minutes and take 54 minutes to get to Ayr station.

By Car from Edinburgh take the A8, A70, A71, M8, and A719 roads. The total distance is 83 miles, with a travel time of 1 hour and 45 minutes.

By Car from Glasgow take the M8, M77, A77 and A719 routes to Ayr. The total distance is 36 miles, with a journey time of 49 minutes.

PRACTICALITIES:

The local **Tourist Information Centre** is based at 22 Sandgate, ☎ (01292) 678-100, **W**: ayrshire-arran.com. You could also contact the Burns National Heritage Park in Alloway, ☎ (01292) 443-700.

FOOD AND DRINK:

Pickwick Hotel (19 Racecourse Road, Ayr) Within the hotel is Mr.Micawbers, a bar and restaurant serving traditional Scottish food. ☎ (01292) 260-111, **W**: pickwickhotel.co.uk. £ and ££

Puddleduck Tearoom (37 High Street, Ayr) Light refreshments, cakes, sandwiches, tea, coffee etc. £

Brig O' Doon Hotel (in Alloway, overlooking the Brig O'Doon) Has two restaurants, a small bar and tea room. ☎ (01292) 442-466, **W**: brigodoon.com. £ and ££

SUGGESTED TOUR:

Circled numbers correspond to numbers on the map.

Leave the **Ayr Train Station** ❶ and wander over to the **Burns Statue Square** ❷, where the poet's likeness surveys the scene. From here you can take the number 205 bus to Alloway. Those with cars can drive the short 2.4-mile distance.

Ask the bus driver to stop at the **Tam O'Shanter Experience** ❸. This is a relatively new Visitor Centre, opened by the Queen in July 1995. Housed within the complex is an extensive gift shop and an attractive restaurant. Two audiovisual theatres bring to life the oldest and best-known tales written by the poet. *Open daily from 9–5. Admission to the shop and restaurant is free, however a charge of £1.50 is levied for the audiovisual presentation, for which a combined ticket to include entry to the cottage and museum can also be obtained.*

A short distance away, you will find the **Burns' Monument** ❹. Opened in 1823, this Grecian-style monument is a conspicuous landmark set in beautiful gardens. It contains some of Burns' mementoes, and a newly-constructed stairway leads directly on to the Brig O' Doon. *The monument is open daily April-Sept., 9–6. Admission £1 for adults and 50p for seniors. Free entry for accompanied children and disabled.*

From the monument, you will notice an attractive old bridge. This is the famed **Brig O' Doon** ❺, possibly dating from the 13th century, over which Tam escaped the pursuing witches in Burns' poem *Tam O' Shanter*. Walk down to it and stroll across its graceful single arch for some nice views.

Return to Alloway Monument Road, where across the way stands **Kirk Alloway** ❻. This is where the poet's father, who spelled his name "Burnes," is buried; and this is where the fictional Tam O' Shanter first encountered the witches and warlocks in their unholy orgy.

From here it is a pleasant ten-minute walk to the **Burns Cottage and Museum** ❼. This "auld clay biggin" with its thatched roof was rebuilt by his father in 1757. Robert Burns was born here two years later and lived in the cottage until the family moved to a nearby farm in 1766. After that the simple structure was used for a variety of purposes, including an alehouse and later, a "temperance refreshment room." In 1881 it was purchased by the Burns National Heritage Trust and was restored to its former glory.

The museum is adjacent to the cottage and houses a superb collection of original works by Burns, including manuscripts, letters and the like. *The cottage and museum are open daily 10–5. The entrance charge is £3.*

Two other structures in Ayr worth seeking out for their connection with Burns are the **Auld Kirk** ❽ and the **Auld Brig** ❾. So board the bus outside the cottage and head back to the High Street in Ayr. The Auld Kirk is a 17th-century church financed by Oliver Cromwell in compensation for

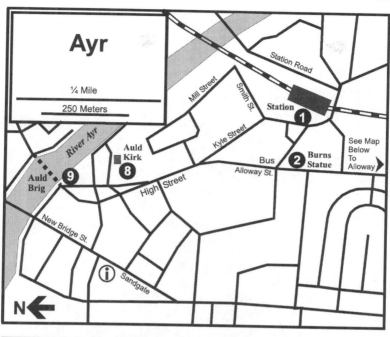

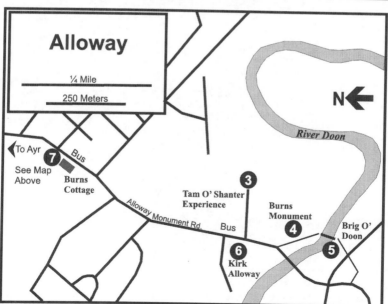

Robert Burns Immortalized in his Cottage

an earlier church he had requisitioned. The poet was baptised by its minister, and he later worshipped here. Nearby is The Auld Brig, a 13th-cen-
tury span immortalised in his poem Twa Brigs. From here you can follow
High Street back to the station.

Brig O' Doon

Lanark

A Daytrip from Glasgow or Edinburgh

Situated in the rolling landscape of the Upper Ward of Lanarkshire, this historic market town is a mere 35 minutes away from Glasgow by car. Lanark was created a Royal Burgh by David I around 1140, although a settlement can be traced back to the Roman period and the siting of Castledykes Fort. Castle Hill Motte, situated at the bottom of Castlegate, was the site of Lanark Castle. The Royal Castle was comprised of a "motte," a fort surrounding an earth mound, and a "bailey," an enclosed court at the foot of the mound. William I (1165–1214) frequently made Lanark Castle his residence, but by the 14th century the castle had fallen into disuse, although the associated medieval street pattern remains today.

Once Lanark had become a Royal Burgh, its prosperity began and continued through to the Victorian era. Many of the town's buildings that can be seen today date from this period. As the centre of Lanark prospered with specialist shops and services, villas were built to house Lanark's growing population. Small industries, such as tanneries, knitwear factories, laundries and confectioners added character to the town. Lanark's clean air and rural situation also attracted a number of institutions such as Bellefield Hospital, established for the treatment of consumption. Today, Lanark continues as a thriving market town with its own auction market and as a commercial and retail centre.

GETTING THERE:

Trains run from Edinburgh's Waverley Station every 2 hours to Lanark. Your journey time will be 1 hour and 45 minutes.

Trains leave Glasgow's Central Station hourly for the 55-minute journey to Lanark Station.

By Car from Edinburgh, take the A8, A70, and A743 routes to Lanark. Your travelling time will be approximately 55 minutes, with a total distance of 33 miles.

By Car from Glasgow, follow the A8, A74, M74, A72, and A73 roads, a total distance of 25 miles, with a journey time of 35 minutes.

PRACTICALITIES:

The local **Tourist Information Centre** is based in the Horsemarket, Ladyacre Road, close to the station. Open all year, ☎ (01555) 661-661, E-mail: Lanark@seeglasgow.com

The Lanimer Festival is the annual week of events in Lanark when the old Burgh boundaries are checked, a custom dating back to 1140. On Lanimer Day (usually in the middle of the week) a colourful procession makes its way through the town to Lanark Cross, where the Lanimer Queen is crowned.

FOOD AND DRINK:

Valerio's (Bannatyne Street, near to the train and bus stations) Seafood restaurant and take away. Established in 1932 as a family-run business, renowned for its traditional fish and chips and real dairy ice cream. ☎ (01555) 665-818. £

SUGGESTED TOUR:

Circled numbers correspond to numbers on the map.

Leaving the **Train Station** ❶, turn right down Bannatyne Street to the High Street. The top of the High Street marks the position of one of Lanark's ancient medieval ports or gateways into the town. The Portvaults public house on the left reminds us of the location of the port. During the medieval period, the High Street or "Hietoun" was a large open area with a number of buildings and rigs running along the boundaries. The "Pudden" Burn ran down the centre of the street. The High Street has gradually narrowed over the years, but the dramatic view down to St. Nicholas' Church and the hills beyond remains.

As you walk along High Street you will notice **The Tolbooth** ❷. The building we see today dates from 1778, but lies on the site of a much earlier tolbooth. Designed as a three-storey building, the present tolbooth was available to the Council and the gentlemen of the town. It contained many functions; a guard house, weigh house, and shops on the ground floor, the sheriff court and Council room on the first floor, and a large room for the use of the gentlemen on the top floor.

As we continue walking down the street, we pass **St. Nicholas's Church**, built in 1774 on the site of an earlier 12th-century chapel. Within the steeple lies the town bell, believed to date from 1130 when it was housed at Old St. Kentigern's and recast in 1659 and 1983. The church has recently been refurbished and restored to the Georgian period, with a lime render and lime wash applied to the stonework.

Follow the map to the end of High Street, where Westport begins. At number 8 you will find **The Royal Burgh of Lanark Museum** ❸, established in 1990 and staffed entirely by volunteers. The aim of the museum is to collect and collate items of historical interest in order to illustrate, by means of annual exhibitions, the ancient and varied history of the Royal Burgh. *Open April–Sept., Fri. and Sat., 10.30–4.40. Also open by appointment for visiting groups. Admission Free.* ☎ *(01555) 666-680.*

Now retrace your steps until you are in front of Greyfriar's Church on **Bloomgate** ❹. Bloomgate formed an important element of the medieval

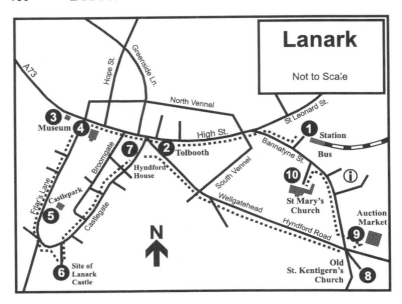

street pattern within the Westport or gateway into the town. The site of the Franciscan Friary lies within Bloomgate beneath the former Assembly Rooms to the rear of Clydesdale Hotel. Greyfriars Monastery was established in 1314 when lands were granted by Robert the Bruce. The Friary consisted of a chapel and a number of single-storey stone buildings with thatched roofs. By 1560 the Friary had been abandoned and had fallen into disrepair. A number of other historic buildings can be seen in Bloomgate.

Walk down **Friar's Lane** ❺ and as you do you will see a fine house rising above the stone wall and mature trees to your left. Castlepark was designed by William Leiper in 1880 in the Japanese style incorporating exposed rafters, timber balconies, and a pagoda-style tower. One of Leiper's best-known works is the Templeton Carpet Factory at Glasgow Green which is said to be influenced by the Doge's Palace in Venice.

Follow the road around until you reach the bowling green at the bottom of Castlegate. Here lies the site of **Lanark Castle** ❻, which dates back to the time of David I, 1124–53. It is believed to have been used by the Romans at a much earlier date. The natural earth mound was surmounted by a timber structure which formed a defensive fortress. Robert the Bruce held a court in the castle in 1321, but shortly after that the castle appears to have fallen into disuse. The mound was used for military drills and grazing until the 18th century when it was reduced in height, and by 1760 a bowling green was established.

Carry on to the end of Castlegate, where just behind Jacks the Ironmongers, you will see the crowstepped gables of **Hyndford House** ❼, the 17th-century town house and former home of the Earl of Hyndford. If you turn back into Hynford Place you will see the site of William Wallace's house, marked with a plaque reading "Here stood the house of William Wallace who in Lanark in 1297 first drew sword to free his native land."

Turn right and continue along Wellgate to Hyndford Road. If you wish to visit New Lanark, you have the option of turning up Braxfield Road along to the village for a 20-minute walk. At the very end of Hyndford Road, situated outside the town is **St. Kentigern's Church** ❽, which was known as the "Out Kirk" or "High Kirk" to distinguish it from St. Nicholas Parish Church within the town. The church is believed to have been established prior to the reign of David I. Local tradition suggests that William Wallace married Marion Braidfute at St. Kentigern's in the 13th century. Now only ruins remain.

Return to Hyndford Road and cross over to the Ladyacre road junction and to the **Lanark Auction Market** ❾. Built in 1867 by Lawrie and Symington, it's characteristic octagonal shape forms a prominent landmark within the town.

Stroll past the **Tourist Information Centre** and cross over the road to **St. Mary's Church** ❿ within St. Vincent Place to the left. Built between 1856 and 1859, the church was largely destroyed by fire in April 1907. St. Mary's was rebuilt in its present form to a design by Ashlin and Colman between 1908 and 1910, incorporating the shell of the former church. The church is a splendid example of the Gothic Revival in the late 13th-century style, complemented by the Presbytery, former school, and adjacent hospital within St. Vincent Place.

Turn left out of St. Vincent Place, along Bannatyne Street and return to the station.

Trip 20

Oban

A Daytrip from Glasgow or Edinburgh

This delightful little port can be reached by travelling on the same train line as you would if visiting Fort William. Soon after you cross the impressive Glen Falloch viaduct, you halt at Crianlarich, where the line splits. The tracks to the left descend to Oban, while those heading towards Fort William would continue climbing northward.

Oban is the unofficial capital of the West Highlands and is often described as the "Gateway to the Isles," as it is the main port for ferries departing to the Inner Hebrides.

The winding streets of Oban, busy with shoppers and holidaymakers, lead down to the picturesque harbour where fishing and pleasure boats rub shoulders.

During the month of August, you will hear the haunting but pleasant sound of the bagpipes being played at competitions held at various venues within the town. Not only that, at Mossfield Park the townsfolk hold their annual Highland Games, where the "porridge"-filled men toss the caber and the women dance the traditional "Highland Fling." It is an extremely memorable experience. Whatever you do don't forget a camera!

GETTING THERE:

Trains depart Edinburgh's Waverley Station via Glasgow's Queen Street Station regularly for the 4-1/2-hour journey to Oban. The earliest train leaving Edinburgh is at 6.30 a.m. and the last one leaves Oban at 6.10 p.m., arriving back at Edinburgh at about 10.20 p.m.

Trains leaving Glasgow's Queen Street Station run every 4 hours for the 3-hour ride to Oban using the Express Scotrail Railways. The earliest train leaving Glasgow is at 8.10 a.m. and the last one leaving Oban is at 6.10 p.m., arriving back in Glasgow at 9.17 p.m. There is no workable service on Sundays.

Always check current timetables as they do have a habit of changing without notice.

By Car from Edinburgh you have to drive via Glasgow, following the A8, A71, M8, A82, and A85 routes. The total distance is 139 miles, with a journey time of 3-1/2 hours.

By Car from Glasgow take the A82 and A85 roads to Oban. The total distance is 92 miles, travelling time 2-1/2 hours.

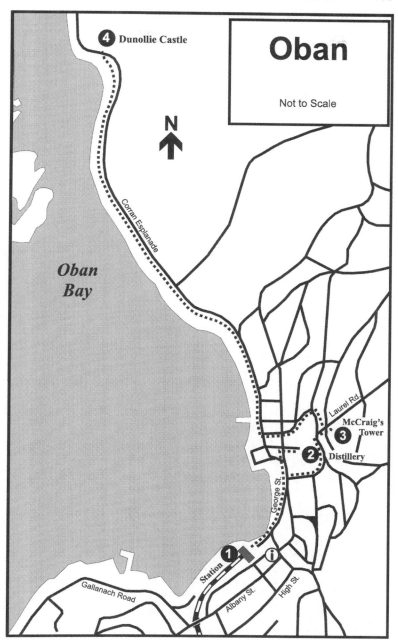

PRACTICALITIES:

You will find the local **Tourist Information Centre** situated at Argyll Square, ☎ (01631) 563-122, **W**: oban.org.uk. This trip can be made anytime, but never on Sundays. Current train timetables are available at any station or by calling Railtrack Information services, ☎ (08457) 484-950, **W**: rail.co.uk

FOOD AND DRINK:

Café Na Lusan (9 Craigard Road, near to the distillery) Internet café serving vegetarian snacks, lunch and dinner to sit in or take away. ☎ (01631) 567-268, **W**: cafenalusan.com. £

Aulay's Bar (8 Airds Place) Local bar with character. Serves bar snacks and lunches. ☎ (01631) 562-596. £

Café Forty-One (41 Combie Street) Continental bistro serving freshly prepared meals with a French/Scottish flavour. ☎ (01631) 564-117. £ and ££

SUGGESTED TOUR:

Circled numbers correspond to numbers on the map.

Leave the **Train Station ❶** and walk along George Street to Stafford Street, where you will find the **Oban Distillery Visitor Centre ❷**. Here you can see one of the six classic malts being made and discover the secrets behind the ancient art of distilling. Not only are you tempted to taste its fine malt whisky produce, but you are treated to an excellent exhibition and a guided tour. *Open all year, Mon.–Fri., 9.30–5. Easter to Oct., also Sat. 9.30–5. July to Sept., Mon.–Fri., 9.30 a.m.–8.30 p.m. and Sun. noon–5. Restricted hours Dec.–Feb. Last tour leaves 1 hour before closing. Admission: Adults £4. Free for children up to 18.* ☎ *(01631) 572-004.*

From Argyll Street, be prepared to walk up a steep set of steps called "Jacob's Ladder" to Ardconnel Terrace and Road, where just behind stands **McCraig's Tower ❸**. This is Oban's most prominent landmark—a coliseum-like structure, built on a hill overlooking Oban Bay. The tower was the idea of philanthropic banker John Stuart McCraig and stands approximately 70 metres above sea level; its circumference is 192 metres, so you can judge for yourself—it's a pretty big building. From the tower, you get some spectacular views of the Firth of Lorne and of the Mountains of Morvern.

Your last visit of the day is to the ruins of **Dunollie Castle ❹**. The simplest way of getting to the castle is by walking along the side of Oban Bay on the Corran Esplanade. This is the most scenic and tranquil route to take, and with a good wind behind you will only take about 10–15 minutes to walk the mile from McCraig's Tower.

The oldest surviving building in Oban is the Castle, which according to Scottish records was captured by the Irish brothers, Loarn, Fergus, and Angus in AD 498. Loarn governed the area around Dunollie—which still bears his name (Lorn as it now known). Originally built in the 7th century, the present ruins date from the 15th century. You have to climb a small but steep hill to reach the ruins, but it's worth it for the view overlooking the Northern entrance of Oban Harbour.

Retrace your steps back to the train station.

Fort William

A Daytrip from Glasgow or Edinburgh

I f you were a film director and wanted to shoot some spectacular scenery, just like the beautiful settings seen in Braveheart, Rob Roy, and Harry Potter, where would you go? The answer is Fort William. Even the train ride from Glasgow will take you through majestic scenery and make you feel relaxed and uplifted.

Dedicated rail fans may prefer to travel a day earlier to experience the Fort William-to-Mallaig Steam Train, riding over what is perhaps the most majestic section of the line. Details are provided at the end of this chapter.

Fort William, also once known as the Black Garrison of Inverlocky, is the largest town in the Highlands and can be found in the shadow of Ben Nevis (Britain's highest mountain) and at the head of Loch Linnhe (one of Scotland's deepest lakes).

It was during 1655 that General George Monck occupied the site of the original timber-framed fort called Inverlocky. After its destruction by the Camerons of Lochiel, the fort was later rebuilt and restored by Colonel John Hill who decided to rename it after their new Dutch monarch—King William III.

Today Fort William is a bustling town that offers something for everyone—shopping, sightseeing, walking, cycling, fishing, and golf.

GETTING THERE:

The quickest way of getting to Fort William by train is by departing from Glasgow's Queen Street station. This will reduce your travelling time by at least 40 minutes.

Trains leave Edinburgh's Waverley Station regularly for the 50-minute ride to Glasgow's Queen Street Station, where you change to the Express Scotrail Railways.

A train leaves Glasgow's Queen Street Station at 8:12 a.m. for the four-hour scenic run to Fort William. The only practical return train departs Fort William at 5:40 p.m., arriving back in Glasgow around 9:17 p.m. There is absolutely no workable service on Sundays or some holidays. Check the current timetables before setting out, as changes are possible.

PRACTICALITIES:

This trip may be made in any season, but never on Sundays or some holidays. Clear weather is essential. The **Tourist Information Centre** in Fort William is located at the Cameron Centre in Cameron Square near the West Highland Museum, ☎ (01397) 703-781, **W**: host.co.uk

Current train timetables are available at any station or by calling Railtrack Information services, ☎ (08457) 484-950, **W**: rail.co.uk

FOOD AND DRINK:

McTavish's Kitchen (100 High Street, near the Museum) Serves Scottish fayre—seafood, Scottish steaks, and haggis. Also a venue for traditional music and dance. ☎ (01397) 702-406, **W**: mctavishs.com. Open all day March to October. £ and ££

The Stables Restaurant (Bank Street, off High Street) Serves a varied menu for lunch, afternoon tea, and dinner. ☎ (01397) 700-730. Open all year. £

Nevis Bank Hotel (Belford Road, east of the station) Meals in a popular hotel with a pub and a restaurant. ☎ (01397) 705-721, **W**: nevisbankhotel.co.uk. £ and ££

SUGGESTED TOUR:

Circled numbers correspond to numbers on the map.

Just before arriving in the town of Fort William, the train takes you past **Ben Nevis**, the highest mountain in Britain. It stands at 4,406 feet and is so tall that, even during the summer months of August, it still has patches of snow on its slopes. A great many visitors to Fort William make the climb every year, but the best advice is that you have to be fit and properly dressed before attempting it.

Upon arrival at the **Fort William Station ❶**, head directly for the **West Highland Museum ❷** on Cameron Square, near the tourist office. One of the most delightful little museums in Scotland, it houses a large collection of historical information and Jacobite memorabilia from Fort William's past. *Open all year Mon.–Sat., 10–5; also on Sun. 2–5 during July–Aug.* ☎ *(01397) 702-169.*

As you now cruise down High Street, have a look at the array of shops on offer, not only for the goods they sell, but also at the age of the buildings they are housed in. One building, established in 1912, houses the **Fine Art Gallery ❸** (46 High Street), home to an exciting range of paintings and prints. Another building to pop into while on High Street is **The Granite House ❹**, Fort William's favourite gift shop for both locals and visitors alike.

Now if you fancy a stroll by the Loch, just follow the map to the end of High Street and turn right onto Station Brae. Walk straight across the zebra crossing and there in front of you is the **Town Pier ❺**. Those of you with "sea legs" can enjoy a cruise along Loch Linnhe from here. The cruiser *Souter's Lass* is at your disposal, with its all-weather lounge offering snacks and refreshments. The trip lasts 1 hour 30 minutes.

Those partial to a "wee dram" (and why not?) need to head for **Middle**

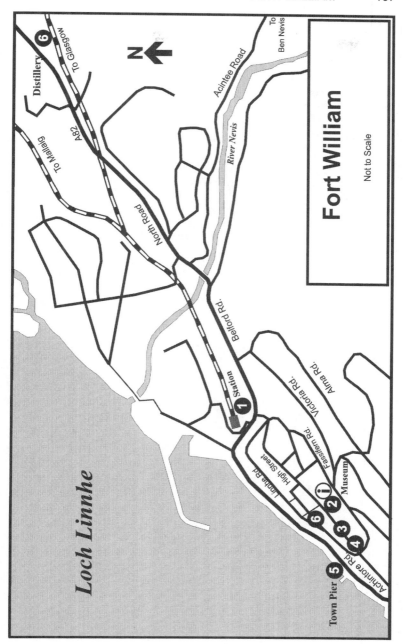

Street ❻ where you will catch the number 45 bus to Corpach, running every 15 minutes. Ask the driver to let you off at Lochy Bridge, as this is where our next visit is located—**The Ben Nevis Distillery and Visitor Centre ❻**. The visitor centre features a permanent exhibition, a video programme featuring Hector McDram, a snack bar, and a shop. While the distillery takes you back through the foundations of its history and, of course, in true Highland tradition, it ends with the sampling of the amber nectar. *Open all year, Mon.–Fri., 9–5.* ☎ *(01397) 700-200.*

Once your tour has finished, walk to the bus stop outside the distillery and catch the number 45 back to Fort William's bus station. From the bus station it is only a short walk to our final attraction of the day, (that is, if you have any time left before catching the 5.40 train to Glasgow). **Ben Nevis Visitor Centre ❼** is a tourist shop situated on Belford Road. Here you can buy a wide variety of souvenirs to take back home with you, ranging from tartans, Scottish foods, Highland Dress, whisky, crafts etc.

Follow the map back to the train station and if you haven't already done so, have a look at *The Jacobite* steam train. Does it look familiar? It should—this train (numbered 75014) is owned and maintained by the same company in Lancashire (where I live) that owns the *Hogwarts Express* (numbered 5972), which was used in the Harry Potter movies.

Talking of steam trains, and as mentioned earlier, you can take an enchanting **ride from Fort William to Mallaig.** The service operates from the middle of June until the beginning of October, Monday to Friday—extended to Sundays throughout August (exact dates can be obtained from the Tourist Information Centre in Fort William). There is only one departure time from Fort William; 10.20 a.m.—arriving in Mallaig at 12.25 p.m. Departure time from Mallaig is 2.10 p.m. Current fares are as follows:

Adult day return—standard £23, 1st class £35
Child day return—standard £13, 1st class £17.50
Adult single—standard £17.50, 1st class £27
Child single—standard £9, 1st class £13.50

Section III

DAYTRIPS IN
WALES

Most of the daytrips in this section can be taken from either Shrewsbury or Aberystwyth, and the remainder from Cardiff, as noted in the text.

Trip 22

Shrewsbury

('Scrobbesbyrig)

Shrewsbury, the county town of Shropshire, is in the English Midlands close to the Welsh border; because of this fact, Shrewsbury makes an ideal base for your daytrips in central and northern Wales.

The first written reference to Shrewsbury is in a charter of 901, where it appears as Scrobbesbyrig (Byrig suggests a fortified settlement). Then in 1086, the Domesday Book contains a description of Shrewsbury. So we know that the town has been in existence for at least 1,100 years.

In the 18th century, Shrewsbury became a stopover for stage coaches travelling from London to Holyhead, providing stabling for over 100 horses every night. The Victorian era brought the railways, and so with them came the demise of the coaching trade, but in their wake provided Shrewsbury with a new role as a major stop on the way to Chester and the North. These days Shrewsbury is a relatively quiet market town whose historic past has a legacy of beautiful black-and-white Tudor buildings, churches, and parks that attract numerous visitors every year.

One of Shrewsbury's famous sons was Charles Darwin, born here on 12th February 1809. His statue now stands outside the public library in honour of his controversial work on the "Origin of Species," first published in 1850.

Just a little way down the River Severn is the town of Ironbridge, where the Industrial Revolution began. Why not pay this important site a visit, you'll enjoy it.

Shrewsbury, with it's narrow cobbled streets and black-and-white buildings, is a town full of intrigue—it is easy to imagine that you have stepped back in time to the era of Tudor England.

GETTING THERE:

Trains from London's Kings Cross Station usually take 3 hours and 30 minutes to arrive at Shrewsbury Station.

Trains depart London's Euston Station every hour for the 3-hour journey to Shrewsbury Station. Train service is less on Sundays.

By Car from London to Shrewsbury, take the following roads: A41, A406, M1, M6, M54, A5, B4380, and A458 for a total distance of 162 miles and a journey time of just over 3 hours.

PRACTICALITIES:

The main **Tourist Information Centre** is in The Square, ☎ (01743) 281-200, **W**: shrewsburytourism.co.uk or shrewsbury.ws. Population of the town itself is 64,400. Market days in the town centre's Market Hall are on Tuesday, Wednesday, Friday, and Saturday. There is an outdoor market on Sundays on the site of the livestock market at Harlescott on the northern edge of town.

FOOD AND DRINK:

The Gallery Tearoom (24–25 Princess Street) Serves light snacks and main meals. Various non-alcoholic beverages. Open Monday to Saturday from 10 a.m. to 4.30 p.m. ☎ (01743) 355-550. £

Three Fishes (Fish Street) A smoke-free pub with meals and good selection of beer. ☎ (01743) 344-793. £

The Cornhouse Restaurant & Wine Bar (59a Wyle Cop) A converted corn house with two levels, serving a large selection of Scottish and International cuisine. ☎ (01743) 231-991, **W**: cornhouse.freeuk.com. ££ and £££

SUGGESTED TOUR:

Circled numbers correspond to numbers on the map.

When you step off the **train** ❶ head south down Castle Gates until you reach:

*SHREWSBURY CASTLE and SHROPSHIRE REGIMENTAL MUSEUM ❷, Castle Street. ☎ (01743) 358-516, **W**: shrewsburymuseums.com. *Open early Feb. to mid-Dec. from 10 a.m. Adults £2; senior's £1; Shrewsbury residents, under 18's, students, and members of the regiments are free.*

The castle was built between 1066 and 1074, during the reign of William the Conqueror. Sometime during the late 18th century, the interior was remodelled as a private house by Thomas Telford. Within the castle you will find the Shropshire Regimental Museum, where you can see some wonderful displays, including uniforms, pictures, medals, weapons, and other militaria from the 18th century up to the present day.

Follow the map along St. Mary's Street and across the English Bridge to **Shrewsbury Abbey** ❸. This magnificent abbey in a tranquil setting has been used in recent years as the home of the fictional character Brother Cadfael—chronicles written by local author Ellis Peters and later adapted for television. The Benedictine Abbey of St. Peter and St. Paul was founded in 1083 by Roger de Montgomery and built on the site of a wooden Saxon church. *Open daily, late March to late Oct., 9.30–5.30; and late Oct. to late March, 10.30–3. Admission free although donations are gratefully received.* ☎ (01743) 232-723.

Retrace your steps and stroll along Town Walls, indicated on the map, until you come to **St. Chad's** ❹. Adjacent to the Quarry, this spectacular

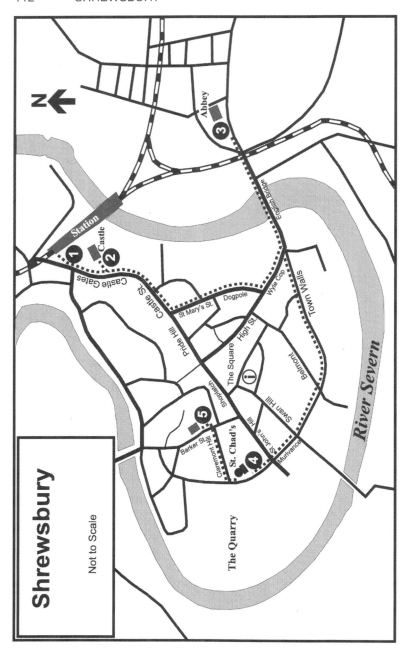

Shrewsbury

Not to Scale

River Severn

The Quarry

N

Abbey

3

Station

Castle

1

2

Castle Gates

Castle St.

Pride Hill

St Mary's St.

Dogpole

Wyle Cop

Town Walls

High St.

The Square

Belmont

i

Swan Hill

Shoplatch

St John's Hill

Mardol

5

Barker St.

Claremont Hill

St. Chad's

4

A Narrow Lane in Shrewsbury

"round" church was designed by controversial George Steuart and built in
1790–92. Charles Darwin was baptised at this unusual and very beautiful
church on November 15, 1809. *Open daily from April to Oct., 8–5; and
from Nov. to March, 8–1. Admission free although donations are gratefully
received.* ☎ *01743 365478.*

From St. Chad's turn right onto the pedestrians-only Claremont Hill,
then left onto Barker Street where **Rowley's House Museum ❺** is located.
It is also known by another name—**Shrewsbury Museum & Art Gallery.** The
museum occupies two adjoining buildings; a 16th-century merchant's
warehouse that is timber-framed and a stone-and-brick building of a 1618
mansion belonging to merchant William Rowley. Apart from looking at a
beautiful Tudor-style building from the outside; from the inside you can
view some wonderful exhibitions. There indeed is something for everyone, including natural history, geology, archaeology, local history, cos-
tume, ceramics, and fine art. *Open year round from 10 a.m., closed
Christmas & New Years' weeks. Admission free.* ☎ *01743 361196.*

Shrewsbury has a wonderful selection of first-class hotels, restaurants, and shops, so if you have selected this beautiful town as your base,
don't head straight back to the train station, have a mooch round and
absorb its fascinating history—you won't be sorry.

Aberystwyth

B eyond the hills of Pumlumon, on the shore of Ceredigion's Bay, stands Aberystwyth—one of Wales favourite seaside towns and the largest settlement along Wales' West Coast, whose name means "Mouth of Winding River."

The town is sheltered in a valley between three hills: Pen Dinas to the south (where there is an Iron Age Fort), Constitution Hill (Craig Glas) to the north, and Penglais to the east. Its strategic position explains the location here of the National Library of Wales—guardian of a treasure trove of literature, maps, and prints—including some of the greatest Celtic literary treasures. The town's proximity to the open hills and the wide choice of family-run accommodation makes the area another perfect base for daytrips in central and northern Wales.

The location here of both the University and the National Library of Wales ensures a healthy mix of new ideas with history and tradition. An area of contrasts, its cosmopolitan flavour goes hand-in-hand with a rural way of life where the pace is relaxed and Welsh, a language once spoken throughout most of the British mainland, is spoken by the majority. The air is clean and fresh, with the environment guarded through centuries of friendly farming practises.

Aberystwyth provides a marriage of both coast and countryside with scenery that you'll never forget. Beautiful sunsets over the bay are enhanced only by the majestic backdrop of the mountains of North Wales or even a glimpse of the resident family of bottlenose dolphins.

There are many attractions to visit while in town, including The Ceredigion Museum, Aberystwyth Castle, The National Library of Wales, Vale of Rheidol Railway, The Arts Centre with Theatre, Concert Hall, Gallery and Craft shop, Café, Bookshop, Cinema and much, much more.

GETTING THERE:

Trains to Aberystwyth leave Shrewsbury at 2-hour intervals, making the journey in 1 hour and 45 minutes. Run by Central Trains, it is said that this one of the more beautiful railway journeys in Britain.

By Car, Aberystwyth is 75 miles southwest of Shrewsbury via the A458 and A483 roads to Welshpool and Llangadfan. Then follow the A470 road and the A489. After that, take the A487 signs to Aberystwyth. The journey takes about 2 hours.

By Coach, a National Express Coach leaves at regular intervals from the Shrewsbury Bus Station, Raven Meadows to Aberystwyth, Plascrug,

Ceredigion. The journey takes 2 hours 15 minutes. Timetables and fare prices will vary—for details ☎ (08705) 808-080.

PRACTICALITIES:

For visitor information contact the **Aberystwyth Tourist Information Centre**, Terrace Road, Aberystwyth, ☎ (01970) 612-125, E-mail aberystwythtic@ceredigion.gov.uk, **W**: ceredigion.gov.uk

The town features several events, including the Aberystwyth Agricultural Show, Trotting Race, and the International Poetry Festival held at the beginning of June; the Musicfest at the Arts Centre, The Aberystwyth Carnival, and the Ten Piece Brass Band Contest held at the end of July; and the Aberystwyth Summer Show and the Aberystwyth Round Table Fun Day held during August.

FOOD AND DRINK:

Yr Hen Lew Du (Bridge Street) The second-oldest pub in town, dating from the 16th century. Traditional Welsh ambiance, serving homemade bar meals throughout the day. ☎ (01970) 615-378. £

Rummers Wine Bar (Trefechan Bridge) is situated on the Harbourside, and was converted from an 18th-century grain warehouse. While relaxing, listen to jazz, rock or traditional music. Open from 7 p.m. ☎ (01970) 624-959/625-177. £ to ££

The Richmond Hotel Restaurant (The Promenade, Marine Terrace) The Hotel's stylish, highly acclaimed, sea view restaurant offers traditional Welsh and British cuisine, using local fresh produce. Vegetarians and those with special dietary needs are catered for. ☎ (01970) 612-201. ££

Singapore Garden Restaurant (Portland Road, off Terrace Road) Newly-opened restaurant situated close to the Tourist Information Centre and the Ceredigion Museum. Specialises in Singapore, Malaysian, and Chinese dishes. ☎ (01970) 611-211/617-617. £ to ££

Brady's Bar (Talbot Hotel, Market Street) This typically Irish bar is situated in the middle of the town centre, just 2 minutes from the beach. A selection of real ales, a comprehensive bar menu featuring snacks and lunches. ☎ (01970) 627-441. £

SUGGESTED TOUR:

Circled numbers correspond to numbers on the map.

Starting at the **Train Station ❶**, follow the map to the **School of Art ❷**. Located in a magnificent Edwardian listed building, the school is part of the University of Wales and presents an active exhibition programme showing works by students as well as touring exhibitions. Displays include art, ceramics, pottery and furniture. *Open Mon.–Fri., 10–1 and 2–5.*

Now walk straight ahead, turning right on Buarth Road/Heol y Buarth. Carry on and turn left on Llanbadarn Road/Ffordd Llanbadarn. As you gently stroll down the road, take time out to breathe in the fresh air and to admire the timeless beauty of the surrounding countryside. In no time at

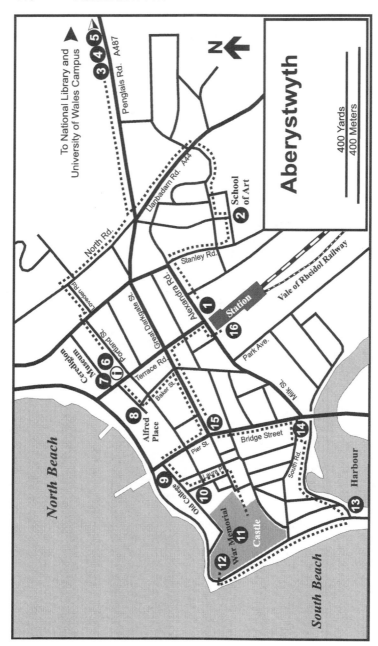

Aberystwyth

400 Yards
400 Meters

To National Library and
University of Wales Campus

Penglais Rd.   A487

Llanbadarn Rd.   A44

School
of Art

North Rd.

Stanley Rd.

Loveden Rd.

Alexandra Rd.

Great Darkgate St.

Portland St.

Terrace Rd.

Baker St.

Ceredigion
Museum

Alfred
Place

Pier St.

Bath St.

Old College

War Memorial

Castle

North Beach

South Beach

Station

Vale of Rheidol Railway

Park Ave.

Mill St.

Bridge Street

South Rd.

Harbour

all, you will have reached Penglais Road/Ffordd Penglais. Turn right and continue walking until you reach the:

*NATIONAL LIBRARY OF WALES—LLYFRGELL GENEDLAETHO ❸, Penglais Hill, ☎ (01970) 632-800, **W**: llgc.org.uk. *Open Mon.–Fri., 9.30–6, Sat. 9.30–5. Closed Sun., public holidays, and first full week of Oct. Admission free. Café.* ♿.

A visit to the National Library is a must. Situated on Penglais Hill, the imposing building is surrounded by beautiful gardens and has a panoramic view over the town, which in itself is worth seeing. However, once inside the library you can enjoy exhibits including illuminated writing and drawings from early Celtic manuscripts, early books and maps, the work of Welsh artists, and the very first Welsh photograph. "A Nation's Heritage," a permanent exhibition located within its Gregynog Gallery, provides a marvellous insight into the heritage and culture of Wales.

A short walk up Penglais Hill will bring you onto the beautifully planted **University of Wales ❹** campus, home to the majority of the university's academic departments, sports centre, halls of residence, and arts centre. The University at Aberystwyth was the first such institution to be established in Wales. When it opened in 1872 there were 29 students, a principal, and a registrar-librarian. Today, the number of students has increased to nearly 8,000 with a staffing level of 1,600. Some of the buildings, such as the Hugh Owen complex, have won awards for innovative architecture. The campus is open to visitors, with sports facilities available at a small charge. Also located on the campus is the:

*ABERYSTWYTH ARTS CENTRE ❺, on campus. ☎ (01970) 622-882. *Open Mon.–Sat., 10a.m.–8p.m.; galleries and shops open 10–5; complex also open Sun. 2–5 in summer. Admission to the exhibitions is free. Café.* ♿.

You can happily spend a few hours at the Arts Centre! Over 400,000 visitors a year are attracted to the Centre's varied programme of festivals, performances by touring companies, as well as excellent art and ceramic exhibitions. Every November and December it holds Wales' largest craft fair. Other facilities include a craft shop, bookshop and café.

Walk down Penglais Hill and head towards North Road/Ffordd y Gogledd. Cross over and stroll down Loveden Road, following the map to the **Aberystwyth Tourist Information Centre ❻** and the:

*CEREDIGION MUSEUM—THE COLISEUM ❼, same complex as the Tourist Information Centre, corner of Bath Street. ☎ (01970) 633-088. *Open Mon.–Sat., 10–5; and on Sun. during school holidays. Admission free.*

This extravagant and exuberant Edwardian building, with its lavish decorations in yellow terracotta and its statues of Edward VII crowning its three principal facades, was built in 1904. Its upper floors catered for theatre, music hall, concerts and public meetings. Early speakers here included David Lloyd George and Mrs. Emily Pankhurst, the suffragette leader. In 1931 it became a cinema.

When this closed in 1976 it was converted into the Ceredigion Museum, an excellent local history museum worth a prolonged visit. It offers its own Oriel Ceredigion exhibition area. Various displays, such as a reconstructed 19th-century cottage and pharmacy, charmingly portray aspects of the area's history. The very attractive Coliseum Gallery forms part of the museum and hosts many touring art and craft exhibitions as well as the museum's own collection. The beautiful mosaic floor of the Bath Street entrance has to be seen to be believed.

Leaving Bath Street, walk down Corporation Street/Stryd y Gorfforaeth until you come to **Alfred Place** ❽. The Public Library, a restrained Edwardian building, dated 1905 and erected with a Carnegie Trust grant, has attractive internal decoration in the Art Nouveau style. The Unicorn Inn (Kane's) is late Georgian. To the right of the simple Italianate English Baptist Chapel (1870) is the entrance to Crynfryn Row and Crynfryn Buildings, early 19th-century working men's cottages saved from demolition. These stand on top of a low sea cliff, hidden from below by houses: its existence is proved by the breakneck flight of steps down from the Row to the Promenade. Victoria House, on the corner of Eastgate and Baker Street, was the Victoria Inn from 1870s to 1910 and had a ship's figurehead of Queen Victoria as its sign. The figurehead, carved about 1840, is a rarity, the only merchant ship figurehead of the Queen to have survived in Great Britain and one of only four in the world.

At the end of Baker Street, turn left onto Great Darkgate Street/Y Stryd Fawr, following it down to Pier Street/Heol y Wig and then turning right. Head towards Aberystwyth's beautiful Promenade, but just as you reach the end, turn left onto King Street. Across the road from the pier is the handsome **Old College** ❾. Designed by JP Seddon in the 1870s, it was originally intended to be a hotel to accommodate the anticipated crowds arriving on the new railway line. However, the enterprise failed and it was sold in 1872 to become the first university in Wales. The building, in high Victorian Gothic style, has many features of considerable architectural interest, which include the splendid oval Seddon Room, the internal Quadrangle with its fine timbered and glazed roof, and the Old Hall beyond it. Today, the Old College houses the Departments of Welsh, Education and Theatre, Film and Television as well as the University's administration.

On the way to Aberystwyth Castle we pass onto **Laura Place** ❿. This fine terrace of Regency houses was built between 1810 and 1820: note the varied designs of fanlights over the doors. On the right is St. Michael's Church, completed in 1890 and the third of the name. A little way down New Street on the left is a former coach house, which has served as the meetinghouse of Unitarians and Quakers. The building with the fine Venetian windows at the top of the Place is the old **Assembly Rooms**, built by George Repton in 1820, a standard requirement in a fashionable watering place, where noble and gentle visitors might attend balls and assemblies, properly regulated by a master of ceremonies. At different times in the later 19th century the rooms served many functions, meeting place of learned societies, concert hall, theatre, public library and then in 1901–07 as the University College chemistry department. Later it was the first home of the National Library of Wales. In 1923 it was converted into the Students Union, which it remained until 1970. Subsequently it has housed the college music department and, at present, the extramural department. The original Assembly Room on the first floor now provides an elegant setting for chamber concerts and is called the Joseph Parry Hall, to commemorate the Welsh composer who was the first professor of music here (1874–80) and whose noble hymn made "Aberystwyth" a household word.

From Laura Place, follow the map to:

*ABERYSTWYTH CASTLE ❶. *Admission Free.*

The Castle is now just a ruin, standing on the rocky headland, but it used to be one of the eight great castles founded by Edward I between 1277 and 1295 to secure his conquests from Llewelyn ap Gruffyd, the last native Prince of Wales. It was commenced by the king's brother, Edmund of Lancaster, in July 1277, but was still incomplete in 1282 when it was captured in a sudden Welsh uprising. Work resumed within months, however, and in 1289 the castle was completed. Provisioned by sea, it was then strong enough to stand a long siege in 1294–95.

The scale of destruction as it stands now makes it difficult to appreciate at first that the castle was a scientifically designed concentric fortress, roughly diamond shaped, with two lines of walls and towers, the inner line close to and overtopping the outer line, with a strongly-defended entrance at the east corner. A barbican barred the approach to the entrance and rock-cut ditches gave further protection on the northeast and southeast sides. Of the outer ward, heavily restored in places, there remains much of the outer northwest gate. The west corner has vanished completely, but much of the southern corners remain. The inner ward is a different story, for most of the curtains and towers have disappeared or been reduced to shapeless lumps of fallen masonry. The principal upstanding remains are those of the great inner bakehouse, which contained the main apartments, and the inner northwest gate tower, which stands to its full height and gives a good indication of the original height of the inner defences.

In the inner courtyard stands the circle of **Gorsedd Stones**, within which are held ceremonies in connection with the National Eisteddfod, which came to Aberystwyth in 1865, 1916, 1952, and 1992. Thirteen stones represent the counties of Wales pre-1974. If you know the Welsh names of the counties and have a taste for cryptography, you can spend an entertaining quarter of an hour deciphering the names carved in the stones in an extraordinary "bardic" alphabet.

Leave the castle by the northwest gate and cross the footbridge onto the Castle Point bm. This area once formed the "third bailey" of the castle and was surrounded by walls and towers. These were in a ruinous state by the mid-14th century and have now disappeared completely, destroyed by the sea encroaching on the headland.

The War Memorial, commissioned and designed by Italian Sculptor Mario Rutelli in 1919, now dominates the point. The Winged Victory or Angel of Peace on top carries both a triumphal wreath and an olive branch. The nude female figure at the base symbolises Humanity freeing herself from the chaos of War. Two rows of bronze plaques record Aberystwyth's lengthy roll of honour in the two World Wars.

After spending some time reflecting, it is time to descend from the headland and onto the Promenade. Follow it to South Marine Terrace/Y Ro Fawr. At the far end of this bear left onto the main wharf of the **Harbour** ⓭. As early as 1280 the constable of the Castle urged that a harbour should be developed as essential to the new town's prosperity. The estuary of the river Rheidol, which before reaching the sea was divided northwards by a single bank, Rofawr, forms the harbour.

For about a century shipbuilding was Aberystwyth's principal industry. Between 1778 and 1880, 278 sailing ships were built, of varying sizes and rigs, from 30-ton sloops to barques of 300 tons or more. They were built mainly on low ground at the north end of the harbour. Shipbuilding brought with it ancillary manufactures, of sails, ropes, blocks, chains, anchors, and a range of chandlery. This industry ceased in the 1880s but boatbuilding continued to 1959, notably at Williams' yard in Trefechan, which specialised in lifeboats during World War II.

Fish was certainly Aberystwyth's earliest export. The smelting of lead ore at furnaces near the harbour in the late 18th century proved uneconomical, but from the mid-18th century to the early 20th, lead ore was the principal export.

Go up steps into South Road, turn right and proceed to the lower end of Bridge Street bo. The present bridge has survived the elements and heavy traffic since 1888, unlike its predecessor, which was destroyed in 1886 by a disastrous flood. The street itself has been less changed by 20th-century developments than any other has!

Two short diversions into side streets to the right as you go up the street are worthwhile: the first into Powell Street/Stryd Powell to see **Tabernacle Chapel** (1880) and the charming little war memorial in the forecourt, another work of Rutelli. The second into Gray's Inn Road/Y Lon Gefn to see **St. Mary's Church.** Begun in 1865 to the designs of William Butterfield, it is the best example in town of Victorian church architecture and has a particularly striking interior.

Retrace your steps to Bridge Street, turn right and walk straight ahead. Then, turning right again, we enter **Great Darkgate Street** ⑮. On the right stands what was once the town's principal inn, the Gogerddan Arms.

Opposite you, you will notice the recently completed replacement town clock, with its modern design and architectural style. The working time mechanism from the original clock tower was carefully restored and is now on show at the Cerdigion Museum.

Farther along and on the right, you will see Chalybeate Street/Y Ffynnon Haearn—this acts as a reminder that a mineral spring, near to the present railway station, was of some repute in the late 18th century.

To take you back to the Railway Station, carry on walking down Great Darkgate Street and turn right down Terrace Road. Once there, there is one last attraction you just cannot afford to miss:

*THE VALE OF RHEIDOL NARROW GAUGE RAILWAY ⑯, ☎ *(01970) 625-819. Runs mid-April to late Oct. Departures at 11a.m. and 2.30 p.m., but from the end of May through the end of Aug. extra times are laid on: Mon.–Thurs., 10.45, 12.15, 2.00, and 3.45. Trains wait 45 minutes before returning and the journey takes 1 hour each direction. Return fares cost: Adult £11, seniors £10, first 2 children £2 each, other children £5.50 each, and dogs £1. Fares and timetables may vary from year to year.*

This extremely popular steam train journey will take you on an 11-3/4-mile scenic tour through the beautiful Rheidol Valley to the well-known attraction—Devil's Bridge. Built in 1902, its original purpose was for carrying equipment and products to and from the lead mines to the valley. Once at Devil's Bridge, there are walks to Mynach Falls, Devil's Punchbowl, and Jacob's Ladder.

Trip 24

New Quay

(Cei Newydd)
A Daytrip from Shrewsbury or Aberystwyth

Just 34 minutes away from Aberystwyth by car is one of Wales's most popular and picturesque seaside destinations—New Quay. Another mode of travel is by bus; this will take you about 45 minutes as there are 11 stops to make before reaching New Quay—on the positive side though, you will be handsomely compensated by the scenic view en route.

One of New Quay's famous visitors was Dylan Thomas, who lived in the town during 1944–45 and wrote his most famous work, *Under Milk Wood*, based on New Quay. Along with the History Trail around town, we will be combining the walk with Dylan Thomas's personal trail—the trail that inspired some of his greatest works.

New Quay has had somewhat of a chequered history; the town's first reference was in the "Cambrian Register" of 1795, where it states "New Quay was a place of notoriety, affording shelter to certain vessels for no other purpose than that of defrauding the revenue, and injuring and beggaring the country by draining it of its health and wealth, to the enriching of our foes in exchange for liquid poison." As evidence of the large scale in which smuggling was carried on, it is stated that the Penwig Side of Church Street was at one time a network of caves, excavated for the sole purpose of hiding contraband goods, mostly brandy and tobacco.

The townspeople were concerned for their safety, so the first steps were taken in 1820 by engaging the services of the famous engineer Rennie to draw out a report and estimate of a proposed new pier. The pier cost between £50,000 and £72,000 to build, but this was inconsequential when compared to lives. New Quay soon became an important centre for fishing and the construction of small vessels. Shortly after, much larger ships were being designed and built in the harbour for people abroad as well as for the coastal trade.

The waning of local industries commenced soon after 1860 with the opening of the Teify Valley railways and the general adoption of steam power.

Today, New Quay is a glorious seaside town, with two main attractions and a wonderful history trail that we can follow. During the summer months a variety of bands will play their instruments on a hill, surrounded by other hills, which in turn creates some fantastic acoustics; you can hear the music for miles and miles — a wonderful experience.

One particular recommendation for anyone visiting New Quay is the excursion on the pleasure boats *Ermol 5* and 6, for a one- or two-hour cruise along the picturesque Ceredigion Marine Heritage Coast. You pass Birds Rock, The Caves, and Seals Bay, giving you the chance to see some of the many sea birds that nest and feed from the cliffs, and also other marine life including Atlantic Grey seals and the awe-inspiring Bottlenose Dolphins and the Harbour Porpoise. Just head towards the pier and buy a ticket.

GETTING THERE:

Trains to Aberystwyth Station leave every 2 hours from **Shrewsbury**. The run takes 1 hour and 45 minutes.

By Bus from Aberystwyth to New Quay, catch the 550 from the bus station, just off Alexandra Road. The first bus sets off at 9.35 a.m. and arrives at Park Street, New Quay at 10.30 a.m. This service operates every half-hour. Your return bus is again the 550 from Park Street.

By Car from Shrewsbury, follow the A458, A483, A44, and A487 routes to New Quay. The total distance is 89 miles and will take 2 hours and 15 minutes.

By Car from Aberystwyth, take the A487 and the B4342 roads to New Quay. The journey takes 34 minutes and has a total distance of 23 miles.

PRACTICALITIES:

The local **Tourist Information Centre** can be found in Paragon House, Wellington Place (near the beach), ☎ (01545) 561-460, **W**: ceredigion.gov.uk. The population of New Quay is approximately 900. Half-day closing is on Wednesdays, although most shops and attractions do stay open all day during the summer season. Also during the summer months, New Quay holds an open-air market every Tuesday, opposite the Quay West caravan park.

FOOD AND DRINK:

The Mariner Restaurant (South John Street) Serves traditional fish and chips. ☎ (01545) 560-467. £

Black Lion Hotel (Dylan's Restaurant) (Glanmor Terrace) Serves bar meals and a speciality board which changes regularly. ☎ (01545) 560-209). £ and ££

SUGGESTED TOUR:

Circled numbers correspond to numbers on the map.

Step off the bus at **Park Street** ❶ and follow the map down Picton Terrace, Penwig Lane, and onto Wellington Place. The trail starts at the **Tourist Information Centre** ❷, where an information board tells you all about Dylan Thomas and New Quay. Opposite is London House, the

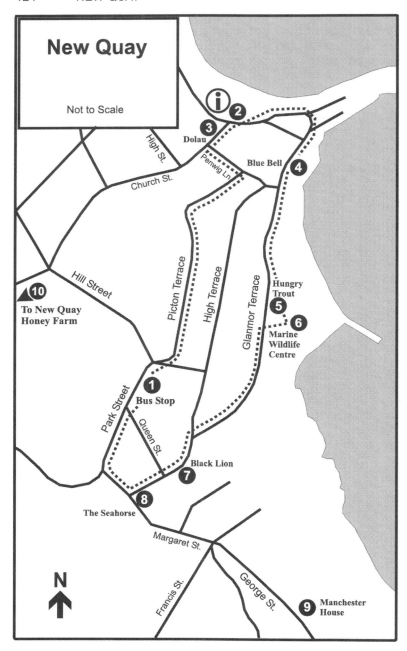

New Quay

Not to Scale

High St.

Dolau

Penwig Ln

Church St.

Blue Bell

Hungry Trout

Picton Terrace

High Terrace

Glannor Terrace

Marine Wildlife Centre

Hill Street

To New Quay Honey Farm

Park Street

Bus Stop

Queen St.

Black Lion

The Seahorse

Margaret St.

Francis St.

George St.

Manchester House

N

home and shop of Dylan's friend Norman Evans, a prototype for the Milk Woods' Nogood Boyo.

Just across the road is the **Dolau** ❸; this was the favourite pub of Caitlin, Dylan's wife. It was also the local of Alastair Graham, Evelyn Waugh's lover; Graham was the basis of Sebastian Flyte in *Brideshead Revisited*.

Stroll over to the **Public Toilets** ❹. This building was once the old lifeboat station. It became known as Cnwc y Glap because the retired sea captains of the town met here everyday to reminisce and gossip. Opposite is the Blue Bell, once run by Auntie Cat, where Dylan and the young Richard Burton drank together.

The Hungry Trout ❺ used to be the post office, where Dylan posted his scripts to London. Jack Lloyd, also the town crier, worked here. As you walk up the hill and look back along the coast towards New Quay, you will see a white bungalow—this is **Majoda**, where Dylan and Caitlin once lived.

Quite close to the RNLI (Royal National Lifeboat Institute) you will find the **Marine Wildlife Centre** ❻.

The Black Lion Hotel ❼, was Dylan's own favourite pub in New Quay, owned by his friend Jack Pat. There's a marvellous collection of Dylan photographs inside. Opposite is Gomer House, where Captain Tom Polly lived, an original inspiration for Captain Cat.

The Seahorse ❽ was called the Commercial in Dylan's day. Before that it was the Sailor's Home Arms, providing the name for Milk Wood's Sailors' Arms.

Look across the road beyond the car park. The chapel you can see is **Towyn**; the minister here was Orchwy Bowen and he was both a poet and a preacher, just like the Rev. Eli Jenkins in *Under Milk Wood*. Opposite Towyn is the Memorial Hall, recalling the Welfare Hall in Dylan's play.

The trail now goes along Margaret Street and George Street. In Dylan's time, both these streets were packed with shops, and to walk along them is to walk through Llareggub (spell it backwards), the fictional town in *Under Milk Wood*. The Costcutter shop was a bakery in Dylan's day, recalling Dai Bread and his two wives. Bethal Chapel became Bethesda in the play. The next house, **Arnant**, was a cobbler's where Dylan liked to sit and gossip, perhaps imagining Jack Black chasing the naughty couples down Goosegog Lane. **Maglona** next door had a barber's in the basement. Did Dylan have his hair cut here, thinking of Mr. Waldo, Llareggub's barber?

The final visit of Dylan's trail is to **Manchester House** ❾. This was a draper's just like the one in Llareggub run by Mog Edwards. Next door, on the left, was Sheffield House, a general ironmonger's of the kind owned by Mrs. Organ Morgan in Milk Wood. On the corner next to the garage, was a sweet shop called the Emporium: the one in Llareggub was run by Myfanwy Price.

We now head back to the bus stop on Park Street, by following the map. The bus to catch is the 550 heading to Synod Inn. Get off near Penlon

Caravan Park (between Cross Inn and Synod Inn). The journey only takes 10 minutes and the attraction—**New Quay Honey Farm** ⓾—is just a half-mile away from the town centre. The Honey Farm is set in an old chapel on a beautiful farm, owned by Gerald and Mariana Cooper, who initially opened a tea room and an exhibition showing the amazing world of the honeybee. Due to the enthusiasm and interest of their customers, they decided to expand the honey shop. They now have on display bees at work, producing honey (all set safely behind glass), a tropical ant colony which shows how social organisation occurs in insects other than bees and wasps, a Meadery showing visitors the production and history of the oldest alcoholic drink known to man (honey wine), a shop that stocks an extensive range of honey and beeswax products, including mead, candles, cosmetics, books, gifts, cards etc., and lastly a tea room converted from part of its 18th-century character. The tea room sells home-made cakes, morning coffee, teas, honey ice cream, and light meals, all at a very reasonable price. On a nice sunny day, take your food out to the picnic area and eat it by the duck pond. *Shop and Tea Room open daily from Easter to Oct., 10–5.30. Exhibition open daily May through Oct., 10–5.30. During Nov. and Dec. the Honey Shop & Tea Room open 11–5, every day except Sun. & Mon. Closed Jan. & Feb. Admission fee to the Exhibition only: Adult £2.65 and children £1.50.* ☎ *(01545) 560-822.*

This daytrip has been an unusual one to take, as we have followed more of a literary trail rather than the normal historical trail, but nevertheless it has been an enjoyable experience. After all, "Variety is the spice of life" and a "Change is as good as a rest."

Aberaeron

A Daytrip from Shrewsbury or Aberystwyth

U nlike some parts of Wales, there are no museums or heritage cen-tres in this little town. You visit Aberaeron either to feed your need for "retail therapy" or merely to enjoy the scenic views by the Quayside.

Only 23 minutes away from Aberystwyth, the town found life between 1807 and 1816, when the harbour and immediate surrounds were built, quickly followed by the construction of an elegant street system flanked by "Late Renaissance" or Georgian houses. When you first enter the town, what strikes you most is the attractive range of colours the hous-es are painted in—duck egg blue, pastille pink, pale yellow etc.—long gone are the boring original grey cement-wash frontages. As soon as you see the houses, it automatically makes you smile and lifts your spirit.

A new age for Aberaeron dawned on the August 1, 1807. On that date Royal Assent was given to "An act to enable the Reverend Alban Thomas Jones-Gwynne, his Heirs and Assigns, to repair and enlarge the Harbour or Port of Aberaeron in the County of Cardigan and to improve the said Harbour and to regulate the mooring of Ships and Vessels there." The far-sighted Rev. Gwynne of nearby Monachdy Mansion had inherited a vast fortune, and, as Lord of the Manor of Aberaeron, initiated on this act to expand this small fishing village into a trading port. Since then, the town has grown and prospered, and in the year 2007 will be celebrating the bicentenary of the Special Act of Parliament signed by King George III.

GETTING THERE:

Trains to Aberystwyth leave every 2 hours from **Shrewsbury**. The trip takes 1 hour and 45 minutes.

By Bus from Aberystwyth to Aberaeron, catch the number 550. The ser-vice runs hourly starting from 9 a.m., but is reduced on Sundays. Return on the 550 from Alban Square.

By Car from Shrewsbury, follow the A458, A483, A44, and A487 road-ways to Aberaeron. The total distance is 89 miles and will take 2 hours and 15 minutes.

By Car from Aberystwyth, take the A487 to Aberaeron. The run only takes 23 minutes and has a total distance of 16 miles.

PRACTICALITIES:

The local **Tourist Information Centre & The National Trust** can be found at The Quay, ☎ (01545) 570-602, **W**: ceredigion.gov.uk. The population of Aberaeron is 1,500. Half-Day closing is on Thursday. Market Day is on Saturday, 10–4.

During the summer months of June, July, and August, the town holds a Country & Western Festival (end of June); a Seafood Festival, and Traditional Summer Fair (middle of July); and the Aberaeron Carnival Day (end of August)—the local TIC will be able to tell you the exact dates and locations.

FOOD AND DRINK:

The Castle Hotel (Market Street) Bar meals, restaurant with Sunday Carvery. Open lunch time and from 7 p.m. onwards. ☎ (01545) 570-205. £

Café & Crafts (Regent Street) Serves fresh coffee, tea, and cakes. Also sells local crafts. ☎ (01545) 571-588. £

The Black Lion Hotel (Alban Square) Homecooked bar meals and a wide selection of real ales. ☎ (01545) 571-382. £

Llond Plat (7 Alban Square, opposite the bus stop) Serves traditional fish and chips to sit down or take away. ☎ (01545) 570-848. £

Hive on the Quay (overlooking the harbour) European cooking in a beautifully situated café/restaurant. Famous for their Honey Ice Creams. Local fresh shellfish a speciality. ☎ (01545) 570-445. £ and ££

SUGGESTED TOUR:

Circled numbers correspond to numbers on the map.

As this particular visit is purely for observing the beautiful scenery and buying gifts in some of the amazing shops, you won't be surprised when I tell you that in the town of Aberaeron there are only two main attractions, and one other on the outskirts. Nevertheless, they all warrant a mention.

Alight from the bus at **Alban Square** ❶ and follow the map through the delightful Market Street and Cadwgan Place to the Harbour and Quay Parade. The **Aberaeron Sea Aquarium** ❷ is inconspicuous in appearance— you might even walk past it without noticing it, just as I did. As with any aquarium, there are lobsters, crabs, eels, and other sea life on display. There is also a large area of white sand where young children can pretend they are on the beach making sand castles. Another room features an audiovisual, again about sea life. *Open daily 9–5 from Easter to the end of Oct. Closed from Nov. to Easter. Admission: Adult £3.50, senior/OAP £2, children £1.25.* ☎ (01545) 570-142.

Exiting the Aquarium, turn right and have a stroll along the Promenade. The fresh sea breeze air will clear away anyone's cobwebs. Those feeling a little bit of nasal congestion will be surprised to find they can instantly breath more easily—wouldn't it be great if we could bottle it and take it home with us!

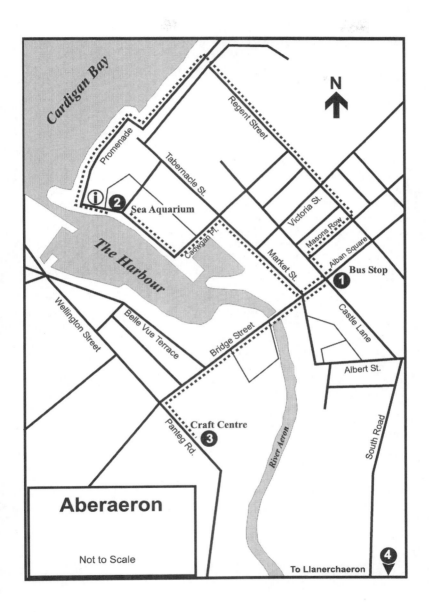

Aberaeron

Not to Scale

Follow the map along Regent Street, Mason's Row, Bridge Street, and Panteg Road, for a two-minute walk to the **Aberaeron Craft Centre** ❸, originally a traditional range of farm buildings that has been tastefully converted into 18 craft workshops. You can actually watch skilled craftsmen and women creating a range of interesting products and gift items, or alternatively just sit and relax in the sheltered courtyard gardens. The Centre is home to an Antiques Shop, Arts and Crafts, a Hobbies Barn, Aeron Pottery, and a restaurant to name but a few. *Open 10–4 all year round. Admission is free.* ☎ *(01545) 570075,* **W**: *crafts.dircon.co.uk*

Retrace your steps back to Alban Square, where you will catch bus number 202 to your last visit of the day, **Llanerchaeron** ❹. The 202 will drop you off on the main road, then be prepared to walk approximately one mile to the mansion. Just ask the bus driver. The bus service runs from 9 a.m. until 7 p.m. The exact timetable is 9, 10 a.m., 12 noon, 2, 3:25, 5:50, and 7 p.m. The journey takes less then 10 minutes. Always check the bus timetables with the Tourist Information Centre, as they do change quite regularly and without much warning.

Llanerchaeron is a small 18th-century Welsh gentry estate that survived virtually unaltered. The house was designed and built by John Nash in 1796. Llanerchaeron was a self-sufficient estate—evident in dairy, laundry, brewery, and salting room as well as the home farm buildings from the stables to the threshing barn.

Today, Llanerchaeron is a working organic farm whose two walled gardens yield home-grown produce. Following extensive restoration to the servants' quarters, service courtyard, and Pamela Ward exhibition, these parts of the house opened to the public for the first time in June 2002. *Open from late March to early Nov., Wed.–Sun., 11–5. Guided tours of the garden and home farm, 2 p.m. every Thurs. in July–Sept.: additional £1. Admission: Adult £4, child £2, family (2+3) £10, adult by bike or foot £3.60, child by bike or foot £1.80, National Trust members free.* ☎ *(01558) 825-147,* **W**: *nationaltrust.org.uk*

On the return journey, you will only need to catch one bus, as the 202 usually connects with the 550 service to Aberystwyth.

Trip 26

Llandudno

A Daytrip from Shrewsbury or Aberystwyth

There is a lot to see and do at Llandudno, so set off on the train good and early to make the most of the day, or alternatively you may decide to stop over an extra night at one of the many guest houses or hotels in town. The local Tourist Information Centre will be able to help you select one.

Although there is much visual evidence to suggest that man has inhabited this part of the coast since 3000 BC, it was primarily the Victorians who created the town for tourists between 1849 and 1912.

Llandudno is Wales's largest resort, uniquely situated between the Great and Little Ormes. The Great Orme is only 4 miles in length, but 679 feet high. It is said that the name "Orme" is derived from an old Norse word for worm or sea serpent and on a misty day it is easy to see why. This huge headland, which the town calls a mountain, was once at the bottom of the sea and so has an abundance of fossil remains of primitive fish, sponges, corals, molluscs, and other invertebrates which can still be found on the land to this day.

During the Victorian era, the Orme seemed big and inhospitable due to the steep slopes and primitive roadways, but soon after the construc-tion of a cable tramway, the first car filled with inquisitive passengers moved off from Victoria Station and up the mountain on July 31, 1902. The service is still in operation today, providing you with an unforgettable scenic journey. Once at the top, you are treated to themed restaurants, bar, gift shops, a country park, and the Great Orme Mines.

At night Llandudno's spectacular crescent bay glistens with a myriad of lights from the elegant Victorian frontage of the Promenade. As the town was developed in the middle of the last century, the Victorian tradi-tion is evident in its architecture with canopied shops and its superbly maintained pier and promenade. Llandudno is certainly a town you will enjoy visiting.

GETTING THERE:

Trains leave Shrewsbury station regularly for the 2-1/2-hour journey to Llandudno.

By Car from Shrewsbury, take the A458, A5, A550, and A55 roadways to Llandudno. The total distance is 80 miles, with a travelling time of 2 hours.

By Car from Aberystwyth, follow the A487 and A470 road signs to

Llandudno. The total distance is 85 miles, with a journey time of 2 hours 15 minutes.

PRACTICALITIES:

The **Tourist Information Centre** can be found at 1–2 Chapel Street, ☎ (01492) 876-413, **W**: llandudno-tourism.co.uk. There are many festivals held in and around Llandudno throughout the summer months, including the Llandudno Victorian Extravaganza & Transport Festival (beginning of May), Sailings to the Isle of Man from Llandudno Pier (end of May), and the Midsummer Music Festival (end of June to July) to name but a few.

FOOD AND DRINK:

Badgers Café & Patisserie (The Victoria Centre, Mostyn Street) Voted one of the top 10 tea rooms in Britain. Speciality cakes, pastries, and food freshly baked each day on the premises. ☎ (01492) 871-649. £

Romeo Ristorante Italiano (25 Lloyd Street) Authentic Italian restaurant pizzeria. ☎ (01492) 877-777. ££

Enochs Fish Restaurant (146 Conway Road, Llandudno Junction) Speciality Fish and Chips. ☎ (01492) 581-145. £

Haulfre Tea Rooms (Great Orme) Opened as a tea room in 1930 by Prime Minister Lloyd George, the original house was owned by Lord Aberconwy's Great-Grandfather Davis Pochin. Serves a variety of pastries, sandwiches, and light lunches. Open 10–5, Easter to October. Closed Mondays in April and October. ☎ (01492) 876-731. £

SUGGESTED TOUR:

Circled numbers correspond to numbers on the map.

Start your tour at the **Train Station ❶**. As on the map, directly opposite the station on Vaughan Street is the **Oriel Mostyn Gallery ❷**. The gallery is regarded as one of the UK's most important, exhibiting opportunities for young and emerging artists. Annually, during March to May, the Gallery holds "The Mostyn Open" where artists internationally can submit their work without supplying their names or curriculum vitae to the judges, for a pecuniary prize of £6,000. If you visit the gallery within these three months, you may just discover the "next" Van Gogh in the making. *Admission Free. Craft Shop. Open Mon.–Sat., 10.30–5.30. Also open Bank Holidays. Closed Dec. 25–26, Jan. 1.* ☎ *(01492) 879-201.*

Follow the map to Trinity Square for your second visit of the day. The **Alice in Wonderland Centre ❸** is not only great for children, but is also great for the child inside you. The "real" Alice (Alice Liddell) spent many summer holidays at her family's residence on the West Shore of town. Large-as-life, animated models relive the story of Alice in Wonderland by Lewis Carroll. The fascinating part of this visit is when you "fall" down the rabbit hole, which has been designed with wheelchair users in mind. *Open Easter through Oct., daily 10–5. Closes an hour earlier on Sun. Open Nov.–Easter, Mon.–Sat. 10–5. Closed Dec. 25–26 and Jan. 1.* ☎ *(01492) 860-*

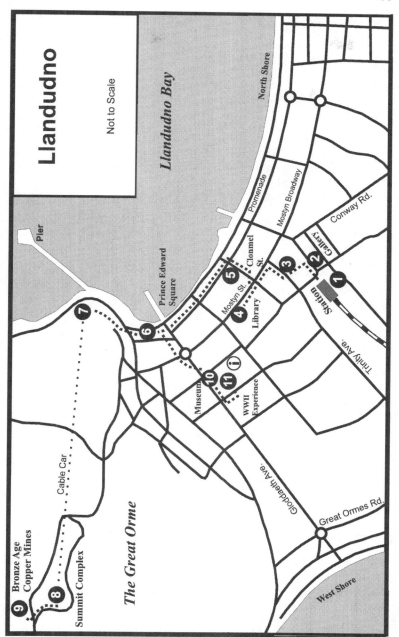

Llandudno

Not to Scale

Llandudno Bay

North Shore

Pier

Promenade

Mostyn Broadway

Conway Rd.

Gallery

Clonmel St.

Prince Edward Square

Mostyn St.

Station

Library

Trinity Ave.

WWII Experience

Museum

Gloddaeth Ave.

Cable Car

The Great Orme

Great Ormes Rd.

West Shore

Bronze Age Copper Mines

Summit Complex

082.

From here, walk along Mostyn Street, with its wealth of cast-iron verandas and porticoes, and past the **Library** ❹, which contains a detailed exhibition on the development of the town and resort.

Back up a little bit until you can see **Clonmel Street** ❺, stroll past the classically designed style of buildings and cast-iron lamp posts to the **Promenade**, where you will enjoy an outstanding view of the Great and Little Orme.

Follow the map left, along the Promenade to **Prince Edward Square** ❻ where you will find a panel celebrating the history of the transport system from the early 19th century to the opening of the Great Orme in 1969.

Carry on walking towards the base of the Great Orme, where a **Cable Car** ❼ will be waiting to take you to the Summit Complex, the Country Park, or the Mines. The ride will only take you 9 minutes for the 2-mile journey, at a cost of £5 for a return ticket for adults and £2.60 for children.

Once at the top, you can pop in to the **Summit Complex** ❽, where you can enjoy an unbeatable panoramic view of North Wales, browse in the gift shop, have a well-earned cup of tea or play a game or two in the Amusement Arcade. For those of you who have come well prepared with binoculars, there isn't a finer place for "twitching" (bird watching). The cliffs of the Great Orme are host to breeding colonies of seabirds such as guillemots, kittiwakes, and razorbills.

The next visit is a must—it is the:

*GREAT ORME BRONZE AGE COPPER MINES ❾, ☎ 01492 870447, **W**: greatorme.freeserve.co.uk. *Open daily from the beginning of Feb. to the end of October, 10–5. Adults £4.50, children £3, family (2+2) £12.50, under 5's free. Visitor Centre. Coffee shop / Secondhand Books. Gift Shop.*

These copper mines you are about to explore were dug 300 years before the Pharoh Tutankhamen lived and died in Egypt. Over 4 miles of tunnels have so far been surveyed, and the archaeologists have found hundreds of animal bones—and also some human remains. The mine tour consists of an introduction to the mines' history and importance via an audiovisual. There is an underground tour exploring the 3,500-year-old passages (it's the only Bronze Age copper mine open to the public in the world). You can also view a prehistoric landscape discovered in 1987, peer down a 470-foot-deep shaft and visit the smelting site, where our prehistoric ancestors turned rock into metal. For the small entrance fee charged, it is an experience of a lifetime.

After your return journey on the cable car, follow the map to Gloddaeth Street, where you will find the **Amgueddfa Llandudno Museum** ❿. The museum and art gallery is administered by the Trustees of the Chardon Trust. Francis Edouard Chardon was a keen collector of objets d'art, paintings, and sculptures from all over the world; when he died he left the house and its contents to the town of Llandudno "for the benefit of the inhabitants and visitors alike." ☎ *(01492) 876-517. Open Easter to Oct., Tues.–Sat., including Bank Holidays, 10.30–1, and 2–5, Sun. 2.15–5. From Nov.–Easter, Tues.–Sat., 1.30–4.30 p.m., closed Christmas. Admission: Adult £1.50, senior/student £1.20, children £0.75p, family (2+3) £3.50 and family (1+3) £2.25.*

If you still have time to spare, bob into **The World War II Home Front Experience** ⑪ on New Street, the next street up from the Museum. This attraction takes its visitors back sixty years to when Britain was at war. For those of you not old enough to have been through the war, this experience gives you the opportunity of living a life during the 1940s—the blackout, the wailing air raid sirens, and sitting in an Anderson shelter that is under attack from German bombers. It's all a bit hair-raising, but at the same time an eye-opening experience.

At the "Home Front" you can find out all there is know about ration vouchers, a war kitchen, the work of an Air Raid Warden, the Home Guard, the Auxiliary Fire Service, and the Women's Land Army. This attraction is a fairly modern history lesson (60 years, instead of 3,500) but nonetheless a very important one. It tells of people managing to live and survive under extreme conditions and not succumbing to the threats of an evil tyrant. That is something we all should remember even in this day and age.

Follow the map back to the train station.

Trip 27

Conwy

A Daytrip from Shrewsbury or Aberystwyth

Only four miles away from Llandudno is one of the best-preserved mediaeval fortified towns in Britain, Conwy. The massive battlemented walls surrounding the town and castle have three double gateways and 21 towers. This great castle was built by Edward I in 1283 and was strategically sited to guard the wide estuary, now crossed by three graceful bridges.

In Conwy town there are over 200 listed buildings, spanning from the Elizabethan, Jacobean, Georgian, and Victorian eras. The Aberconwy House, dating from 1400, and Plas Mawr (the Great Hall) built between 1576 and 1585, can still be visited today.

On the lively quay at Conwy stands a house claimed to be the smallest house in Britain. It consists of just 2 rooms and measures 6 feet across, by 10 feet 2 inches to the eaves.

Conwy is a beautiful Welsh town, only 7 minutes away from Llandudno, so why not combine the two daytrips together and make one great day out!

GETTING THERE:

Trains leave Shrewsbury every hour for the 2-1/2-hour journey to Conwy.

Trains leave Llandudno train station every hour for the 18-minute journey to Conwy.

By Car from Shrewsbury, follow the A458, A5, A483, A541, A550, and A547 roadways to Conwy. The total distance is 78 miles, with a travelling time of 2 hours.

By Car from Aberystwyth, take the A487, A470, A5, and B5106 roads. The total distance is 82 miles, with a travelling time of just over 2 hours.

By Car from Llandudno, follow the A546 to Conwy. The total distance is just 4 miles and the journey time only 7 minutes.

PRACTACALITIES:

The local **Tourist Information Centre** is situated within Conwy Castle's Visitor Centre, ☎ (01492) 592-248, **W**: llandudno-tourism.co.uk. During July, Conwy holds the annual Bluegrass Festival, and during August the town plays host to the River Festival.

FOOD AND DRINK:

Anna's Tea Room (9 Castle Street) Specialises in home cooking, soups, lasagne, scones, cakes, tea, coffee etc. Open 10–5. ☎ (01492) 580-908. £

Archies at Langleys (Aberconwy Park, near Conwy Marina) Bistro serving International and English food. ☎ (01492) 580-404. £ and ££

SUGGESTED TOUR:

Circled numbers correspond to numbers on the map.

Leave the **Train Station** ❶ and turn right onto Rosemary Lane. Follow the map through Lancaster Square (the centre of a variety of activities in Conwy throughout the year—i.e. Morris Dancing and Christmas Carol singing) and onto the High Street, where we stop for our first visit. **Plas Mawr** ❷ or the "Great Hall" was built for an influential Welsh merchant named Robert Wynn during 1576–85. The tall, lime-rendered walls reflect the status of its builder, as does its richly decorated interior.

Plas Mawr is an architectural gem, the finest surviving town house of the Elizabethan era to be found in Britain. It stands as a symbol of a prosperous, buoyant age, epitomised by the style and taste of Robert Wynn, a remarkable and well-travelled courtier and trader who rose to pre-eminence amongst the Welsh gentry. The interior of the house is magnificent, with its glorious decorated plasterwork ceilings and friezes, and skilful carpentry. Visitors can take an audio tour of the house that describes the restoration and the life of the Tudor gentry. *Open   April–Sept., 9.30–6. Closed Oct.–March. Admission: Adults £4.10, reduced rates £3.10, family ticket (2+3) £11.30.* ☎ *(01492) 580-167.*

A little farther up the street, on the corner of High Street and Castle Street is **Aberconwy House** ❸, which is the only 14th-century, medieval merchant's house in Conwy to have survived the turbulent history of the walled town for nearly six centuries. The rooms have been decorated to depict the different eras of the house's past. An audiovisual presentation helps you relive a bygone era. *Open daily March–Nov., 10–5. Admission: Adult £2, child £1, family (2+3) £5, pre-booked group £1.80, National Trust members free.* ☎ *(01492) 592-246,* **W**: *nationaltrust.org.uk*

Follow the map along Castle Street and take the first turning on your right—this will lead you to St. Mary's Churchyard where you will see the tombstone with the epitaph "We are seven." Retrace your steps and turn right back onto Castle Street. As you stroll along, you will notice on the opposite side the **Teapot World Museum** ❹. Housed within this building is an extraordinary collection of teapots from all eras, dating from the mid-18th century to the present day. There are also a few rare teapots on display. Open daily Easter–Oct. Admission: Adult £1.50, children/ seniors/students £1, family (2+2) £3.50. ☎ (01492) 596-533.

Keep on walking straight a head, until you reach:

*CONWY CASTLE ❺, ☎ (01492) 592-358, **W**: cadw.wales.gov.uk. *Open daily March–May, 9.30–5; June–Sept., 9.30–6; Oct.–March, Mon.–Sat. 9.30–4 and*

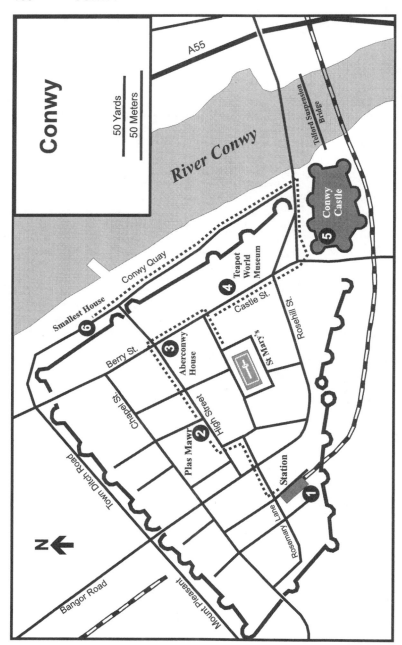

Conwy

50 Yards
50 Meters

River Conwy

A55

Telford Suspension Bridge

Conwy Castle 5

Conwy Quay

Teapot World Museum 4

Smallest House

6

Castle St.

Rosehill St.

Berry St.

Aberconwy House 3

St Mary's

Chapel St.

High Street

Plas Mawr 2

Town Ditch Road

Rosemary Lane

Station

1

Mount Pleasant

Bangor Road

N

Sun. 11–4. Closed Dec. 24, 25, 26, Jan. 1. Admission: Adults £3.50, reduced rate £3, family ticket (2+3) £10. Also available: joint ticket for Conwy Castle, with Plas Mawr. Gift Shop. Guidebook available. Guided Tours available (must book in advance).

The Castle was constructed between 1283 and 1289 by the English monarch Edward I at a cost of £15,000 in an attempt to contain the Welsh within his "iron ring" of castles. Conwy Castle is a huge, gritty, dark-stoned fortress, which evokes an authentic medieval atmosphere. Its circuit of walls is over three quarters of a mile long and is guarded by no less than 22 towers. After visiting the castle why not try and "walk the town walls."

In comparison to other great Edwardian castles, Conwy is relatively straightforward in design, a reflection of the inherent strength of its siting. The castle, a World Heritage Site, has soaring curtain walls and eight huge round towers, which radiate an intimidating presence undimmed by the passage of time.

Within the castle is an exhibition on medieval chapels and a large gift shop selling a variety of quality souvenirs.

Exit the castle and turn right onto Castle Square, then left onto Conwy Quay. We leave one massive structure and enter one of the smallest—that of the **Smallest House in Great Britain** ❻. This little red house has just two rooms and measures 6 feet across, and 10 feet, 2 inches in height. It was originally built as a fisherman's cottage and amazingly, its last occupant measured 6' 3" in height—the mind boggles as to how he lived there. *Open April–Oct.*

Follow the map back to the train station.

Bangor

A Daytrip from Shrewsbury or Aberystwyth

Bangor City sits close to the Menai Straits, a stretch of water separating the charming Isle of Anglesey from mainland Britain. The city's name was derived from the word "Bangori," which means "binding part of wattle fence," and has been in existence since AD 525, when a nobleman by the name of Deiniol was given the land to build a dwelling place and church on by the King of Gwynedd's son Maelgwn. Deiniol enclosed his land by driving posts into the ground and weaving branches between them—hence the phrase "binding part of wattle fence."

Today, situated in the heart of the city, stands the enchanting Cathedral Church of St. Deiniol, which Queen Elizabeth II visited during her Golden Jubilee in 2002.

After centuries of plight, Bangor eventually found prosperity when it became a major seaport and began shipping slate throughout the world. Evidence can still be seen at Penrhyn Castle, located on the outskirts of Bangor and definitely worth a visit. Now owned by the National Trust, this mock Norman Castle was originally built by the Pennant Family, who had made vast fortunes by exporting slate from Bethesda Quarries. Lavishly decorated with stunning views, the castle has a Victorian walled garden, a fine collection of steam engines and grand master paintings on display.

GETTING THERE:

Trains depart Shrewsbury station hourly for the 3-hour ride to Bangor.

By Car from Shrewsbury, take the A458, A5, and A5122 roadways to Bangor. The total distance is 82 miles with a journey time of just over 2 hours.

By Car from Aberystwyth, follow the A487, A470, and A5 roads to Betws-y-coed. The total distance is 88 miles, with a travel time of 2-1/2 hours.

PRACTICALITIES:

The local **Tourist Information Centre** is in the Town Hall on Deiniol Road. ☎ (01248) 352-786, **W**: gwynedd.gov.uk. Bangor's half-day closing is on Wednesday, although during the summer season hardly any shops close early. Bangor's population is approximately 17,000. Open-air market held every Friday. The Bus Station is near to the Museum and Library—you can't miss it.

FOOD AND DRINK:

You'll pass a good number of excellent cafés and restaurants along the route of this walking tour. Just a couple are mentioned below:

La Bella Vita (166 High Street) Italian flavour—serving pizza and pasta dishes. ☎ (01248) 362-920. £ and ££

Penrhyn Castle Tearoom (Penrhyn Castle, near Bangor) Licensed tea room, serving light meals and snacks. ☎ (01248) 371-381. £

SUGGESTED TOUR:

Circled numbers correspond to numbers on the map.

Leave **Bangor Railway Station ❶** and follow the pedestrianized High Street to your first visit, the:

*CATHEDRAL CHURCH OF ST. DEINIOL ❷, ☎ 01248 353983. *Open daily Mon.–Fri., 7.30–6, Sat. 10–1, Sun. services from 7.30 a.m.–12.30 p.m. and 2.30–6p.m. Free to enter. Gift Shop.*

St. Deiniol is the oldest cathedral foundation in the United Kingdom, being founded as a church in AD 525 and a cathedral in AD 546. It is due to this fact that Queen Elizabeth II selected this cathedral to represent Wales in a National Service of Thanksgiving on June 11, 2002, during her Golden Jubilee.

This beautiful cathedral definitely warrants a visit. The Stewards on duty are particularly helpful and will offer to show you around, but if you decide to stroll around on your own, then buy a guide book at the cost of only £2. Not only will the book guide you through St. Deiniol's chequered history, but it will also act as a keepsake and remind you of a happy daytrip to Bangor.

Back to the map. Follow it to Fford Gwynedd (Gwynedd Road) where next to the Library, you will find **Bangor Museum & Art Gallery ❸**. The museum has three floors; on the ground floor you will find the Gallery containing paintings, sculptures, photography, and temporary exhibitions. Also on the same floor there is an activities room and shop. The first floor is home to a traditional Welsh kitchen, furniture, and a section where you can learn about the local history. The second floor is filled with archaeological finds and various costumes from bygone days. *Open Sat. 10.30–4.30; Tues.–Fri. 12.30–4.30. Closed Sun., Mon., public holidays, and the Christmas period. Free.* ☎ *(01248) 353-368.*

For your last visit of the day you will need to catch the number 5 or 5X bus to Llandudno and ask the driver to drop you off at the main gates of:

*PENRHYN CASTLE ❹. ☎ *(01248) 353-084. Open March–Nov., Wed.–Mon. Closed Tues. Castle opening times during March to June and Sept. to Nov., noon–5; Aug. 11–5. Garden & Stable-Block exhibition opening times March to June and Sept. to Nov. 11–5; July and Aug. 10–5. Admission: Adult £6, child £3, family (2+3) £15, group 15+ £5. Garden & Stable Block only: Adult*

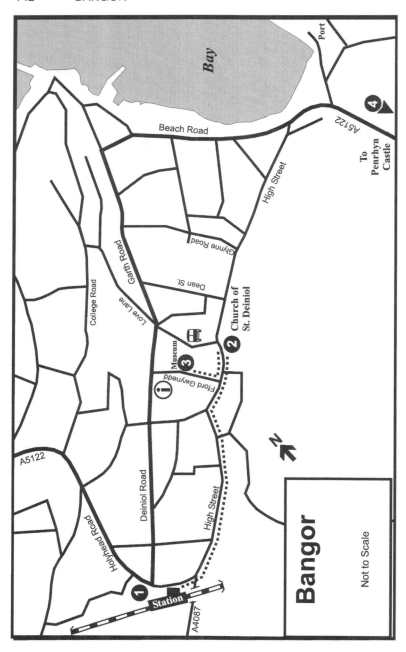

Bay

Port

A5122

To Penrhyn Castle

Beach Road

High Street

Glynne Road

Garth Road

Dean St.

Love Lane

College Road

Church of St. Deiniol

Museum

Ffordd Gwynedd

A5122

Deiniol Road

High Street

Holyhead Road

Station

A4087

Bangor

Not to Scale

£4, child £2.

Built for the Pennant family by the architect Thomas Hopper during the 19th century, the castle is an elaborate example of neo-Norman architecture. The Pennant family commissioned Hopper in the 1830s to build their "stately home" and designer furniture out of Welsh slate. Everywhere you look there is slate—floors, fireplaces, staircase, and even a one-ton slate bed made for Queen Victoria.

The castle is set in 45 acres of breathtaking parkland, overlooking the Menai Straits and the Snowdonia Mountains.

As well as the extravagant décor of the castle to see, you can also visit the old stable blocks where there are two Railway Museums, a Dolls' Museum, two exhibition Galleries, and a shop. The Gallery is home to one of the best art collections in Wales and exhibited paintings include the works by Rembrandt, Gainsborough, and Canaletto.

This visit has something for everyone—from young to old, you won't be disappointed. You can catch the same bus back to Bangor (5X) from the main gate.

The Cathedral Church of St. Deiniol

Trip 29

Caernarfon

A Daytrip from Shrewsbury or Aberystwyth

On leaving Bangor, we head 9 miles south by bus to the fortified town of Caernarfon. Very few towns in Britain can claim to be inhabited without a break since pre-Roman times, but Caernarfon can boast such a feat. The town's roots go far back as AD 78, when the fort of Segontium was built high on the hill above Caernarfon - today, the excavated ruins and museum are open to the public.

During 1283, the English monarch Edward I built Caernarfon Castle as a symbol of power and strength over the Welsh. It was not only constructed as a military stronghold, but also as a royal palace and seat of government. Caernarfon's royal connections go from ancient Celtic chieftains to modern times with the investiture (a ceremony at which a sovereign confers honours) of Prince Charles, the present Prince of Wales, in 1969.

It is imperative that this town not be missed as it is an extremely historic and beautiful one to see. Near to where the castle stands, the Menai Straits run into the Seiont River, bringing with it an array of sailing vessels. Sit on the side of the Quay, eat your sandwiches and watch the world go by.

GETTING THERE:

Trains leave Shrewsbury every few hours for the 3-hour trip to Bangor, where you change to a bus for Caernarfon.

By Car from Shrewsbury, follow the A5 and A4086 roads for the 2-1/4-hour journey to Caernarfon. The total distance is 85 miles.

By Car from Aberystwyth, take the A487, A470, A4085 (junction for Porthmadog—take the 2nd exit at the roundabout), and A4086 roads. The total distance is 74 miles, with a travel time of about 2 hours.

From Bangor Bus Station take any of the number 5 buses to Caernarfon. They run every 20 minutes, with a travelling time of one-half hour. The same bus number brings you back.

PRACTICALITIES:

The local **Tourist Information Centre** is located on Castle Street, ☎ (01286) 672-232, **W**: gwynedd.gov.uk. Caernarfon's population is approximately 10,000. Market days are on Saturdays and Mondays during the summer months. Half-day closing is on Thursday.

FOOD AND DRINK:

Macsen Café/Restaurant (11 Castle Square) Air-conditioned coffee shop and licensed restaurant, serving morning coffee, light snacks, and an à la carte menu; using the freshest produce for their Welsh and Vegetarian fayre. ☎ (01286) 676-464. £ and ££

The Little Tea Pot (13 Stryd y Castell—Castle Street) Smoke-and-chip-free zone. A wide selection of home baked cakes and gateaux on offer, as well as the traditional Welsh Cream Teas. Speciality, croissants, and bagels with various fillings, such as smoked salmon. ☎ (01286) 678-444. £

Bechdan Bach (Castle Square) Open for daytime snacks and light meals—mainly serving sandwiches and baguettes. ☎ (01286) 677222. £

The Battered Cod—Takeaway and Café (28 High Street) Eat in or take out, traditional fish-and-chip shop. ☎ (01286) 675-576. £

Stones Bistro (4 Hole in the Wall Street) Relax in a 300-year-old building and taste the delicious Welsh Lamb. You can also enjoy a candlelit supper with a more international flavour. ☎ (01286) 671-152. ££

SUGGESTED TOUR:

Circled numbers correspond to numbers on the map.

Get off at the **Bus Station ❶** on Penllyn and follow the map along Castle Ditch until you come to the entrance of:

*CAERNARFON CASTLE ❷, ☎ (01286) 677-617, **W:** caernarfon online.co.uk. *Open daily March–May, 9.30–5; June to end of Sept., daily 9.30–6. Winter months, Mon.–Sat. 9.30–4 and Sun. 11 a.m. to 4 p.m. Closed Dec. 24–26, Jan. 1. Parking, toilets and gift shop. Admission: Adult £4.50, reduced rate £3.50, and family ticket (2+3) £12.50. Within the castle is the* **Royal Welsh Fusiliers Museum,** ☎ *01286 673362, open daily June–Sept., 9.30–6. Early closing Oct.–May (please ring for times). Admission free.*

Caernarfon Castle was built as a symbol of English dominance during 1283 by Edward I. Architecturally, the castle has a majestic aura surrounding it—it was no accident that Edward tried to re-create the walls of Constantinople, the imperial power of Rome, and the "dream-castle—the fairest that man ever saw." Edward succeeded with his dream, for he built a fortress with unique polygonal towers, intimidating battlements, and colour-banded masonry.

During 1294, Madog ap Llywelyn (from a junior line of the ruling dynasty of Gwynedd) rebelled against the Edwardian settlement, burned down part of the castle, and damaged the town walls. By the following year, the English had reclaimed the castle and made it defendable again.

The **Royal Welsh Fusiliers Museum**, based within the castle, re-enacts some of the fighting scenes of that era—it is well worth asking the castle administration which dates these are held, but as a point of rule, they usually take place during the May and August Bank Holidays.

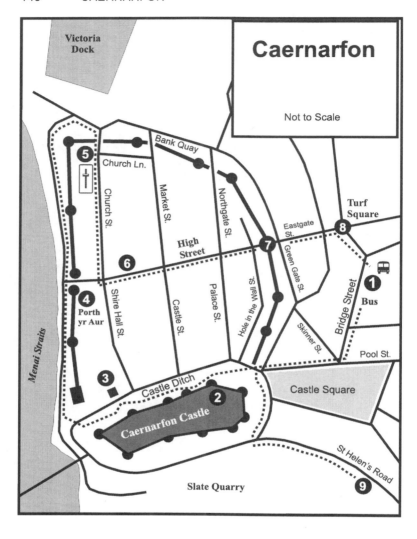

Caernarfon

Not to Scale

Victoria Dock

Menai Straits

Church Ln.

Bank Quay

Church St.

Market St.

Northgate St.

High Street

Eastgate St.

Turf Square

Green Gate St.

Shire Hall St.

Castle St.

Palace St.

Hole in the Wall St.

Skinner St.

Bridge Street

Bus

Pool St.

Porth yr Aur

Castle Ditch

Caernarfon Castle

Castle Square

St Helen's Road

Slate Quarry

Carry on walking along Castle Ditch until you see an imposing, classical building—the **County Hall** ❸. Although a County Hall has been in this vicinity since the 13th century, the present building with its Ionic columns dates from the 1860s and is currently used as the County Court (the statue of Justice on the roof gives it away).

Turn right, following the town walls along the Promenade until you pass through the arches of **Porth yr Aur** ❹ (meaning Golden Gate), which houses the Royal Welsh Yacht Club. In 1933, Group Captain Lionel Brabazon-Rees, a club member, boarded his 34-foot ketch *May* and sailed to Miami, Florida—making him the first man to sail the Atlantic single-handed.

Continue to follow the map to Bank Quay and then turn right through an archway. Immediately to your right you will find **St. Mary's Church** ❺. Henry of Ellerton, one of the castle's master masons, initially founded this as a garrison church in 1307 and incorporated it into the town walls. Even though the building underwent some extensive renovation during the early 19th century, many of the original features remain, including the arcades over the nave and the rare Jesse Window in the southern wall.

Pass the church and turn left on to **High Street** ❻. You are now entering the traditional commercial centre of town. Looking up the street you can appreciate the impact of the iron grid pattern of the old town as laid out by Edward I. It was divided into 56 equal blocks of 80 x 60 feet, called Burgages, each one rented to an individual burgess (borough magistrate or governor), who paid an annual rent of one shilling. The distance between each street is 160 feet, i.e. 2 burgages.

Walk straight ahead and through the arch of the main entrance to the town. To your right is **Porth Mawr** ❼ on Eastgate Street. In medieval times there was a curfew on the town's inhabitants; those not inside the town walls by 8 p.m. would be locked out as the drawbridge closed in Porth Mawr. Above the gateway was the Exchequer to the Chancery of North Wales, the old tax office, which during 1763 was taken over as the Town Hall. Unfortunately alterations over the years have meant that much of the original gate has disappeared and what we see today is mainly from the Victorian era.

Carry on under Porth Mawr to **Turf Square** ❽, the site of the town pillory and stocks that were instituted in the 13th century, with the proviso that the victim's body was to suffer no harm. This form of punishment remained in use until 1837.

After all that walking, it's time to put your feet up and enjoy the scenic views of the Menai Straits and the mountains of Snowdonia. Head towards St. Helen's Road, where you can catch the:

*WELSH HIGHLAND RAILWAY ❾, ☎ (01766) 516-073, **W**: festrail.co.uk. *Running daily April through Oct., approximately every 3 hours starting from 10.30 a.m. All Day Return ticket: Adult £8, concession £6.50, and fami-*

ly (2+2) £16. Half-way return journey: Adult £4, concession £3.25, family £8.

The one-hour-and-15-minute return train journey takes you past some stunning views of the Menai Strait and the mountains of Snowdonia. The Welsh Highland Railway in Caernarfon is one of North Wales' newest tourist attractions, with trains steaming out of the town for the first time on the re-opened line in October 1997. Backed by the Millennium Commission, the year 2000 saw the line extend along the original track bed for the first time in 60 years, from Dinas to Waunfawr, one of the gateways to the Snowdonia National Park.

Follow the map back to the bus station.

Caernarfon Castle

Porthmadog

A Daytrip from Shrewsbury or Aberystwyth

This busy little town, home to the Ffestiniog Railway and gateway to the country's breathtaking Snowdonia National Park, has only been in existence for less than 200 years. William Maddocks, who had a lifelong interest in this part of North Wales, turned his attention to the adjoining town Tremadog, which in 1806 was nothing but marshland in the Glaslyn Estuary. With his enthusiasm and the rapidly growing slate trade business, Maddocks began to reclaim the land with the thought that it would be the last staging post on the London-to-Ireland route.

Between 1808 and 1825, Maddocks built an embankment, known as the "Cob," and the harbour (hence the town's name, which translates as "Madog's Port"), which started to bring prosperity to the town. It is estimated that during the 1870s over a thousand vessels used the harbour in any one year and at its very peak in 1873, over 116,000 tons of Blaenau slate left Porthmadog for all parts of the world.

Today Porthmadog is a bustling town full of individual shops and places to eat. Steam railway buffs just love the place because of the Ffestiniog and Welsh Highland Railways.

GETTING THERE:

Trains depart Shrewsbury every couple of hours for the 3-hour trip to Porthmadog.

Trains leave Aberystwyth frequently for the approximately 3-hour ride to Porthmadog—this includes a change at Machynlleth.

By Car from Shrewsbury follow the A5 and A487 roads to Porthmadog. The total distance is 80 miles, with a journey time of 2 hours.

By Car from Aberystwyth, take the A487, A470, and again the A487 routes to Porthmadog. The total distance is 59 miles, a journey of 1-1/2 hours.

PRACTICALITIES:

You can find the **Tourist Information Centre** close to the Maritime Museum on Stryd Fawr, ☎ (01766) 512-981, **W**: gwynedd.gov.uk. Half-day closing in Porthmadog is on a Wednesday. The population of the town is about 4,000.

FOOD AND DRINK:

Llechan Las Welsh Bistro (10 Bank Place) Serves traditional Welsh meals including local game and seafood. ☎ (07780) 837-667. £ and ££

Cadwaladers Ice Cream (43/47 High Street) Offers a choice of coffee's, baguettes, rolls, pastries, and ice cream sundaes. £

The Royal Sportsman Hotel (131 High Street) Serves traditional and international menus cooked to order—uses fresh ingredients. Eat in the Orchard Restaurant, Tavern Bar or garden. ☎ (01766) 512-015. £ and ££

SUGGESTED TOUR:

Circled numbers correspond to numbers on the map.

Leaving the **Train Station ❶**, walk in a southerly direction down High Street until you reach Ganolfan, where you turn right on to Oakley Wharf. Towards the end of the wharf you will find the **Porthmadog Maritime Museum ❷**. A hundred or so years ago the small ports of Gwynedd, which included the Menai Straits and Caernarfon to name but two, were crammed with working sailing ships, hundreds of them owned and built locally, engaged both in coastal and oceanic trades. The beautiful three-masted schooners that came from the shipyards of Porthmadog, known to contemporaries as the Western Ocean Yachts, gained an enviable reputation in the slate trade and in the salt fish trade. The largest vessel to come from the local shipyard at Port Dinorwic in 1878 was the 875-ton wood barque *Ordovic*, but many large wooden sailing ships built in the Canadian Maritimes and the United States were owned and managed in Gwynedd throughout the last century. At the museum you can discover the story of the world-famous "topsail" schooners, their builders, and about the men who sailed in them. *Open daily May through Sept., 11–5. Small admission charged.* ☎ *(01766) 513-736.*

As you leave Oakley Wharf, turn to your immediate right and head towards Harbour Station and the **Ffestiniog Railway ❸**. This unique steam-hauled narrow-gauge train was built in the 1830s to haul slate from the quarries of Blaenau Ffestiniog to the harbour at Porthmadog, where it was then loaded onto ships. Originally using horse traction uphill and gravity down, the line developed suitable steam engines in 1863 and began a passenger service in 1865. As the slate industry declined after the turn of the century, the line turned increasingly to the tourist trade for its survival. This lasted until the beginning of World War II, after which the railway was abandoned. In 1954 it was taken over by a dedicated group of voluntary preservationists, who began a short passenger service in 1956, only to be frustrated by the construction of a pumped-storage hydroelectric facility that put part of the line under water.

This setback was overcome by a spectacular detour, adding greatly to the railway's scenic beauty. In 1982 the railway was totally restored all the way from Porthmadog to Blaenau Ffestiniog, a distance of 13.5 miles.

The railway twists and climbs its way through the foothills of Snowdonia National Park, climbing over 700 feet and doubling around

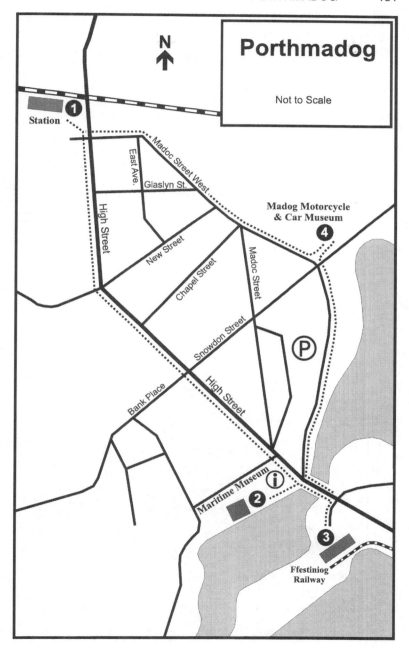

Porthmadog

Not to Scale

N

Station ❶

Madoc Street West

East Ave.

Glaslyn St.

High Street

New Street

Chapel Street

Madoc Street

Snowdon Street

Madog Motorcycle & Car Museum ❹

Ⓟ

Bank Place

High Street

Maritime Museum ❷

ⓘ

❸ Ffestiniog Railway

itself in a great horseshoe bend. The 1-hour journey passes pastures and forests, lakes and waterfalls, always providing breathtaking vistas along the way.

The Ffestiniog Railway offers two classes of service, Third and First. *Fares charged for 3rd class All Day; Adult £14, seniors £11.20, family(2+2) £28. 3rd Class Half-way Trip; Adult £8.50, seniors £6.80, family £17. For 1st Class seating in the Observation Car, there is an additional charge of £2.50 single or £5 return. Snacks and drinks are always available in both classes.* ☎ *(01766) 516-073,* **W**: *festrail.co.uk*

Follow the map along the sea front to the **Madog Motorcycle & Car Museum** ❹ located on Snowdon Street. This museum has a wonderful collection of British-built cars and motorbikes. On display are toys and models from the last century, classic cars, and a display of memorabilia of all kinds. *Open from Easter to Oct., 10–5. Admission: Adults £2, seniors £1.50, children £1, under 5 free.* ☎ *(01758) 713-330.*

To get back to the train station, follow the map along Madoc Street West.

Along the Ffestiniog Railway

In an Observation Car of the Ffestiniog Railway

Trip 31

Portmeirion

A Daytrip from Shrewsbury or Aberystwyth

Just three miles South of Porthmadog is the spectacular Italianate village of Portmeirion, created by the architect Clough Williams-Ellis between the years 1926 and 1976. He had one purpose in mind, and that was to show how a naturally beautiful location could be developed without spoiling it. Clough died on the April 8, 1978.

Today, Portmeirion is owned by a registered charity, the Second Portmeirion Foundation. The grounds are designated as a Conservation Area and most buildings are listed Grade II. The village attracts over 240,000 visitors a year from all over the world; the admission charge levied at the tollgate contributes directly to the maintenance of the grounds and buildings.

During 1966–67, Portmeirion was used as the setting for one of UK's and USA's most famous television series, *The Prisoner*. Many daytrippers of a certain age will remember Patrick McGoohan, who played "Number Six" in the series—a retired secret service agent not allowed to roam free in the world with the knowledge in his head and so was sent to a top-secret establishment for the rest of his life, known as The Village—a safe house, where Second World War spies "retired" until the war was over.

Within the village itself are many wonderful restaurants and shops to mooch around in. With Portmeirion being only 2 hours from either Shrewsbury or Aberystwyth, you can easily make a full day of it—but don't forget your camera—this daytrip is a memorable one!

GETTING THERE:

Refer to the train information in the **Porthmadog** chapter (page 000). From the Australia Pub in Porthmadog catch the **Bus Express 98** which leaves for Portmeirion at 10.10 a.m. and 2.10 p.m. The return bus departs Portmeirion at 12.06 p.m. and 4.30 p.m.

By Car from Shrewsbury follow the A5 and A487 roads to Portmeirion, 1.5 miles west of Penrhyndeudraeth, signposted at Minffordd. The total distance is 79 miles, with a journey time of 2 hours.

By Car from Aberystwyth, take the A487, A470, and again the A487 routes to Portmeirion, as above. The total distance is 57 miles, a journey time of about 1-1/2 hours.

PRACTICALITIES:

The **Portmeirion Village** can be contacted on ☎ (01766) 770-228, **W**: portmeirion.com. The nearest **Tourist Information Centre** is in Porthmadog on Stryd Fawr, ☎ (01766) 512-981, **W**: Gwynedd.gov.uk

A WARNING—Do not go onto the estuary without first checking the tide times. Also there are many steps and steep paths and the woods and beach are not accessible to wheelchairs.

FOOD AND DRINK:

Castell Deudraeth Bar & Grill (Portmeirion) Brasserie style menus based on fresh local produce including lobster, crab, and scallops from the Lyn Peninsula, rock oysters brought in daily from the shores of Anglesey, Welsh beef and lamb hill-farmed from the farms around Bala. ££

Cadwaladers Ice Cream Parlour (Portmeirion) Uses fresh local dairy produce create its traditional ice creams. Tea and coffee also served. Open March to November, 10–5. ☎ (01766) 522-478. £

The Town Hall Restaurant (Grade II listed building in Portmeirion) Also known as Hercules Hall, it was designed to house a Jacobean ceiling, panelling, and mullioned windows salvaged from Emral in Flintshire. Self-service restaurant with seating both inside and outdoors. Offers a choice of hot and cold meals as well as snacks from 10–5. £ and ££

SUGGESTED TOUR:

Circled numbers correspond to numbers on the map.

Portmeirion has 45 points of interest, and far too many to mention here. However, I will point out to you just some of the key buildings and areas that were used in *The Prisoner* episodes, so you can have your photograph taken in the very spot where Patrick McGoohan stood.

To help guide you around this vast village I would suggest accessing the Portmeirion website and print out the Guidebook, or alternatively you can buy the Guide Book from the Portmeirion Gift shop once there.

Portmeirion is a beautiful and unique attraction, one that should not be rushed. Even though the location sites from *The Prisoner* are highlighted as the tour in this chapter, be sure to visit every magnificent piece of architecture within the village.

Leave the car park to the **Tollgate** ❶, where you will pay your admission charge (see details at the end of the tour text). Follow the map to the **Battery Square** ❷. The surface is delightfully cobbled and surrounded by a pair of archway-linked buildings—**The Round House** ❸ and **Lady's Lodge** ❹ will be easily recognisable to *The Prisoner* show fans as Number 6's residence and the village store. The Round House is a Grade II listed building and is one of a pair of Baroque shops linked by an overhead walkway. In actual fact the house is too small to accommodate a spacious lounge, bedroom, bathroom, and kitchen as was seen in the series, so all the interior shots had to be filmed at the MGM Studios. The building now houses Number Six, the Prisoner Shop. The other Baroque shop—Lady Lodge,

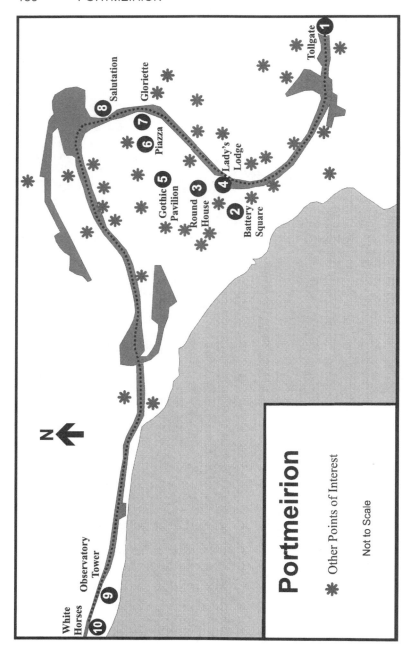

Portmeirion

* Other Points of Interest

Not to Scale

has a beautiful semi-circular mural above the bay window by Hans Feibush. Originally Lady Lodge was built as a lock-up garage, but was converted in the early 1960s into the Battery Stores and then The Peacock. Both signs are featured in *The Prisoner*. The shop is now called Siop Bach (little shop) and above it is the Lady Lodge Beauty Parlour.

Directly across the road from Lady Lodge, below the dome, is a pan-tiled loggia housing a gilt statue of Buddha, which Clough Williams-Ellis managed to salvage from the film set of the Inn of the Sixth Happiness, starring Ingrid Bergman.

Follow the map to **The Gothic Pavilion** ❺, which was built to front the Gloriette beyond its pool and fountain. The lawn in front of the Gothic Pavilion is where the human chess game was played in *The Prisoner* through laying white squares on the grass.

Straight in front of you is the **Piazza** ❻. This part of the Portmeirion Village was prominently used in the making of the series. You can easily see why—a beautiful fountain pool, surrounded by exotic plants and flowers, where you can sit and think and imagine that you too are part of that fabulous television series, set somewhere in a secret location, far, far away. Also a part of this masterpiece, two gilt Burmese dancers stand on Ionic columns, and just beyond, the majestic Gloriette. The "Dance of the Dead" episode was filmed at the Piazza.

The first episode of *The Prisoner* was titled "'Arrival," where the mysterious Rover Mark II made its debut at the top of the **Gloriette** ❼. As you may remember, Rover was the 7-foot inflatable balloon that appeared from nowhere and chased McGoohan across Portmeirion's beach. During the series over 5,000 balloons were used, mainly because they kept popping. To keep Rover from floating away the makers of the series had to fill the balloon with a mixture of helium and air for buoyancy and a pint or two of water to hold it down. In the episodes "The Chimes of Big Ben" and "Free for All," Rover grew two "babies"—absolutely mind boggling, but anything was possible in this surreal TV show.

Follow the map to **Salutation** ❽. This Grade II listed building, erected sometime between 1842 and 1858, is now the Salutation Restaurant and a shop specialising in Portmeirion Pottery. Clough's daughter Susan and her husband Euan designed and painted the colourful mural of vines and cupids with fountain and white doves on the courtyard side of this building. Prisoner fans will recognise it as the café area used in the television series.

Stroll along to the **Observatory Tower** ❾. This part of the beach was used in the film scenes for "The Queen's Pawn (Checkmate)" and features the Tower/Camera Obscura in the rear shot. At the foot of the Observatory Tower is a Coade stone figure of Nelson, given to Clough by Sir Michael Duff from Caernarfon. Close by is a weeping beech tree given to Clough by his friends on his 80th Birthday.

The last visit of our Prisoner tour is to the **White Horses** ❿ on the map. This 18th-century building was originally a fisherman's cottage.

White Horses is so called because with a spring tide and a south-westerly gale, crested breakers batter its walls and occasionally even break and enter. Clough for a short time used it as a workshop for weaving and dyeing until 1966 when he converted White Horses into habitable accommodation by adding two bedrooms raised on arches above the beach footpath. One of the first residents to stay at White Horses was Patrick McGoohan in 1966–67 while filming *The Prisoner.*

Open every day of the year from 9.30–5.30. Admission: Adult £5.30, seniors £4.20, children £2.60 (under 5 free), and family (2+2) £12.60. ☎ *(01766) 770-000,* **W**: *portmeirion.com*

Aerial View of Portmeirion Village

Isle of Anglesey

Three Daytrips from
Shrewsbury or Aberystwyth

We leave the cosmopolitan City of Bangor and head in a southerly direction, across the Menai Bridge and onto the tranquil Isle of Anglesey. Robin Ddu, the 16th-century bard, prophesied that the Menai Straits would be bridged, but it took the genius of Thomas Telford to complete the task. Telford was born the son of a shepherd in a tiny cottage by the Megget Water at Glendinning, Dumfries on August 9, 1757. He built canals, roads, bridges, aqueducts, docks, and harbours throughout Britain, but the Menai Suspension Bridge is widely regarded as one of his finest achievements.

The Menai Bridge was finally opened to the public on 30th January 1826, but unfortunately Telford died only eight years later on 2nd September 1834. The bridge is the largest in Britain and is 1,500ft in length.

The Isle of Anglesey nestles on the northwest corner of Wales, with 125 miles of spectacular coastline, all designated as areas of outstanding natural beauty. Everywhere you look, you can see field upon field of luscious green grass with new spring lambs jumping around each other, playing an imaginary game of "tick."

There are no high-rise blocks here and the traffic on the roads is practically non-existent, just land as far as the eye can see.

The island is 60 miles in circumference, contains about 200,000 acres, 74 parishes, and 2 market towns—Beaumaris and Llangefni. The ancient name for Anglesey was Insula Opaca, based on the quantity of wood with which it was overgrown, and on its principal commodities of corn, cattle, fish, and fowl; all of which it produced with such abundance that the Welsh call it Mam Cymru—i.e. the Mother of Wales.

There are many beautiful little towns to visit on the island, including **Beaumaris** (page 161), **Benllech** (page 166), and **Holyhead** (page 170), just to mention a few. All are accessible via public transport.

Another draw to the island is what the Welsh call Llanfair P.G., otherwise known to the rest of the world as Llanfairpwllgwyngyllgogerychwyrndrobwllllantysiliogogogoch—the place with the longest name in the UK.

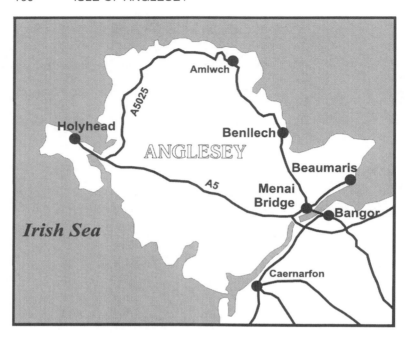

The Menai Bridge

Beaumaris

A Daytrip from Shrewsbury or Aberystwyth

As you enter this elegant little town via the coastal road, you will be treated to a spectacular scene—hundreds of sailing yachts anchored in the bay, belonging to the members of the Yachting Centre, who annually hold the two-week Menai Strait Regatta during August.

Its history, like many of the Welsh towns, started late in the 13th century when Edward I began building the castle, which was the last in a series along the North Wales Coast. The castle was sited on a "beautiful marsh" or Beau Mareys (Beaumaris).

Beaumaris Castle is regarded as the "great unfinished masterpiece" as its construction was not fully completed. Edward I ran out of money and supplies before the fortifications reached their full height. Despite this fact, the castle is nonetheless an awesome sight, and thought of as one of the finest of all the great Edwardian strongholds.

To this day, the town still shows its medieval origin in its layout and by its many buildings of interest. For example, Tudor Rose, built in the main street in 1400 or so, is one of the oldest houses in Anglesey; and close to that you have the "Ye Olde Bull's Head Hotel," an ancient inn visited by such illustrious traveller's as Dr. Johnson and Charles Dickens.

Beaumaris is one of the prettiest towns in Wales, and so to fully appreciate its beauty and perfect location, you should climb to the top of the hill directly opposite the castle's park and have a look.

GETTING THERE:

Trains depart Shrewsbury via Chester for the 2-1/2-hour ride to Bangor, where you change to a bus (see below).

By Bus from Bangor, catch numbers 53,57, or58, which run hourly for the 22-minute journey into Beaumaris's Castle Street. The service on Sundays runs every 2 hours from 9.27 a.m. until 9.18 p.m. For return journeys, catch the same bus numbers.

By Car from Shrewsbury, follow the A483, A5, A487, and A4080 roads to Beaumaris. The journey time is 2 hours 17 minutes, with a total distance of 89 miles.

By Car from Aberystwyth, take the A487, A4080, and A545 routes to Beaumaris. The total distance is 85 miles, with a travel time of about 2-1/4 hours.

PRACTICALITIES:

For information contact **The Beaumaris Chamber of Trade and Tourism,** ☎ (01248) 810-317, **W**: beaumaris.org.uk, located in the Town Hall. The best way to see the town is on foot. Although a good dry day is always favourable, Beaumaris can be visited at any time of the year. If you do get stuck in a shower, just bob into one of the many cafés and ask for a "cream tea" until it passes.

The town of Beaumaris has a population of approximately 2,000. Half-day closing is on a Wednesday, although during the summer months most shops do remain open until about 5.30 p.m.

FOOD AND DRINK:

The Spinning Wheel Tea Rooms (Castle Street, near the Castle) Speciality Welsh Cream Teas, although other light meals and sweets are also served. Set in comfortable and pleasant surroundings. £

The Bulkeley Hotel (Castle Street) A grand hotel, with a sweeping stair-case on your right as you pass through two sets of huge double doors. On Sundays they open up one of the many lounges to host a weekly antiques fair. Serves a variety of foods; soups, cream teas, à la carte menu etc. ☎ (01248) 810-415. £ and ££

Ye Olde Bull's Head Inn (Castle Street) A coaching inn, the Bull's Head is one of the oldest buildings in the town. Pub grub served; soup, steak, welsh lamb, etc. ☎ (01248) 810-329. £

The Sailors Return (Church Street) Built on the old Town Wall—the remains of which are still visible, the Sailors Return was first opened during the 1800s, with probably one small room serving beer from a wooden barrel into an enamel jug. A small but varied selection of food on offer; soup, garlic mushrooms, steak, gammon, fish, curry etc. ☎ 01248 811-314. £

SUGGESTED TOUR:

Circled numbers correspond to numbers on the map.

Get off the bus at Castle Street, where straight ahead of you is:

***BEAUMARIS CASTLE ❶**, ☎ (01248) 810-361. *Open daily 9.30–5 from end of March to the end of May; end of May through Sept., daily 9.30–6. In Oct., daily from 9.30–4; end of Oct. to end of March, Mon.–Sat., 9:30–4 and Sun. 11–4. Closed Dec. 24, 25, 26, Jan. 1. Admission: Adults £2.50, reduced rate £2, family ticket (2+3) £7. Gift shop. Mostly ৬.*

Beaumaris Castle has a magical feel to it. For all its tranquil setting now—swans and ducks swimming idly on the moat—when you start to cross the draw bridge, you immediately find yourself thinking about the people who once inhabited it.

King Edward I began building his last and largest castle in 1295, on an entirely new site. Due to the designer's creative genius, it is probably the most sophisticated example of medieval military architecture in Britain.

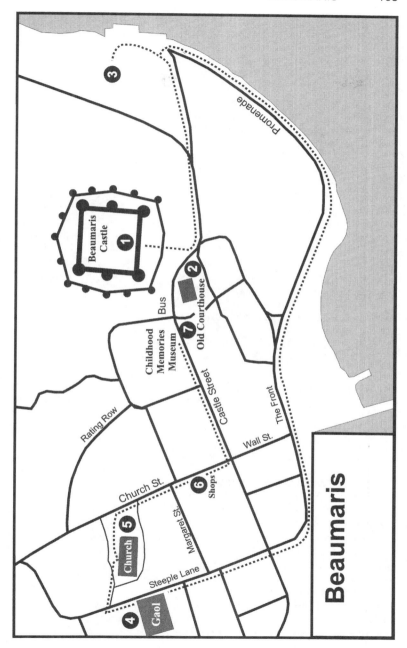

Beaumaris

Beaumaris Castle ①

③

Promenade

Bus

Childhood Memories Museum

Old Courthouse ②

⑦

Rating Row

Castle Street

The Front

Wall St.

Church St.

Shops ⑥

Margaret St.

Church ⑤

Steeple Lane

Gaol ④

The designer, Master James of St.George, had many years of experience in castle-building, both in Wales and on the Continent, and so armed with so much knowledge he engaged 2,600 men to start construction. Across the 18-foot-wide moat is a low curtain wall of the outer ward, its circuit punctuated by 16 towers and two gates.

Visitors to the castle should not miss the little chapel in the tower of that name. Its vaulted ceiling and pointed windows make it one of the highlights of the castle. Also in this tower is a fascinating exhibition on the "Castles of Edward I" in Wales, which provides much background to the building of Beaumaris itself.

As you leave the castle, directly in front of you on Castle Street is the **Old Courthouse** ❷, a building with an atmosphere all of its own. Since 1614, when the Courthouse was built, all types of prisoners have faced trial here. For many of them it was a case of life or death. Some of the prisoners sentenced at the Courthouse included Hugh Hughes in 1786, cruelly whipped through the streets of four towns on the island for stealing food. Another man sentenced there was William Murphy, who in 1910 murdered his mistress on Christmas Day after she left him for someone else. Although it may seem gruesome, this visit is very interesting. *Open daily, Easter to Sept., 10.30–5. Small admission charge.* ☎ *(01248) 811-691.*

Follow the map around the green (used as a car park in high season) and head towards the end of the Promenade, where you will find a little rusty gate that gives access to the **bottom of a hill** ❸. Climb to the top and be rewarded with some fantastic views of Beaumaris town, the castle, the straits, and Snowdonia—definitely well worth the effort.

Retrace your steps back down the hill and stroll along the front of the Promenade, right the way around onto Steeple Lane. Just past Rosemary Lane, on your left you will find **Beaumaris Gaol** ❹, a massive building with dimly-lit corridors, spartan cells, and places of punishment. It is a hands-on experience, where, if you feel inclined, you can sit in the stocks and handle the chains and fetters last worn by prisoners centuries ago. *Open daily, Easter to Sept., 10.30–5. A small entrance fee is charged.* ☎ *(01248) 810-921.*

Follow the map to **St. Mary and St. Nicholas Church** ❺. The south porch of this 14th-century church houses the empty coffin of Princess Joan, wife of Llywelyn Fawr. Joan died at Llywelyn's court in Aber in February 1237 and was brought across Lavan Sands to be buried at Llanfaes Friary (then situated on land on the outskirts of the present town of Beaumaris). When the friary buildings were demolished in 1539 during Henry VIII's Dissolution of the monasteries, many of the monuments there were hastily dispersed or destroyed. The lid of Joan's coffin was taken to the church in Beaumaris, while the coffin itself was left in a field alongside the Llanfaes-to-Beaumaris road. Early this century the lid and coffin were brought together once again, but the whereabouts of Joan's body remains a mystery.

Exit the church at Church Street and walk along until you reach lilac buildings in the shape of a **square** ❻. Those of you with shopping in mind will find a cobbled square of craft and gift shops selling the most ornate and unusual ceramics and metal ware.

After spending a few pounds on gifts for friends back home, follow the map back along Castle Street and head towards the Castle. Just before reaching it, on the right-hand side of the street, you will find the **Museum of Childhood Memories** ❼. Located within a Georgian building are over 2,000 exhibits illustrating the happier side of family life over the past 150 years. The museum was opened during 1973 and is home to teddy bears, nursery furniture, push-along toys, the Prince of Wales corridor—a historical memory lane, audiovisual items and much, much more. *Open Mon.–Sat., Easter to Nov. 1, 10.30–5.30; Sun. noon to 5. A small entrance fee is charged. Gift Shop.* ☎ *(01248) 712-498.*

After your last visit of the day, catch the return bus to Bangor from Castle Street.

Beaumaris Castle

Benllech

A Daytrip from Shrewsbury or Aberystwyth

On the North Coast of Anglesey, only 10 miles from Bangor, is the popular seaside resort of Benllech. Set in a crescent-shaped bay, with fossil-studded cliffs, is the fine beach of golden sand. When the tide is out you can walk right across, uninterrupted, to the picturesque Red Wharf Bay—have a bit of lunch at the Ships Bell and stroll back again.

As a young girl, I spent my holidays in Benllech, and because the whole community is so friendly and welcoming, my mother relocated and now lives in the town.

You won't find any museums or galleries in Benllech. What you will find here is a wide variety of shops, hotels and pubs all situated within easy walking distance of each other and the beach.

If you want a day of relaxation by the sea, then the quaint little Welsh town of Benllech shouldn't be missed. You can combine this visit with Beaumaris and/or Holyhead.

GETTING THERE:

Trains depart Shrewsbury station hourly for the 3-hour ride to Bangor, where you transfer to a bus (see below).

By Bus from Bangor to Benllech, catch the number 62 from the bus station. The first bus leaves at 7.45 a.m., the next 8.45 a.m. and then every 15 and 45 minutes past the hour until 1.45 p.m., then 2.45 p.m., 3.45 p.m., 4.45 p.m., 5.15 p.m., 5.45 p.m., 7.15 p.m., 8.35 p.m., 9.35 p.m. and the last one 10.35 p.m. On Sundays there is a limited service—11.50 a.m., 2.45 p.m., 4.35 p.m., 7.05 p.m. and the last one at 9.20 p.m. The journey time is 27 minutes.

By Car from Shrewsbury, take the A5, A55, and A5025 roads to Benllech. The total distance is 92 miles, with a journey time of 2-1/2 hours.

By Car from Aberystwyth, follow the A487, A470, A4085, and A4086 road signs to Benllech. The total distance is 89 miles, with a travel time of about 2-1/2 hours.

PRACTICALITIES:

The **Tourist Information Centre** representing Benllech is 18 minutes away at the station site in Llanfairpwllgwyngll or Llanfair PG for short, ☎ (01248) 713-177, **W**: anglesey.gov.uk, E-mail: llanfairpwll.tic@virgin.net. The bus number 62 runs via Llanfair PG from Bangor to Benllech.

Half-day closing is on Thursday. The nearest market is held in

Llangefni on Thursdays and Saturdays. Llangefni is 6.4 miles away from Benllech. Choose a nice, warm day for this visit, as you want to gain the most from walking on the beach. Also, ask the local tourist office for a timetable for the incoming and outgoing tides—you don't want to land on the beach only to find that the tide is in and you can't walk over to Red Wharf Bay.

FOOD AND DRINK:

Wendon Café (The Promenade) Serves traditional meals, all-day English breakfast, lunches, and dinner. £

The Jolly Fryer (Corner of Beach and Bangor roads) Traditional fish and chip meals. £

The Breeze Hill Hotel (Bangor Road) Serves a wide variety of pub lunches and dinner. Traditional meals cooked to a high quality. ☎ (01248) 852-308. £ and ££

The Bay Court Hotel (Beach Road) Open from 8 a.m. until late, serving breakfasts, lunch, and dinner. Well-cooked food and large portions. Friendly, relaxed atmosphere. ☎ (01248) 852573. £

The Talent House Restaurant (Bangor Road) Specialises in Peking and Cantonese cuisine to take out or eat in. ☎ (01248) 853-889. £ and ££

SUGGESTED TOUR:

Circled numbers correspond to numbers on the map.

As mentioned earlier, this particular visit isn't noted for museums or similar attractions; it is instead a popular seaside resort which you can enjoy sitting on a deckchair on the golden sands. You can easily combine a trip to Benllech with a trip to Beaumaris and/or Holyhead as they are all situated on the same coastal road.

Ask the bus driver to let you off at the **stop** ❶ nearest to the Glanrafon Hotel on Bangor Road. Only a few yards away is the town centre's precinct with its array of gift shops. In the same square you will suddenly smell the delicious aroma of home-baked bread—pop in and buy some Welsh "Bara-brith."

As you complete walking round the precinct, there are some steps leading back onto Bangor Road, directly opposite Benllech Church. Saunter down them, cross over the road and turn left. Stroll past the chemist, which is also a well-stocked gift shop, and pop into a delightful shop called **Classy Things** ❷. For the avid "Beanie Bear" collector, this shop is paradise. Here you can buy the "rare" beanies for less than £10. Also stocked within the shop are other collectors' pieces, such as fairies, cards, pottery, and much, much more.

Come out of the shop and turn right, continue walking along Bangor Road past The Talent House restaurant and the Benllech Hotel, then turn right onto Beach Road. From here, it is only a 10-minute walk to the beach, but you do have to command a steep downwards slope to reach it, remembering that you have to climb back up afterwards. If you are not

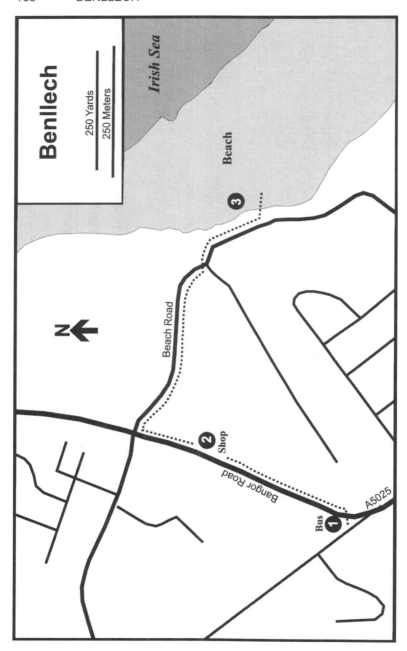

100% fit and able, I would suggest calling a taxi— ☎ (01248) 853-600.

When the tide is out, the **beach** ❸ stretches for miles, right across to Red Wharf Bay. The stroll across the beach is a beautiful and relaxing way to de-stress yourself—just breathe in the sea air and listen to the gentle lapping of the waves on the shore.

After having a spot of lunch or high tea in The Ships Bell at Red Wharf Bay, retrace your steps and make your way back to the town centre where you can catch the same numbered bus back to Bangor. All the fresh, unpolluted air will make you sleep like a log when you arrive back at your hotel tonight.

Benllech Beach

South Stack at Holyhead (see Page 173)

Holyhead

A Daytrip from Shrewsbury or Aberystwyth

The largest town on Anglesey is Holyhead, perched on Holy Island and connected by a causeway built in the Regency period of the 1820s by Thomas Telford. The grey-stone port is the terminal of the ferry services to Dublin and Dun Laoghaire and is a major attraction with its delightful promenade, traditional shops, and surrounding countryside.

Anglesey is comparatively flat when looking back over the Menai Straits to the peaks of Snowdonia. The highest point on the island is Holyhead Mountain, which rises 700 feet above sea level.

There have been many civilisations that have left their mark on Holyhead—Vikings, Druids, and finally the Romans. St. Cybi is a 13th-century church in Holyhead that was built on land where once a Roman Fort stood. The Romans were also responsible for founding copper mining in the island, and the industry flourished right up to almost the present day.

Holyhead has prospered and grown over the years, thanks to its close proximity to the Irish coast. It takes little more than an hour and a half to cross by ferry to Dun Laoghaire, and as early as 2000 BC the town was busy with boats discharging axes from Ireland. Since the formation of the Single European Market, the port has offered an ideal link from the Continent to Ireland.

It has been recorded that more than 2.5 million passengers pass through Holyhead each year, making the future of this town extremely bright.

GETTING THERE:

Trains leave Shrewsbury hourly and take 2 hours and 40 minutes to arrive at Holyhead.

By Car from Shrewsbury, take the A5 and A55 roadways to Holyhead. The total distance is 105 miles with a journey time of 2 hours and 40 minutes.

By Car from Aberystwyth, follow the A487, A470, A4085, A55, and A5154 routes to Holyhead. The total distance is 102 miles, with a travelling time of about 2-1/2 hours.

PRACTICALITIES:

The local **Tourist Information Centre** is situated at Terminal 1, Stena Line, ☎ (01407) 762-622, **W**: angelsey.gov.uk. The main terminal building is adjacent to Turkeyshore Road. The population of Holyhead is approximately 12,500. Anyone requiring wheel chair hire can contact the Red Cross. ☎ (01248) 430-588.

Market days are on Fridays and Saturdays.

FOOD AND DRINK:

The Harvest Moon (Newry Street) Vegan Café serving local produce, situated in the heart of the town. £

The 79 Public House (Market Street) Serves bar snacks and three-course meals at lunch time and evening. Has speciality board, which is changed regularly. Open from 12 noon. £ and ££

The Kings Arms (Public house on Victoria Road) As the 79, serves bar snacks and three-course meals. Open from 12 noon. £ and ££

SUGGESTED TOUR:

Circled numbers correspond to numbers on the map.

Leave the **Train Station** ❶ and stroll along Victoria Road to the **War Memorial** ❷. The monument was designed and executed by L.F. Roslyn, R.B.S of London. Roslyn used imperishable materials such as Cornish granite and bronze and built it to a simple yet dignified design. The panels on either side are a tribute to the Navy and to the Army, representing also "Freedom" and "Honour." The bronze wreaths represent "Victory" and the swords symbolise "Sacrifice." The Memorial was unveiled by H.M. Lord Lieutenant Commodore Sir R. Williams Bulkeley Bt., K.C.B. on September 15, 1923.

Follow the map the **Ucheldre Centre** ❸ on Millbank. The Ucheldre has been transformed from a convent chapel into an award-winning arts and exhibition centre and is regarded by many as one of the jewels in the crown of Anglesey. Visitors to the Centre are delighted by the range of what is on offer—Welsh folk dancing, traditional Celtic music, outdoor Shakespeare, mime, dance, talks, concerts, and shows by well-known touring companies and broadcasting personalities. Also on offer at the Ucheldre is some wholesome home-cooked food, which can be found in a beautiful contemporary kitchen. If that doesn't appeal to you, you can stroll around the landscaped gardens with its amphitheatre and sculpture or browse in either the bookshop, music shop, or gift shop. *Open Mon.–Sat., 10–5, Sun. 2–5. The Ucheldre Kitchen is open weekdays 10–4.30, Sun. 2–4.30. Admission free.* ☎ *(01407) 763-361.*

Back to the map and follow Victoria Road straight up to Salt Island where the **George IV Arch** ❹ is located. Built during 1822–24 by Thomas Harrison, an architect from Chester, it commemorates George IV's landing at Holyhead on August 7, 1821 en route to Ireland; the royal yacht was delayed by bad weather and eventually the king had to travel on the new post office steam packet, a decision that earned him popularity. Public subscription paid for the monument, and it was inserted into the 1821 scheme designed by the renowned engineer John Rennie; this resulted

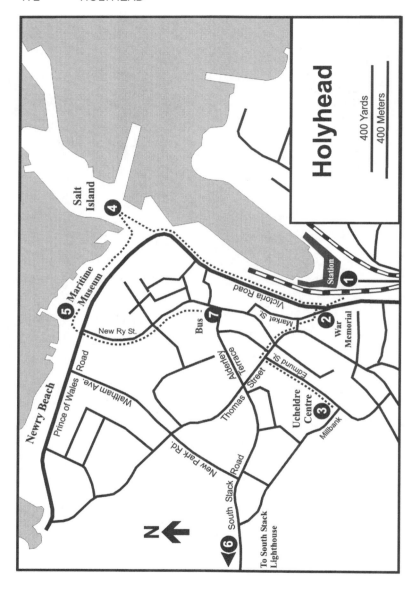

from an Act of Parliament to improve the harbour, and it included Admiralty Pier, Harbour Office, and Customs House. The Doric structure in the form of a gateway is traditionally known as the Triumphal Arch. The monument is built of Mona marble from Red Wharf quarry and is now a Grade II listed building. It was unveiled by the Marquis of Anglesey on August 6, 1824.

Follow the new harbour round to the right and on to Newry Beach. The **Maritime Museum** ❺ is housed in the oldest lifeboat station in Wales. The original station was built in 1858 and cost £410 to construct it from local stone; it had no windows and was lit by oil lamps. Some 144 years later, it is now home to the museum, which is entirely run by willing volunteers. The museum houses a display of models, photographs, and artefacts relating to the maritime history of Holyhead and district from Roman times until the present. *Open Easter to end of Sept., Tues.–Sun., 1–5. Closed Mon. Café & Gift Shop. During the closed season, private parties are accommodated by contacting the Secretary,* ☎ *(01407) 764-374. Admission: Adults £2, children 50p, family £5, seniors £1.50. Museum* ☎ *(01407) 769-745.*

If you are fit and able you cannot leave Holyhead without paying a visit to **South Stack** ❻, an historic **lighthouse** located on a small island reached via a descent of 400 steps down the steep mainland cliffs. For obvious reasons, those with heart or respiratory conditions are advised not make the visit. Built in 1808, the lighthouse has guided many vessels around the dangerous rocks. Inevitably though, many strayed off course to their doom, the most well-known being the *Royal Charter,* which went down on a stormy day in 1859 with over 450 passengers and crew while on its way from Australia to Liverpool. Bullion and valuables worth almost half a million pounds were recovered from the wreck, and the story was used by Charles Dickens in his essay The Uncommercial Traveller.

To visit South Stack, which is only 3 miles away from Holyhead, a special bus service is in operation between the months of April and October, Monday through Saturday. The number 22 bus runs from **Summer Hill** ❼, in the centre of town, at 10:50 a.m., 2:30 p.m., and 5 p.m., and arrives at the lighthouse 15 minutes later. *Open daily Easter to Sept., 10:30–5.30. Admission: Adults £2.50, students/seniors £2, children £1.50, and family ticket £6.50. Tickets may be purchased from the South Stack kitchen or at locations displaying the South Stack logo. A minimum height requirement of 1 metre is required for entry to the tower.* **W**: *lighthouse-visits.co.uk*

Cardiff

(Caerdydd)

Proclaimed the Capital of Wales in 1955, Cardiff has been populated since the Romans arrived in AD50. Its name is derived from the Roman General Aulus Didius—"Caer Didi." The Romans left in the 5th century, and little is known about the people who inhabited the area until the 11th, when the Normans arrived.

Cardiff's wealth and prosperity began with the Industrial Revolution when the local landed gentry (the Bute Family) took a huge gamble in creating the Cardiff Dock, and by building the Glamorganshire Canal, which connected the Dock with Merthyr Tydfil, enabling Cardiff to export coal and iron from the Welsh Valleys. At its peak in 1913, more than 13 million tons of coal left the City.

Today Europe's youngest city is an exciting place to visit, a rich blend of ancient and modern, where Victorian and Edwardian architecture is complemented by some of the most innovative of new developments. For the very reasons mentioned, you could also consider Cardiff as a base for the following daytrips to Newport (page 179) and Tenby (page 183).

GETTING THERE:

Trains leave Shrewsbury Station every 20 minutes for the 2-hour run to Cardiff's Central Station.

Trains depart London's Paddington Station hourly, arriving at Cardiff's station in 2 hours.

By Car from Shrewsbury, take the A458, A5112, A49, B4367, A4113, A4110, A49, and M4 roadways to Cardiff. The total distance is 110 miles, with a journey time of about 2-1/2 hours.

By Car from Aberystwyth, follow the A487, B4337, A482, A476, A48, M4, and again the A48 routes to Cardiff. The total distance is 111 miles, with a travelling time of just over 2-1/2 hours.

By Car from London, follow the M4 route to Cardiff. The total distance is 152 miles, taking just under 3 hours.

PRACTICALITIES:

The local **Tourist Information Centre**, ☎ (029) 2066-7773 or (029) 2022-7281, **W**: cardiff.gov.uk, is on Wood Street, near the Central Train Station. Open every day, all year. Cardiff's population is approximately 300,000. The indoor market is open every day except Sundays.

FOOD AND DRINK:

Cardiff has a wide variety of restaurants and pubs in all price ranges, and is noted for its distinctive local beer, Brains. A few dining suggestions are:

Benedicto's (4 Windsor Place, just off Queen St., near the Park Hotel) International cuisine in elegant surroundings. ☎ (029) 2037-1130. X: Sun eve. £££

Old Orleans (17 Church Street, just off High St.) Lively bar/restaurant with American Deep South theme. Menu includes Cajun and Creole dishes. ☎ (029) 2022-2078. £ and ££

Giovanni's (38 The Hayes) Authentic Italian cuisine — a family-run business since 1983. ☎ (029) 2022-0077. X: Sun. ££

Celtic Cauldron (Castle St., near the Castle) Small and busy restaurant providing a true taste of Wales. ☎ (029) 2038-7185. £

SUGGESTED TOUR:

Circled numbers correspond to numbers on the map.

Beginning at **Central Station ❶**, follow the map past the Tourist Information Centre (also known as Cardiff Visitor Centre) and onto Westgate Street where you will find the **Millennium Stadium ❷**. This magnificent piece of modern architecture dominates Cardiff's skyline. For a relatively small entrance fee, you can see where pop icons such as Robbie Williams have performed and where sports stars in Rugby and Football have played. You can even visit the VIP areas, sit in the Royal Box and see where HRH the Queen, Prince Philip, the Princess Royal and the Prince of Wales sat during Rugby World Cup 1999. *Open daily Mon.–Sat., 10–6, Sun. 10–5. Closed Good Friday, Dec. 24–26 and 31, Jan. 1. Adults £5, children (5–16yrs)*

£2.50, concessions £3, children (under 5yrs) free; family ticket (2 adults & 3 children) £15. ☎ *(029) 2082-2228,* **W**: *Cardiff-stadium.co.uk*

Follow Westgate Street to Castle Street and:

*****CARDIFF CASTLE ❸**, ☎ *(029) 2087-8100,* **W**: Cardiff-info.com/castle. *Open March–Oct., daily 9.30–6; Nov.–Feb., daily 9.30–5. Closed Dec. 25–26, Jan. 1. Admission prices of Grounds and Tour of interiors (approx. 50 minutes): Adults £5.25, children & seniors £3.15, family £14.75. Admission charges for the Grounds only (no tour): Adults £2.60, children & seniors £1.60, family £7.40. Last entry an hour before closing. Tea Room and Gift Shop.*

The Castle is really three in one—part Roman, part medieval castle, and part 19th-century mansion. Norman Lord Robert Fitzhamon arrived in town in 1091 and built a fort out of timber. This was replaced by a stone keep during the 12th century and strengthened over the years against Welsh attacks. Then, in 1865 after succumbing to centuries of ruination, the Third Marquis of Bute commissioned the architect William Burgess to restore the castle to a quite lavish specification. This attraction is a must see!

Now follow Kingsway to the **City Hall ❹**, built in 1905 of Portland

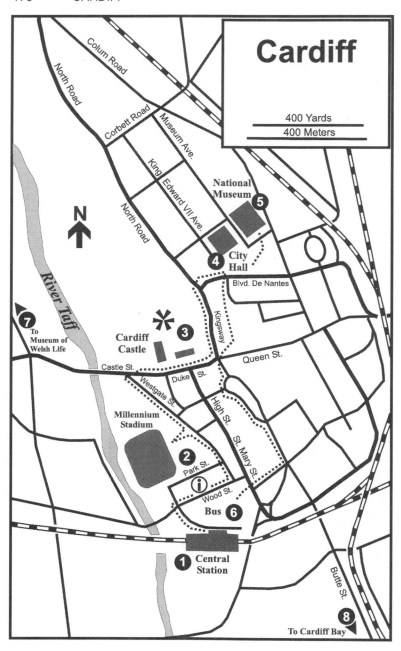

Cardiff

400 Yards
400 Meters

Colum Road

North Road

Corbett Road

Museum Ave.

King Edward VII Ave.

North Road

National Museum **5**

City Hall **4**

Blvd. De Nantes

N

River Taff

7
To Museum of Welsh Life

Kingsway

Cardiff Castle **3**

Queen St.

Castle St.

Westgate St.

Duke St.

High St.

St. Mary St.

Millennium Stadium

2

Park St.

ⓘ

Wood St.

Bus **6**

1 Central Station

Butte St.

8
To Cardiff Bay

stone in a style from the Renaissance period. At the very top, a fierce Welsh dragon stands guard over the ornate 194-foot clock tower and dome. Just behind City Hall, you will find Cathays Park, a central garden surrounded by some of Europe's finest Neo-Classical buildings named the **Civic Centre**. Built in 1897, the Civic Centre is often compared to the architecture in Washington DC.

Practically next door is the **National Museum and Gallery** ❺, housing a wealth of exhibits from Impressionist drawings and paintings to Swansea porcelain. The evolution of Wales offers a dazzling tour through the last 4,600 million years, using robotics and audiovisual effects. Upstairs is home to a superb *Art Collection, full of wall-to-wall paintings from some of our most famous artists, including Renoir, Monet, Cézanne, Van Gogh, Turner, plus many more. *Open Tues.–Sun., 10–5. Closed Dec. 25, Jan. 1. Admittance is free. Shop, restaurant.* ☎ *(029) 2039-7951.*

We now head to the **Bus Station** ❻, where we can hop on a number of different buses and visit attractions just outside of Cardiff town.

ST. FAGAN'S:

Bus number 32A takes you directly to the main entrance of the Museum of Welsh Life. The bus runs hourly, beginning at 9.50 a.m. and returns to Cardiff at 22 past the hour. On Sundays the service operates hourly starting from 11.12 a.m. and returns at 38 past the hour. The actual travelling time is only 20 minutes.

MUSEUM OF WELSH LIFE ❼, St. Fagan's, ☎ (029) 2057-3500, **W**: cf.ac.uk/nmgw/mwl. *Open daily 10–5, remaining open until 6 from July–Sept. Closed Dec. 24–25. Admission free.*

The 100-acre parkland where the museum stands was donated to the people of Wales by the Earl of Plymouth. It was opened on 7th July 1948 and quickly established itself as Wales' most popular heritage attraction. Here, craftspeople demonstrate their traditional skills in a mill, bakery, saddlery, and tannery. There is so much to see at this museum, it would be advisable to buy a guide booklet—that way you won't miss a thing.

CARDIFF BAY:

As the bay is only a mile away, you can either walk or catch a number 8 bus from Wood Street bus station.

Hailed as the "**Waterfront City**" ❽, the bay has a vast amount of attractions to see, so the most important first port of call is the **Cardiff Bay Visitor Centre**, ☎ (029) 2046-3833, where you can study a large scale model of the bay and obtain all the information needed to navigate the area's many interesting sights.

The main attraction is **Techniquest**, the UK's first purpose-built science discovery centre. This visit in particular is aimed at children, although most adults would find it interesting as well. *Open every day except for Christmas, Mon.–Fri. 9.30-4.30; weekends and Bank Holidays 10.30–5. Last* *admission 45 minutes before closing. Adults £6.30, children 5–16 and concessions £4.30, family ticket (2 Adults & 3 Children) £17.50. ☎ (029) 2047-5475, **W**: techniquest.org. Gift Shop. Café.*

In the Museum of Welsh Life

Newport

A Daytrip from Cardiff

The gateway linking England and Wales is Newport, a county borough covering 84 square miles that comprises the third-largest urban area in Wales. Newport is situated at the mouth of the River Usk and dates back to a Celtic settlement 2,000 years ago. During the 12th century the Normans settled in the town and built a castle beside the Usk, the remains of which can still be seen today.

The town grew rapidly during the 19th-century Industrial Revolution, from a small seaport to one of the most important places in the country for coal export.

An important part of Newport's history is the Chartist Uprising of 1839. The Chartists fought for the vote for all men over the age of 21 years, secret ballots, wages for the members of Parliament, and the abolition of the property qualification for Members of Parliament. Twenty-two Chartists were shot dead for their beliefs and suffered for principles we now take for granted.

Today, the town is home to some exciting and fascinating pieces of art, sculptures, and historical artefacts, such as the "In the Nick of Time" collapsible clock and Tredegar House, to name but two.

GETTING THERE:

Trains depart Cardiff every 15 minutes for the 12-minute journey to Newport.

Trains leave Shrewsbury station hourly for the two-hour run to Newport town.

By Car from Cardiff, follow the A4161, A48, and A4042 routes to Newport. The total distance is only 12.4 miles, with a travelling time of just 22 minutes.

By Car from Shrewsbury, take the A458, A5112, A49, A4110, A40, and A4042 roads to Newport. The total distance is 98 miles, with a journey time of 2-1/2 hours.

By Car from Aberystwyth, follow the A44, A470, A479, and A40 roads to Newport. The total distance is 98 miles, journey time about 2-1/2 hours.

PRACTACALITIES:

The local **Tourist Information Centre** is housed within the Museum and Art Gallery on John Frost Square, ☎ (01633) 842-962, **W**: newport.gov.uk.

Newport and the County borough has a population of 139,000. Market days are held on Saturdays.

FOOD AND DRINK:

There are plenty good restaurants and pubs in Newport, including:
The Rat and Parrot Pub (6–8 Cambrian Road, close to the train station). Serves a variety of traditional bar meals. ☎ (01633) 265-409. £

O'Neills Pub (22–24 Dock Street) A popular local pub with good food. ☎ (01633) 240-091. £

Café Delice (11 Skinner Street) Serves sandwiches, light meals, cakes etc. ☎ (01633) 250-911. £

Bar Piazza (15 John Frost Square) Modern type café/bar, serving light meals. ☎ (01633) 213-212. £

SUGGESTED TOUR:

Circled numbers correspond to numbers on the map.

Leave the **Train Station** ❶ and cross over the Queensway road and onto Cambrian Road. At the top of the road on your left-hand side stands the **Murenger Public House** ❷, a Grade II listed building from the 16th century, possibly the town house of the first High Sheriff of Monmouthshire, Sir Charles Herbert.

Cross over the road and follow the map down High Street and over to Skinner Street, here you will find the **Chartist Statues** ❸, which were commissioned for the 150th anniversary of the Chartist uprising of 1839. Not too far away on your right-hand side, you will pass the **Westgate Hotel** ❹, which was stormed during the Chartist uprising—the bullet holes are still visible in the entrance pillars.

Continue walking along the pedestrianised street and you will see in close proximity to each other, the statue of The Bell Carrier, the Chartist Murals, and the D-Day Memorial Stone.

Now turn left and onto John Frost Square, standing in the far corner is the **"In the Nick of Time" Clock** ❺. Nine meters high, the collapsible clock was commissioned by Newport council for the Garden Festival in Ebbw Vale in 1992. The clock is a fascinating piece of art, for when it "chimes," the whole structure looks as though it is breaking in half.

Also located within John Frost Square is the **Newport Museum & Gallery** ❻, which houses a variety of displays depicting local history, the natural sciences, and archaeology. The collection of the Roman town of Caerwent is particularly interesting, as is the story of the Chartist Uprising of 1839, which has been well illustrated with relics and documents. *Open Mon.–Thurs., 9.30–5, Fri. 9.30–4.30, Sat. 9.30–4. Admission free.* ☎ *(01633) 842-962.*

Follow the map to Dock Street, where on your right you will pass **"This Little Piggy"** ❼, a life-size pig cast in bronze and produced by Sebastian Boyesen during 1993/94.

You want to retrace your steps a few yards until you are at the bus sta-

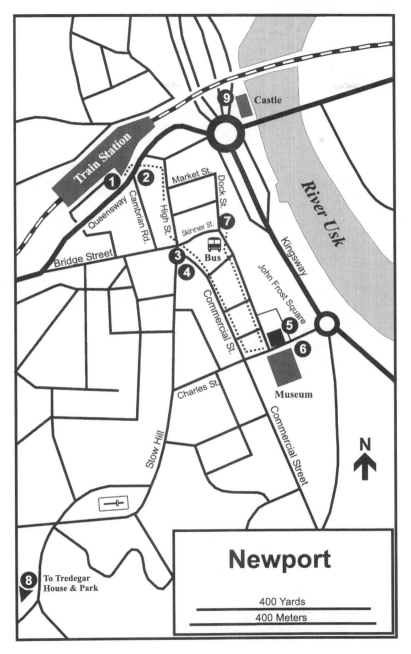

Newport

400 Yards
400 Meters

tion. From this point, catch the bus numbered 15 or 30, which leaves every 20 minutes for the 17-minute run, and ask the driver to let you off at:

*TREDEGAR HOUSE and PARK ❾, ☎ (01633) 815-880. *Park open daily throughout the year from 9 until dusk. House open Easter to the end of Sept., Wed.–Sun. and Bank Holidays, 11.30–4. Admission: Adult £5.10, senior/child £3.75.*

For over 500 years, Tredegar House was the ancestral home of the Morgans, but now is one of the finest examples of Restoration Architecture in Wales. Set in 90 acres of award-winning gardens and parklands, visitors to the house can discover what life was like for those who lived "above" and "below" stairs. You have a stunning sequence of staterooms, elaborately decorated with carvings, gilding and fine art paintings contrasting significantly with the extensive domestic quarters.

The "County House" picture is made complete by the lakeside walks, beautiful walled gardens, the orangery, and the magnificent stable block.

Throughout the year, the house is host to many events, including outdoor classical concerts, children's activity days, fairs, and theatre productions. Up close, you can watch a variety of craftspeople demonstrating their skills; making traditional musical instruments, stained glass, leather work, pottery, and woodland gifts.

Get on bus number 15 or 30 for your return journey back to Newport Bus Station.

Before getting back on the train, you may just have time to visit the ruins of **Newport Castle** ❾, a 14th-century Grade II listed building, erected between 1327 and 1386 by Hugh d'Audele or his son-in-law Ralph, earl of Stafford. The castle, as indicated on the map, has been virtually squeezed out of existence due to the demands of modern transport; most of it lies under roads and only the east side survives, sandwiched between a road and a railway bridge. Constructed on the bank of the River Usk in order to guard the river crossing, the castle can still be toured today. *Admission free.*

Retrace your steps back to the train station.

Tenby

A Daytrip from Cardiff

With four excellent beaches and a rich maritime heritage, it's little wonder the Welsh name for Tenby is "Dynbych-y-Pysgod," meaning "Little Fort of Fish." Tenby is both a mediaeval walled town and one of Wales' favourite seaside resorts. Its ancient harbour is surrounded by Regency houses in pastel colours, making it a perfect focus for artists and photographers from all over the world.

In the Middle Ages, Tenby carried on a prosperous sea trade with France and Spain, Ireland and England. One of the wealthy merchants' houses now belongs to the National Trust and so can still be visited today.

The town became a resort two hundred years ago, when the attractions of the sea began to compete with the fashionable people of Regency and early Victorian times wanting spas, balls, theatres, and the all-round social life that accompanies it. The seafaring natives were expected to serve the visitors' every pleasure.

Tenby is in a corner of Carmarthen Bay, sheltered by Caldey Island, an ancient religious settlement and today the home of the Cistercian community of monks, who welcome visitors to the seclusion and rugged beauty of their refuge.

I have personally visited this beautiful town on many occasions and have always thoroughly enjoyed my time here. One of the most memorable visits is that to Caldey Island and the monks—you feel you're in completely different world!

GETTING THERE:

Trains depart Cardiff's Central Station every 2 or 3 hours for the 3-hour run to Tenby.

By Car from Cardiff, take the A470, M4, A477, and A478 roads. The total distance is 99 miles, with a journey time of 2 hours.

By Car from Aberystwyth, follow the A487 to Cardigan, then the A478, A4218, and A4139 roads to Tenby. The total distance is 70 miles, with a travelling time of about 1 hour and 45 minutes.

PRACTICALITIES:

The local **Tourist Information Centre** is located in The Croft on the front of the North Beach, ☎ (01834) 842-402, **W**: virtualtenby.co.uk. The population of Tenby is approximately 5,000. A market is open from

Monday to Saturday. There is no half-day closing. Every September, Tenby plays host to the Arts Festival. The bus timetables change annually in July.

FOOD AND DRINK:

The town has a wide selection of restaurants, pubs, and cafés, especially in the budget range. Some choices are:

Bluberrys (The High Street) The menu has a Continental air, serving baguettes, pizzas, cappucinos, pastries etc. Open daily from 10 a.m. ☎ (01834) 845-785. £

The Plantagenet (next to the Tudor Merchant's House, Quay Hill) Set in a 13th-century building, The Plantagenet is Tenby's oldest house. The Quay room serves hot croissants, freshly squeezed juices, cappucinos etc. The Restaurant offers a home-made menu consisting of fresh fish and seafoods, vegetarian dishes, Welsh organic steaks, lamb, duck etc. ☎ (01834) 842-350. £ and ££

Caldey Island Tea Gardens (Caldey Island) A comprehensive selection of light refreshments are served. ☎ (01834) 844-453. £

SUGGESTED TOUR:

Circled numbers correspond to numbers on the map.

On leaving the **Train Station** ❶, follow the map along Park Road and Upper Park until you reach the **Town Walls** ❷ and the **Five Arches** ❸ located on South Parade and St. Florence Parade.

The Town Walls probably date from the rebuilding of Tenby in 1260. They incorporate the Five Arches, originally the South West Gate. You can still see the slots in one arch where the iron portcullis was lowered and raised. The gate has recently become the logo of the Walled Towns Friendship Circle, a group initiated in Tenby involving 130 towns from 22 countries.

Now turn left onto St. Georges Street, right onto Tudor Square, and then the first left into a mediaeval alleyway known as Quay Hill. Here you will find the well-restored 15th-century building called the **Tudor Merchant's House** ❹. The narrow three-storey house, with its fine Flemish chimneys and fireplaces, is a great example of a wealthy merchant's house. The family would have lived on the first and second floors with the servants preparing food on the ground floor and the merchant conducting business from the room nearest the street. *Open daily March to Sept., 10–5, Sun. 1–5, closed Wed.; Oct. and Nov. open daily except Wed. and Sat., 10–3, Sun. noon–3 p.m. Admission: Adult £2, child £1, family (2+3) £5, group (15+) £1.60 and NT Member free.* ☎ *(01834) 842-279,* **W**: *nationaltrust.org.uk.*

Now turn right and walk along Bridge Street and up to Castle Hill. It's a rather steep climb to the remains of **Tenby Castle** ❺, but once there you will be rewarded by breathtaking views of the Gower Peninsula; and beyond Caldey Island the north coast of Devon. The castle was first documented in 1153, but now only the watchtower has survived. Also on the

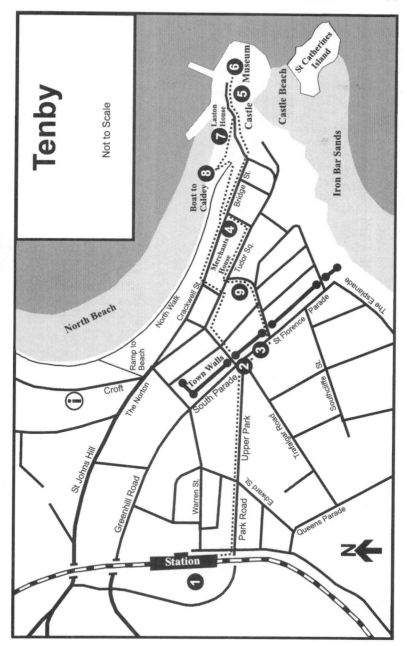

hill is a close replica of the original Victorian bandstand. Easy footpaths wind around the hill and up to a statue of Prince Albert, who is seen frequently sporting a seagull on his head.

Right at the top of the hill is the **Tenby Museum and Art Gallery** ❻, which was founded in 1878 and is one of the oldest independent museums in Wales. The museum and art gallery is housed in part of the remains of Tenby Castle and, although looking deceptively small from the outside, the museum has six spacious galleries, research facilities, and a gift shop. Exhibits include local rocks, shells, animal and plant life that were admired by great scientists of the 19th century. Also on display are the works of local artists including Augustus John and Charles Norris. *Open Mon.–Fri., 9–5. Admission: £2.* ⅄.

Make your way down the hill and back to the Harbour. Located here is the rounded white **Laston House** ❼, which once provided hot and cold baths and fashionable assembly rooms. Later it was to become the studio of a pioneering photographer who produced Tenby's earliest postcards. The Greek inscription above the door means "The sea washes away the ills of man."

From the harbour, return tickets can be obtained from a kiosk for the 20-minute boat trip to the beautiful **Monastery Island of Caldey** ❽. The island has been the home of monastic communities for 1,500 years, with the present order of Reformed Cistercians settling in the 1920s and devoting their lives to the service of God. Today, the community of around 20 monks lead their lives according to the austere Rule of St. Benedict and attend 7 services each day in the simple dignity of the monastery church— the first being at 3.15 a.m. A Holy Mass for visitors is held every Tuesday at 2.20 p.m. in St. David's Church. In addition they maintain a prime herd of beef cattle, bake shortbread in the monastery ovens, and produce delicious hand-made chocolate. One of their most interesting business ventures is the manufacture of the famous range of Caldey perfumes and toiletries, inspired by the profusion of wild island flowers, gorse, and herbs.

Not far from the landing bay is the village, featuring a pond, gift shop, and tea gardens. A small museum occupies the Post Office. While in Caldey, take time to visit **St. Illtud's Church**, with it's leaning spire and pebble floor. The Ogham stone, on the south side of the nave, dates from the 6th century. The **lighthouse** is well worth the uphill walk, the nearby cliff top affording fantastic views and an ideal picnic site.

Perhaps it is the long monastic heritage that gives Caldey its pervasive air of peace and tranquillity—coupled with its breathtaking natural beauty and freedom from excessive commercialism; a day out here will reward the more thoughtful visitor with memories of a deeper, more lasting kind. *A fleet of boats runs to the Island from Tenby Harbour from Easter to Oct. The boats run every 15 minutes between 9.30 a.m. and 5/6 p.m., Mon.–Fri. Also on Sat. from mid-May to mid-Sept. between 11 a.m. and 4 p.m. The Island is closed on Sundays. Crossing time 20 minutes. Boat tickets cost £7 for adults and £3.50 per child.*

Follow the map to **St. Mary's Church** ❾, just off Tudor Square. Built 800 years ago, and greatly extended in the 14th and 15th centuries, this is one of Wales' largest and finest parish churches. Its 152-foot spire looks beautiful when floodlit at night. To the right of the altar steps is the tomb of Tenby Mayor Thomas White, who is famous for concealing the young Henry Tudor from Richard III in the cellar under what is now Boots the Chemist. Without such an act, Britain may never have seen Tudor times.

As indicated on the map, retrace your steps back along Park Road to the train station.

Section IV
APPENDIX

A SCOTTISH TIMELINE

1000 BC:	The Iron Age.
500–100 BC:	The Celts arrive.
43 BC–AD 383:	Roman Britain.
AD 96	The Pictish people were first mentioned in Roman literature. The name "Pict" is said to have derived from the Latin word meaning "Fighter."
AD 123	The Roman Emperor Hadrian starts work on building a border wall.
AD 360:	Roman Literature describes the warring tribe based in Ireland as the "Scots."
AD 368:	The Pict, Scot and Saxons attack the Romans in London and plunder their treasures.
AD 503:	The Scots leave Ireland and build their kingdom of Dalriada in Argyll on the west coast of Scotland.
AD 563:	St. Columbia sails from Ireland to Argyll founding monastries and spreading Christianity.
AD 597:	St. Columbia died.
AD 794:	Vikings invade Scotland.
AD 843:	The first step in creating a united Scotland was by uniting the Scots and the Picts as one nation.
1005	Malcolm II kills Kenneth III and becomes king.
1018:	Kingdom of Scotland is born when Malcolm II defeated the Saxons at the Battle of Carham.
1034:	Duncan kills his grandfather Malcolm II and becomes king of a united Scotland.
1040:	MacBeth kills Duncan and becomes king.
1057:	Malcolm III kills MacBeth and becomes king.
1124:	After the death of Edgar and Alexander I, David I becomes king of a united Scotland.
1272:	William Wallace was born.
1296:	Annexation of Scotland by England. Scotland's Coronation Stone—the "Stone of Destiny" was removed to Westminster Abbey, London, by the English King Edward I. The stone was permanently returned in 1996.
1297:	The Battle of Stirling Bridge.
1298:	The Battle of Falkirk.
1305:	William Wallace was captured and executed.

1306:   Robert the Bruce crowned.

1314:   The Battle of Bannockburn resulted in Scottish independence.

1320:   The Declaration of Arbroath was drawn up to urge the Pope to recognize Scottish Independence—the Pope accepted the declaration.

1329:   Robert the Bruce died.

1411:   University of St. Andrews was founded.

1451:   University of Glasgow was founded.

1494:   University of Aberdeen was founded.

1502:   King Henry VII's daughter married James IV of Scotland. This gave rise to the Union of the Crowns in 1603.

1512:   Under the terms of a treaty with France, all Scottish citizens became French and vice versa.

1559:   John Knox's sermon in Perth started the Reformation in Scotland.

1582:   University of Edinburgh founded.

1603:   James VI of Scotland becomes James I of England, bringing about the Union of the Crowns.

1625:   Charles I becomes king on the death of his father.

1637–42:   Charles tries to enforce a new prayer book on the Scots, resulting in a civil war breaking out in England.

1682:   The National Library of Scotland was founded.

1692:   The massacre of Glencoe. Clan Campbell, siding with the king, murders members of Clan McDonald.

1695:   Bank of Scotland was founded and is still operating today.

1707:   Act of Union is passed—Scotland formally united with England to form Great Britain. In doing so, the Scottish Parliament voted itself out of existence.

1744:   The world's first golf club was founded (the Honourable Company of Edinburgh Golfers).

1745:   Prince Charles Edward Stuart—Bonnie Prince Charlie—returns to Scotland.

1826:   Scotland's first commercial railway was opened between Edinburgh and Dalkeith.

1860:   Scotland hosted the first Open Golf Championship.

1870:   The first Rugby International was played between Scotland and England.

1896:   Opening of the only underground railway in Scotland—the "shooglie."

1937:   The Queen Elisabeth—the largest ocean liner ever built, was launched in Clydebank.

1943:   During the Second World War, over 1,000 people were killed over two days in Clydebank and Southern Glasgow, during the only sustained German Luftwaffe attack on Scotland.

1964:   Her Majesty Queen Elisabeth II opened the longest sus-

	pension bridge in Europe, the Forth Road Bridge.
1967:	The QE2, the last of the great Clyde-built passenger liners, was launched in Clydebank.
1975:	The first oil was piped ashore from the North Sea at Peterhead.
1988:	Scotland's worst terrorist incident occurred when a bomb exploded on board a Boeing 747 airliner on course from Frankfurt to New York. It crashed on the village of Lockerbie in Dumfriesshire, killing a total of 275 people.
1999:	After 292 years, a Scottish Parliament was re-instated, following the devolution of powers from London through the Scotland Act, 1997.

A WELSH TIMELINE

1000 BC:	The Iron Age.
500–100 BC:	The Celts arrive.
43 BC–AD 383:	Roman Britain.
AD 383:	The Macsen's Legions withdrawal—the Welsh Nation began.
AD 400–600:	The Saxon invasions.
AD 516:	The Battle of Mount Badon.
AD 550–650:	Saxon Influence—More than 300 years of fighting between the native Celts and the ever-increasing numbers of Germanic peoples resulted in Britain sorting itself out into three distinct areas; the Britonic West, the Teutonic East, and the Gaelic North. These areas later became Wales, England, and Scotland.
AD 600:	The Welsh Language begins its written history.
AD 425–664:	The age of the Celtic Saints. A Welsh missionary named Patrick went to Ireland and became their Patron Saint.
AD 615:	The Battle of Chester and the split in the Brythonic Kingdoms.
AD 633:	Wales becomes a separate cultural & linguistic unit.
AD 664:	The death of Cadwaldr.
AD 720:	Links between Wales and Britany are severed.
AD 768:	Celtic Church reunites with Rome.
AD 784:	The King of Mercia builds Offa's Dyke.
AD 844-77:	The reign of Rhodri Mawr (Rhodri The Great).
AD 890:	Welsh rulers acknowledge the overlordship of Alfred of Wessex.
AD 937:	The Battle of Brunanburgh.
AD 960:	The "Annales of Cambriae."

1039–63:	The reign of Gruffudd Ap Llewelyn. The only Welsh ruler to unite the ancient kingdoms of the whole of Wales under his authority.
1066–77:	The Normans come to Wales. The defeat of the English King Harold at the Battle of Hastings in 1066.
1137–1282:	The reign of Owain Gwynedd.
1169:	According to legend, Prince Madog of Gwynedd, accompanied by a group of followers, made landfall on what is now Mobile Bay, Alabama in America, some time in 1169. The explorers then travelled up the Missouri, where a remnant inter-married with the Mandan Indians of North Dakota and left behind some of their customs and their language.
1200–40:	Llywelyn ap Iorwerth, grandson of Owain Gwynedd, reigned for 46 years as Prince of Wales and married Joan, the daughter of King John of England in 1205.
1216:	Death of King John.
1216–72:	Henry III of England gave the young Prince Edward, who was was born on June 17 1239, control of all the crown lands in Wales. Edward I took the throne in 1272, determined to crush any resistance to his rule in Wales.
1277:	Llywelyn ap Gruffudd was forced to give up most of his lands after being confined to the west of the River Conwy. From 1258, King Edward began building English castles, garrisoned by English mercenaries and settlers, which led to a massive revolt led by Llywelyn.
1282:	An English knight called Cilmer killed Llywelyn, so all resistance ended quickly.
1294–1400:	After the death of Llywelyn ap Gruffudd, Madog ap Llwelyn, Llywelyn Bren, Lord of Senghenydd, and Owain Lawgoch (Owen of the Red Hand) raised the flag of rebellion.
1307:	Death of Edward I.
1399:	Richard II surrenders to Bolingbroke at Flint Castle.
1404:	Owain summoned a Parliament and declared himself Prince of Wales.
1409:	The Charter of Brecon. Henry V retook most of the lands captured by Glyndwr.
1485:	The final battle of the War of the Roses was fought in August 1485 at Market Bosworth in the English Midlands. Henry Tudor, the only surviving Lancastrian claimant to the English throne, was of Welsh decent. Owain Tudor of Penmynedd in Anglesey, had secretly married Catherine, widow of Henry V. At the battle at Bosworth, Henry Tudor ascended the English throne after defeating Richard III.
1536:	The Act of the Union.
1603:	James I becomes ruler of the Kingdom of Great Britain—a union of the crowns of Scotland and England was made.

1664:   The Conventicle Act prohibited groups of more than 5 people from assembling for religious worship other than that prescribed by the established church. It had the effect of furthering emigration to North America, where Welshmen became prominent in municipal government and the universities.

1681:   William Penn given proprietary rights to Pennsylvania.

1768:   Copper Ore mined at Mynydd Parys, Anglesey.

1788:   The first Welsh people to arrive in Australia. Perhaps the most famous of all the Welsh immigrants to arrive "Down Under" was Joseph Jenkins, who left Wales because of a nagging wife and whose exploits as "The Jolly Swagman" of the popular song has earned him a prominent place in the pantheon of Australian folk heroes.

1790–1800:   The great era of canal building in Wales.

1826:   Thomas Telford built two suspension bridges over the River Conwy and the Menai Straits.

1839:   The Newport Rising.

1867:   The Great Reform Act gave the vote to every male householder in the counties with premises rated at £12 or more.

1870:   The Education Act sets up Board Schools.

1872:   Aberystwyth, Wales' first University opens.

1881:   Welsh Rugby Union established.

1890:   David Lloyd George, the Manchester-born, Welsh-speaking solicitor, is elected to Parliament.

1905:   Cardiff elevated to City status.

1907:   The National Library and the National Museum of Wales open.

1913:   At the Lancaster Pit, near to Caerphilly, an explosion killed 439 mine workers.

1914:   World War I begins. Welsh volunteers marched happily to the colours (and to their deaths) singing their stirring hymns.

1915:   Lord Rhondda, who introduced food rationing to Britain during the war and who directed the supply of munitions from the United States to Britain, survived the sinking of the Lusitania.

1916:   David Lloyd George, raised in the little village of Llanystumdwy, Gwynedd, became the first Welshman in British history to achieve the position of Prime Minister.

1920:   The University College of Swansea established.

1925   After World War I, with its massive loss of life that affected whole Welsh-speaking communities, the language began a precipitous decline, and with it, a distinct way of life. In an attempt to stop the rot, Plaid Cymru (the Party of Wales) was founded. It took the party over 40 years to gain its first seat in Parliament.

1939–45:	World War II.
1946:	Lloyd George introduced the revolutionary National Insurance Act of 1946, where workers were able to insure themselves against ill health or unemployment.
1947:	Welsh Gas Board established.
1948:	The Council of Wales established.
1953:	An important figure in the literary history of Wales— Howell Elvet Lewis—dies.
1953:	Dylan Thomas, the famous Welsh poet, died in New York City.
1955:	Cardiff selected as the capital city for Wales. Wales could now think of herself as a real nation with its own capital city, on equal footing with other small nations throughout Europe.
1964:	James Griffiths became the first Secretary of State for Wales.
1966:	The Aberfan Disaster. 144 children and their teachers were buried in their Junior School, near Merthyr Tydfil, after a pile of slag (waste from the collieries) softened by rain, slipped unnoticed down the mountainside.
1967:	The Welsh Language Act.
1969:	The Investiture of Prince Charles. Ever since Edward I made his son Prince of Wales in 1300, the title Prince of Wales has been automatically confirmed upon the first-born son of the sovereign.
1969:	"The Mighty Atom"—Jimmy Wilde dies. Born at Tylorstown, Rhondda, Jimmy was the smallest and lightest boxing world champion ever. He was the only boxer from Britain to be accepted in the USA as the finest in his division (fly weight) and was rated by four American sports writers as the greatest boxer ever.
1974:	Local Government reorganized. Also, for the first time in the long history of Parliament, Welsh MPs were allowed to take their oaths of allegiance to the British Crown in the Welsh language as well as in English.
1984:	The Miners' Strike.
1997:	The Government published its white paper, "A Voice for Wales," which outlined its proposals for the devolution in Wales.
1998:	The Government of Wales Act, which established the National Assembly for Wales and the Transfer of Function order 1999, which enabled the transfer of the dissolved powers and responsibilities from the Secretary of State for Wales to the Assembly.

GLOSSARY— SCOTTISH TO ENGLISH

Abune above, over
Adae difficulty, fuss, ceremony
Agate against
Aheid ahead
Aiblins perhaps
Atween between
Auld old
Aye yes, always
Ayont beyond
Backspeir question
Bairn child, kid
Baurley-bree whisky
Bawbees money
Ben the Hoose in the other room
Blashie wet and windy
Blether talk nonsense
Bonalie farewell drink
Bonny pretty
Bowster-cup nightcap
Brig bridge
Brose porridge made with meal, water, salt, & butter
Burn stream
Dinnae don't
Dram glass of Scotch
Fae from
Gang go

Hen Mrs.
Laddie boy
Lassie girl
Nicht night
Philabeg kilt
Plottin het scalding hot
Polis police
Quaich a drinking cup
Quean girl
Retour return, return journey
Richt right
Saicont second
Saut salt
Scrieve write
Sicht sight
Simmer summer
Syne doun wash down food with drink
Tattie potato
Tent listen to, notice, care for, attention
The day today
Twa two
Wean child
Wee small
Yin one

GLOSSARY—WELSH TO ENGLISH
Pronunciation guide is in italics

Aber *(ab-er)* estuary
A chi? *(a chee)* and you?
Bont *(bon-t)* bridge
Bore da *(boreh-da)* good morning
Capel *(kap-el)* chapel
Castell *(kah-stell)* castle
Croeso *(kro-ee-soh)* welcome

Cyfarchion *(cuv-ar-ch-ion)* greetings
Da boch/Hwyl *(dah bok/hooeel)* goodbye, so long
Dau *(die)* two
Dim diolch *(dim-dee-olch)* no thank you
Dinas *(dee-nas)* fort

Diolch *(dee-olch)* thank you
Fford *(for-th)* road
Iechyd da *(yek-id-da)* good
health
Lawn diolch *(ee-awn dee-olch)*
fine, thanks
Llan *(ch-lan)* in the parish of,
church of saint
Nag di *(nag ud-ee)* no
Nod-da *(nos da)* good night
Noswaith dda *(nos-waith tha)*
good evening
Os gwelwch yn dda *(os-g'well-ooch-un-tha)* please

Prynhawn da *(prun-hawn da)*
good afternoon
Schd ych chi? *(shwd eech chee)*
how are you?
Shwmae *(shw-mai)* hello
Sut *(scwd)* how
Traeth *(traa-ith)* beach
Tre *(treh)* town or hamlet
Tri *(tree)* three
Y *(uh)* the, of the
Ydi *(ud-ee)* yes
Ydi'r banc ar agor? *(ud-eer banc ahr ag-ohr)* is the bank open?
Yn *(in)* in

Acknowledgements

Daytrips Scotland & Wales is dedicated to my family — husband and travel partner Garry, son Jonathan, and daughter Frances, who have made this book possible by their patience, silence, enthusiasm and understanding. A sincere "thank you" goes to my mother Christine, her friend Leonard, mother and father-in-law Margaret and John who provided encouragement and help over the years.

A great big "thank you" is extended to Earl Steinbicker, creator of the DAYTRIPS series, for his kind words of wisdom and inspiration, and for supplying the photos otherwise not credited.

Special recognition is extended to all the Tourist Information Centres mentioned in the book for being extremely personable and attentive. In particular:

The Aberdeen and Grampian Tourist Board for supplying the beautiful photographs of Elgin.

The National Trust for Scotland for the front cover photo of the Glenfinnan Monument and for the photograph of the Statue of Robert the Bruce at the Bannockburn Heritage Centre in Stirling.

The Snowdonia Press in Porthmadog, Wales for the aerial photograph of Portmeirion Village.

John Cave, Holyhead's local historian and Hon. Sec. of the Holyhead Maritime Museum, Wales, for supplying the photographs of South Stack.

Jackie Nightingale, Town Clerk's Assistant in Beaumaris, North Wales, for all the helpful advice given.

Neil Cane and Sheila Ropke in the Statistical Directorate and Cartographics Department at the National Assembly for Wales for supplying me with land area statistics.

… and our many friends throughout Scotland and Wales.

Photographs of the Menai Bridge, Beaumaris Castle, Benllech Beach on Anglesey, Bangor Cathedral, Caernarfon Castle in Wales, and the Highland Cattle in the Cairngorms taken by the author and Jonathan David Duddle.

Index

Special interest attractions are listed under their category headings.

Aberaeron 127-130
Aberdeen 55-60
Aberystwyth 114-121
Air travel 12-13
Alloway 91
ART MUSEUMS:
Aberdeen Art Gallery,
   Aberdeen 60
Aberystwyth Arts Centre,
   Aberystwyth 117
Amgueddfa Llandudno Museum,
   Llandudno 134-135
Bangor Museum & Art Gallery,
   Bangor 141
Fine Art Gallery, Fort William 106
Glasgow School of Art, Glasgow
   88
Inverness Museum & Art Gallery,
   Inverness 62
National Gallery of Scotland,
   Edinburgh 22
National Museum & Art Gallery,
   Cardiff 177
McManus Galleries, Dundee
   49-51
Oriel Mostyn Galley, Llandudno
   132
Paisley Museum, Paisley 90
School of Art, Aberystwyth 115
Shrewsbury Museum & Art
   Gallery, Shrewsbury 113
Tenby Museum & Art Gallery,
   Tenby 186
Aviemore 65-68
Ayr 93-97

Bangor 140-143
Beaumaris 161-165
Benllech 166-169
Blair Atholl 52-54
BOAT TRIPS:
Fort William 106
Linlithgow Canal Centre,
   Linlithgow 28-30
Monastery Island of Caldey,
   Tenby 186
Northcoast Marine Adventures,
   The, John O'Groats 83

BRASS RUBBING:
Brass Rubbing Centre,
   Edinburgh 25
BritRail Pass 11
Bus travel 10

Caernarfon 144-148
Cairngorms, The 65-68
Car travel 11-12
Car rental 12
CASTLES:
Aberystwyth Castle Ruins,
   Aberystwyth 119
Beaumaris Castle, Beaumaris
   162-164
Blair Castle, Blair Atholl 54
Caernarfon Castle, Caernarfon
   145
Cardiff Castle, Cardiff 175
Conwy Castle, Conwy 137-139
Dunbar Castle Ruins, Dunbar 40
Dunollie Castle Ruins, Oban 104
Edinburgh Castle 22
Elgin Castle Ruins, Elgin 74
Inverness Castle, Inverness 62
Lanark Castle Ruins, Lanark 100
Newport Castle Ruins, Newport
   182
Old Wick Castle Ruins, Wick 79
Penrhyn Castle, Bangor 141-143
St. Andrews Castle Ruins, St.
   Andrews 44
Shrewsbury Castle 111
Stirling Castle 36
Tenby Castle Ruins, Tenby 184
Urquhart Castle, Drumnadrochit
   64
CATHEDRALS & CHURCHES:
Abbey Church, Dunfermline 32
Auld Kirk, Ayr 91
Cathedral Church of St. Deiniol,
   Bangor 141
Church of the Holy Rood,
   Stirling 36
Elgin Cathedral Ruins, Elgin 76
Glasgow Cathedral, Glasgow 85
Holy Trinity Church, St. Andrews
   46

Kirk Alloway, Alloway 91
Monastery Island of Caldey,
    Tenby 186
Paisley Abbey, Paisley 90
St. Andrew's Cathedral, Aberdeen
    56
St. Andrew's Cathedral Ruins, St.
    Andrews 46
St. Chad's Church, Shrewsbury
    111
St. Giles' Cathedral, Edinburgh
    24
St. Giles' Kirk, Elgin 74
St. Kentigern's Church, Lanark
    101
St. Machar's Cathedral, Aberdeen
    56-60
St. Mary & St. Nicholas Church,
    Beaumaris 164
St. Mary's Church, Aberystwyth
    120
St. Mary's Church, Caernarfon
    147
St. Mary's Church, Lanark 101
St. Mary's Church, Tenby 187
St. Michael's Church, Linlithgow
    28
St. Nicholas Church, Lanark 99
St. Nicholas Kirk, Aberdeen 60
Shrewsbury Abbey, Shrewsbury
    111

CHILDREN:
Museum of Childhood,
    Edinburgh 25
Museum of Childhood
    Memories, Beaumaris 165
Churches—see Cathedrals &
Churches

COLLEGES & UNIVERSITIES:
King's College, Aberdeen 56
Marischal College, Aberdeen 56
Old College, Aberystwyth 118
St. Salvator's College, St. Andrews
    46
University of Wales, Aberystwyth
    117
Conwy 136-139

Drumnadrochit 64
Dunbar 39-42
Dundee 48-51
Dunfermline 31-34

Edinburgh 20-26
Elgin 73-77

Food and drink 13-14
Fort William 105-108

GARDENS:
Biblical Garden, Elgin 76
Cruikshank Botanical Gardens,
    Aberdeen 60
Tredegar House & Park, Newport
    182
Glasgow 84-88
Glossaries 194-195

HISTORIC HOUSES:
Abbot House Heritage Centre,
    Dunfermline 32
Aberconwy House, Conwy 137
Andrew Carnegie Birthplace
    Museum, Dunfermline 32
Argyll's Lodging, Stirling 36
Burns' Cottage & Museum,
    Alloway 91
Georgian House, Edinburgh 26
John Knox House, Edinburgh 25
John Muir Birthplace, Dunbar 40
Merchant's House, Tenby 184
Plas Mawr, Conwy 137
Provand's Lordship, Glasgow 87
Provost Skene's House, Aberdeen
    60
Rowley's House Museum,
    Shrewsbury 113
Smallest House in Great Britain,
    Conwy 139
Thunderton Hotel, Elgin 74
HISTORY MUSEUMS:
Atholl Country Life Museum,
    Blair Atholl 54
Bangor Museum & Art Gallery,
    Bangor 141
Ceredigion Museum,
    Aberystwyth 117-118
Coats Observatory, Paisley 91
Dunbar Town House Museum,
    Dunbar 40
Dunfermline Museum,
    Dunfermline 34
Elgin Museum, Elgin 76
Inverness Museum & Art Gallery
    62
Linlithgow Museum & Heritage
    Centre 28
Maritime Museum, Aberdeen 56
McManus Galleries, Dundee
    49-51
Museum of Edinburgh 25

Nairn Museum, Nairn 70
National Museum & Art Gallery,
   Cardiff 177
Newport Museum & Gallery,
   Newport 180
Paisley Museum, Paisley 90
People's Palace, Glasgow 87
People's Story Museum,
   Edinburgh 25
Portmeirion Village 154-158
Preservation Trust Museum, St.
   Andrews 46
Provost Skene's House, Aberdeen
   60
Royal Burgh of Lanark Museum,
   The, Lanark 99
St. Andrews Museum, St.
   Andrews 47
Shrewsbury Museum & Art
   Gallery, Shrewsbury 113
Sma Shot, Paisley 90
Tenby Museum & Art Gallery,
   Tenby 186
Tenement House, Glasgow 87
West Highland Museum, Fort
   William 106
Wick Heritage Centre, Wick 81
Holidays 16
Holyhead 170-173

Internet 17
INDUSTRIAL:
   Ben Nevis Distillery, Fort William
      108
   Caithness Glass Visitor Centre,
      Wick 81
   Madog Motorcycle & Car
      Museum, Porthmadog 151
   Maritime Museum, Aberdeen 56
   Moray Motor Museum, Elgin 77
   Oban Distillery Visitor Centre,
      Oban 104
   Pulteney Distillery, Wick 79
   Sma Shot, Paisley 90
   The Mill, Blair Atholl 54
   Verdant Works, Dundee 51
Inverness 61-64

John O'Groats 82-83

Linlithgow 27-30
Llandudno 131-135
Loch Ness 61, 64
LITERARY INTEREST:
   Brig O' Doon, Alloway 91

Burns' Cottage & Museum,
   Alloway 91
Burns' Monument, Alloway 91
New Quay 122-125
Scott Monument, Edinburgh 22
Writer's Museum, Edinburgh 24
Tam O'Shanter Experience,
   Alloway 91

Mail 16
MARITIME INTEREST:
   Maritime Museum, Aberdeen 56
   Maritime Museum, Holyhead 173
   Northcoast Marine Adventures,
      The, John O'Groats 83
   Porthmadog Maritime Museum,
      Porthmadog 150
   RRS Discovery and Discovery
      Point, Dundee 49
Money 16

Nairn 69-72
NATURE PRESERVES:
   Aberaeron Sea Aquarium,
      Aberaeron 128
   Benllech Beach, Benllech 169
   Ben Nevis, Fort William 106
   Cairngorm Reindeer Centre,
      Aviemore 66
   Culbin Forest, Nairn 70
   Glenmore Visitor Centre,
      Aviemore 68
Newport 179-182
New Quay 122-126

Oban 102-104

Paisley 89-92
Palaces—see Stately Homes &
   Palaces
Porthmadog 149-151
Portmeirion 154-158
Pubs 15

Rail/bus passes 10
RAILFAN INTEREST:
   Ffestiniog Railway, Porthmadog
      150-151
   Mallaig Rail Trip, Fort William 108
   Strathspey Railway, Aviemore 68
   Vale of Rheidol Narrow Gauge
      Railway, Aberystwyth 121
   Welsh Highland Railway,
      Caernarfon 147-148
Rail travel 9

Restaurants 15

St. Andrews 43-47
St. Fagan's 177
Scotland 19-108
Shrewsbury 110-113
SPORTS:
British Golf Museum, St. Andrews
44
Millennium Stadium, Cardiff 175
Royal and Ancient Golf Club, St.
Andrews 44
STATELY HOMES & PALACES:
Blair Castle, Blair Atholl 54
Cardiff Castle, Cardiff 175
Dunfermline Palace Ruins,
Dunfermline 32
Linlithgow Palace, Linlithgow 28
Llanerchaeron Estate, Aberaeron
130
Palace of Holyroodhouse,
Edinburgh 25
Penrhyn Castle, Bangor 141-143
Plas Mawr, Conwy 137
Tredegar House & Park, Newport
182
Stirling 35-38

Telephones 17
Tenby 183-187
THEME EXHIBITIONS:
Aberaeron Sea Aquarium,
Aberaeron 128
Alice in Wonderland Centre,
Llandudno 132
Bannockburn Heritage Centre,
Stirling 38
Beaumaris Gaol, Beaumaris 164
Cairngorm Reindeer Centre,
Aviemore 66
Camera Obscura & World of
Illusions, Edinburgh 24
Castle Garrison Encounter,
Inverness 62
Elgin Museum, Elgin 76
Gladstone's Land, Edinburgh 24
Great Orme Bronze Age Copper
Mines, Llandudno 134
Loch Ness Exhibition Centre,
Drumnadrochit 64
Museum of Welsh Life, St. Fagan's
177
New Quay Honey Farm, New

Quay 126
Oban Distillery Visitor Centre,
Oban 104
Old Town Jail, Stirling 38
People's Story, The, Edinburgh 25
Pulteney Distillery, Wick 79
Royal Burgh of Stirling Visitor
Centre, Stirling 36
RRS Discovery & Discovery Point,
Dundee 49
Scotch Whisky Heritage Centre,
Edinburgh 24
Sensation, Dundee 49
Tam O'Shanter Experience,
Alloway 91
Techniquest, Cardiff 177
World War II Home Front
Experience, Llandudno 135
Timelines 188-193
Tourist information 18

Universities—see Colleges &
Universities
UNUSUAL MUSEUMS:
Anthropological Museum,
Aberdeen 56
Camera Obscura & World of
Illusions, Edinburgh 24
Coats Observatory, Paisley 91
Linlithgow Canal Centre 28-30
Moray Motor Museum, Elgin 77
Museum of Childhood,
Edinburgh 25
Museum of Childhood
Memories, Beaumaris 165
Museum of Piping, Glasgow 88
Museum of Welsh Life, St. Fagan's
177
Madog Motorcycle & Car
Museum, Porthmadog 151
Royal Welsh Fusiliers Museum,
Caernarfon 145
Writer's Museum, Edinburgh 24
Shropshire Regimental Museum,
Shrewsbury 111
Teapot World Museum, Conwy
137
Techniquest, Cardiff 177
Verdant Works, Dundee 51

Wales 109-186
Weather 15
Wick 78-81

Daytrips
• OTHER EUROPEAN TITLES •

Daytrips LONDON

By Earl Steinbicker. The perfect companion to Daytrips Scotland and Wales. This long-time favorite guide explores the metropolis on 10 one-day walking tours, then describes 45 daytrips to destinations throughout southern England — all by either rail or car. 7th edition, 352 pages, 61 maps, 32 B&W photos, glossaries and a menu translator. ISBN: 0-8038-2056-9.

Daytrips GERMANY

By Earl Steinbicker. 60 of Germany's most enticing destinations can be savored on daytrips from Munich, Frankfurt, Hamburg, and Berlin. Walking tours of the big cities are included. 6th edition, 352 pages, 68 maps, 36 B&W photos, glossaries and a menu translator. ISBN: 0-8038-2033-X.

Daytrips SPAIN & PORTUGAL

By Norman P.T. Renouf. 50 one-day adventures by rail, bus, or car — including many walking tours, as well as side trips to Gibraltar and Morocco. All the major tourist sights are covered, plus several excursions to little-known, off-the-beaten-track destinations. Revised 2nd edition, 382 pages, 51 maps. ISBN: 0-8038-2012-7.

Daytrips IRELAND

By Patricia Tunison Preston. Covers the entire Emerald Isle with 55 one-day self-guided tours both within and from the major tourist areas, plus sections on shopping. Expanded 2nd edition, 400 pages, 57 maps. ISBN: 0-8038-2003-8.

SEVENTH EDITION

Daytrips
LONDON

55 one day adventures by rail or car, in and around London and southern England

EARL STEINBICKER

Now in its Seventh Edition – The perfect companion to Daytrips Scotland and Wales.

Daytrips FRANCE

By Earl Steinbicker. Describes 48 daytrips — including 5 walking tours of Paris, 24 excursions from the city, 5 in Provence, and 14 along the Riviera. 5th edition, 304 pages, 60 maps, glossaries and a menu translator. ISBN: 0-8038-2006-2.

Daytrips ITALY

By Earl Steinbicker. Features 40 one-day adventures in and around Rome, Florence, Milan, Venice, and Naples. 4th edition, 288 pages, 45 maps, glossaries and a menu translator. ISBN: 0-8038-9372-8.

Daytrips HOLLAND, BELGIUM & LUXEMBOURG

By Earl Steinbicker. Many unusual places are covered on these 40 daytrips, along with all the favorites plus the 3 major cities. 3rd^{d} edition, 272 pages, 45 maps, plus Dutch and French glossaries and a menu translator. ISBN: 0-8038-2009-7.

Daytrips
• AMERICAN TITLES •

Daytrips NEW YORK

By Earl Steinbicker. Completely rewritten and sporting many new maps for its eighth edition, Daytrips New York now features 10 walking tours of the Big Apple itself. Beyond that, the book describes some 40 one-day adventures in nearby New York State, Connecticut, New Jersey, and Pennsylvania. 338 pages, 68 maps, and 27 B&W photos. ISBN: 0-8038-2021-6.

Daytrips WASHINGTON, D.C.

By Earl Steinbicker. 50 one-day adventures in the Nation's Capital, and to nearby Virginia, Maryland, Delaware, and Pennsylvania. Both walking and driving tours are featured. 368 pages, 60 maps. Revised 2nd edition. ISBN: 0-8038-9429-5.

Daytrips PENNSYLVANIA DUTCH COUNTRY & PHILADELPHIA

By Earl Steinbicker. Completely covers the City of Brotherly Love, then goes on to probe southeastern Pennsylvania, southern New Jersey, and Delaware before moving west to Lancaster, the "Dutch" country, and Gettysburg. There are 50 daytrips in all. 288 pages, 54 maps. ISBN: 0-8038-9394-9.

Daytrips SAN FRANCISCO & NORTHERN CALIFORNIA

By David Cheever. 50 enjoyable one-day adventures from the sea to the mountains; from north of the wine country to south of Monterey. Includes 16 self-guided discovery tours of San Francisco itself. 336 pages, 64 maps. ISBN: 0-8038-9441-4.

Daytrips HAWAII

By David Cheever. Thoroughly explores all the major islands — by car, by bus, on foot, and by bicycle, boat, and air. Includes many off-beat discoveries you won't find elsewhere, plus all the big attractions in detail. 2nd edition, 288 pages, 55 maps. ISBN: 0-8038-2019-4.

Daytrips NEW ENGLAND

By Earl Steinbicker. Discover the 50 most delightful excursions within a day's drive of Boston or Central New England, from Maine to Connecticut. Includes Boston walking tours. Revised 2nd edition, 320 pages, 60 maps. ISBN: 0-8038-2008-9.

IN PRODUCTION: Check www.daytripsbooks.com or
☎ 1-800-206-7822 for availability.

Daytrips EASTERN AUSTRALIA

By James Postell. 60 adventures from Sydney, Melbourne, Brisbane, and in the Outback, Gold Coast, Sunshine Coast, and the Tropical North. Many of these are to little-known destinations. The big cities are covered, as well.

Daytrips QUÉBEC

By Karen Desrosiers. Besides a dozen do-it-yourself walking or driving tours of Québec City and Montréal, there are easy excursions to nearby locations selected for their travel appeal, plus daytrips to the Charlevoix Coast, the St. Lawrence Valley, the Laurentians, the Eastern Townships, and Northeast Québec.

Extraordinary Places ... Close to London

By Elizabeth Victoria Wallace. Features some unexpected treasures for the more adventurous traveler.

Hastings House
Daytrips Publishers

2601 Wells Ave., Suite 161, Fern Park, FL 32730
(☎ orders toll-free: 1-800-206-7822)
Internet: www.daytripsbooks.com
E-mail: Hastings_Daytrips@earthlink.net

ABOUT THE AUTHOR:

Judith Frances Duddle has always had a keen interest in travelling and thoroughly enjoys the carefree style of daytripping. Even when she worked for the British Government for 13 years, she enjoyed getting away on weekends and taking trips to Scotland and Wales. Living in the North West of England, it only takes two hours travelling time to reach Wales, where her family now live.

During 1992, Judith was involved in a car accident that left her disabled. Far from extinguishing her thirst for living life to the full, the experience has actually enhanced it. Judith started writing about her true-life experiences, and the articles about her have been published in British magazines and local papers. She has also appeared on National Television and been interviewed on Regional Radio Stations.

Made in the USA
Middletown, DE
23 November 2018